THE FOUNDING
OF THE
FEDERAL REPUBLIC
OF GERMANY

THE FOUNDING
OF THE
FEDERAL REPUBLIC
OF GERMANY

By John Ford Golay

 THE UNIVERSITY OF CHICAGO PRESS

Library of Congress Catalog Number: 57-11205

THE UNIVERSITY OF CHICAGO PRESS, CHICAGO 37
Cambridge University Press, London, N.W. 1, England
The University of Toronto Press, Toronto 5, Canada

© *1958 by The University of Chicago. Published 1958*
Composed and printed by THE UNIVERSITY OF CHICAGO
PRESS, *Chicago, Illinois, U.S.A.*

FOR MY PARENTS

This is an essay in the promotion of international understanding. I have tried to show how the constitutional foundations of the new German Federal Republic originated in German constitutional and political developments in the past, the present needs and interests of the Western German people, and the influences brought to bear by the Western Allied governments. I hoped to do this in such a way that English-speaking readers who are unfamiliar with these developments would be able to see Western Germany's new constitution and present-day problems as the Germans themselves see them.

Some aspects of the establishment of the Federal Republic have been omitted. The question of revision of the boundaries of the southwestern Länder was not settled until some time after the Basic Law took effect. It seemed best not to enlarge and complicate this study by giving a partial account of the negotiations on this problem. The arrangement made for the government and support of the isolated Western sectors of Berlin is an important (and dramatic) episode in the story of Western Germany, but justice could not be done to it here. It is a subject for a study in itself. An account of the constitutional court would perhaps better have been presented as a part of the chapter on the federal structure of the Basic Law. It had also to be discussed in connection with basic rights, the field of law in which the practice of judicial review began in Germany. To avoid repetition, I decided to confine discussion of the court to that chapter.

Except in discussing certain federal provisions of the Basic Law and the German party system, I have not attempted to carry the story beyond 1950. Even if time had been available for this task, it could not have been undertaken, because most of the recent intergovernmental documents have not been released for study. Hence, the important amendments to the Basic Law covering the rearmament of Western Germany and included in Appendix A are not commented upon in the text.

All of the German documents and records on the drafting and negotiation of the Basic Law have either been published or are available for study in the archives of the Bundestag at Bonn. Of the Allied documents, the most important have been published, except for the records of the London conference of 1948 and certain of the meetings of the military governors and their advisers in 1948 and 1949. For the latter, I have relied on my own recollections and General Lucius D. Clay's account of these meetings in his book, *Decision in Germany*. As will be seen from the list of references appended to his book, General Clay drew upon all the documents not yet released to the public.

The text of this book has been "cleared" for publication by the historical division of the Department of State. I should add that Dr. G. Bernard Noble and his staff, whom I must thank for the trouble they took to read and check my manuscript, bear no responsibility for any error of fact or interpretation that it may contain.

The mountainous documentary and other literature that must be sifted and read and the numerous problems of evaluation and interpretation that arise necessarily make any contemporary historical study a collaborative work. I owe much to Professor Agnes Headlam-Morley of Oxford University, who counseled me wisely and gave generously of her time during the preparation of this study. I must also mention the inspiration of the teaching and example given me in earlier days by the former Master of my College, Lord Beveridge, and Professors G. D. H. Cole and K. C. Wheare of Oxford University.

The expert assistance afforded me by library staffs in many places was indispensable to this undertaking. I am particularly indebted to Herr Kurt Wernicke, director of the library and reference service of the Bundestag in Bonn, who for many months put at my disposal all the materials and facilities of his admirably organized and staffed *Abteilung III*. I must also thank for their services the library of Bonn University, the Wiener Library, London, the periodical section of the library of the Royal Institute of International Affairs, London, the library of the London School of Economics, the law and reference libraries of the office of the United States High Commissioner, Germany, and the library of Hampton Institute, Hampton, Virginia.

On points of German law and politics, I was much enlightened by conversations and correspondence with my friend Herr Werner Blischke of the library and reference service of the Bundestag. I am also indebted to him for a laborious review of the manuscript for errors of fact and reference. Needless to say, he bears no responsibility for any that remain.

My friend and former colleague, Mr. James E. King, Jr., formerly executive secretary to the United States High Commissioner, Germany, and Professors Otto Wirth and Helmut Hirsch of Roosevelt University, Chicago, read the book in manuscript and made many helpful suggestions.

Finally, I must thank my chief collaborator, my wife, who typed the manuscript in draft four times and, when she could overcome my resistance, corrected my spelling, punctuation, and grammar.

J. F. G.

ROOSEVELT UNIVERSITY
October 1957

TABLE OF CONTENTS

CHAPTER I

THE DECISION TO ESTABLISH A WESTERN GERMAN GOVERNMENT

> The French knew that we were ready to proceed in the three zones, but otherwise were determined to go ahead in two.
>
> LUCIUS D. CLAY

1. FOUR-POWER DISUNITY

The establishment of the Federal Republic of Germany resulted from the failure of the four powers—Great Britain, the United States of America, the Soviet Union, and France—to unite in the first two years of postwar occupation to carry out policies treating Germany as a political and economic whole. It is certain that, at least initially, none of the powers desired the ultimate consequence of their disunity: the division of Germany into two states, incorporated within the spheres of influence and the defensive system of opposing blocs of powers. But they were impelled step by step in that direction by conflicts arising from the incompatibility of their purposes and interests in Germany and elsewhere.

The disagreements in Germany extended to nearly every aspect of the occupation. But the two which were perhaps most fateful for four-power unity concerned the reconstruction of the German economy and the satisfaction of reparations claims. The heads of government of Great Britain, the United States, and the Soviet Union, meeting at Potsdam in July–August, 1945, had given a large share of their attention to both problems. Their agreement provided that Germany was to be treated as "a single economic unit."[1] To produce a balanced economy and reduce the need for imports, there was to be an "equitable distribution of essential commodities between the several zones."[2] Central German administrative departments, acting under the Allied Control Council, were to be estab-

1

lished for transport, finance, communications, foreign trade and industry.[3] A level of economic activity was projected which would "maintain in Germany average living standards not exceeding the average of standards of living of European countries," excluding Great Britain and the Soviet Union.* Reparation was to be made by the appropriation of German industrial equipment and Germany's assets abroad—the Soviet claims to be met in the first instance by removals from the Soviet zone of occupation and the claims of the Western Allies and of other countries by removals from the Western zones. The Soviet Union was also to receive a share of equipment "unnecessary for the German peace economy" from the Western zones, for part of which it was to provide in exchange food and coal and other materials.[4] But "payment of reparations," the agreement went on, "should leave enough resources to enable the German people to subsist without external assistance. In working out the economic balance of Germany, the necessary means must be provided to pay for imports approved by the Control Council in Germany. The proceeds of exports from current production and stock shall be available in the first place for payment for such imports."[5]

Conditions for a collision of interests already existed in this agreement. Apart from its other ambiguities, it left two vital points unclarified: the total sum of reparations to be exacted (at the Crimea Conference, the Soviet Union had proposed $20 billion, of which it was to receive half) and what part, if any, was to be taken from current production. In the short run, anyway, the restoration of the economy—even at the modest level provided by the agreement—and the satisfaction of reparations claims on the scale envisaged by the Soviet Union were incompatible objectives. The partial accomplishment of either would have required flexibility, a disposition to com-

---

* Potsdam Agreement, Sec. III, par. 15(b). The Allied Control Authority plan for reparations eventually agreed upon on March 28, 1946, would, its authors estimated, reduce "the level of industry as a whole to a figure about 50 or 55 per cent of the pre-war level in 1938" (see par. 16 of the plan). [11] The accuracy of the estimate has been disputed. (See J. P. Nettl, *The Eastern Zone and Soviet Policy in Germany* [Oxford: Oxford University Press, 1951], p. 49.) At any rate, the United States and United Kingdom governments recognized in August, 1947, that "neither the Bizonal area nor all of Germany can regain economic health under the plan as it now stands." Their revised level of industry plan for the Bizone (BIB/P[47]81/1, August 29, 1947) provided for the retention of industrial plant "sufficient to approximate the level of industry in Germany in 1936, a year that was not characterized by either boom or depressed conditions."

promise, and the closest co-operation between the occupying powers.

For the Americans and the British, reconstruction of the economy took priority. Their zones of occupation in the first two years were in a worse state than the Soviet zone, lacking food and raw materials, with their industries unable to produce exports to pay even for the most essential supplies to maintain the health of the people. These deficiencies the American and British governments were obliged to make good at the cost to them of hundreds of millions of dollars a year. Hence these two powers from the start exerted pressure in the Allied Control Council to secure the common use of German resources for the benefit of all the zones, a single export-import program for the whole of Germany, the elimination of barriers to the movement of trade and persons between the zones, and the establishment of the central German administrative agencies. American and British representatives were to press these demands repeatedly in the Allied Control Council and at meetings of the Council of Foreign Ministers in Paris (September, 1946), Moscow (March–April, 1947), and London (November–December, 1947).

The Soviet Union, on the other hand, gave priority to reparations. When it became clear that the Russians were taking not only industrial plant, but an increasing share of products and materials from their zone, both as reparations in kind and in the form of exports, the Western powers asked for an accounting by the Soviet Union of reparations withdrawals from its zone and insisted anew upon the common utilization of resources and the conduct of export-import operations for the whole of Germany. They saw themselves left indefinitely to bear the costs of subsidizing their zones, while the Soviet Union recouped its losses from both Eastern and Western zones.[6] The Russians refused to meet either request. They could not agree, they said, to any pooling of resources until all the productive facilities of each zone had been brought into operation, nor to exports and imports for all Germany until a trade balance had been achieved in each zone.[7] On the initiative of the United States military government, deliveries of reparations to the Soviet Union from the Western zones were stopped in the spring of 1946.

The views of the French government, which had not been a party to the Potsdam Agreement, produced a further disagreement affecting the treatment of Germany as a political and economic whole. The French repeatedly vetoed moves by the other three powers to establish central German administrative agencies, on the ground that this would prejudge settlement of the question of control of the Ruhr and the Rhineland[8] and the future organization of government in Germany. Self-government in Germany, they held, should be resumed first at the local and state level and be restored at the center only at a later stage and under restricting conditions.[9] The Soviet Union, for its part, refused to recognize the unilateral act of the French integrating the Saar with the French economy and insisted that it too should be given a share in the control of the Ruhr.[10]

The United States government in July, 1946, "pending quadripartite agreement . . . to treat all of Germany as an economic unit," offered to combine its zone of occupation with that of any or all of the other powers for administration as a single economic area.[11] The British government accepted this offer, and by midsummer, 1947, the zones of these two powers had been united under the joint administration of the American and British military governors, with an indirectly elected German bizonal economic council and German administrative agencies for economics, food and agriculture, transport, communications, civil service, and finance acting under military government supervision. The French did not join in this undertaking, because they feared its effect upon the "maintenance of co-ordinated action by the four occupying powers."[12] The Soviet Union denounced it as a contravention of the Potsdam Agreement.[13]

On this issue and the pooling of resources and an export-import program for all Germany, freedom of movement between the zones, a central German administration, control of the Ruhr, and reparations,[14] the Council of Foreign Ministers adjourned without reaching agreement at Moscow in April, 1947, and again in London in December, 1947.

Since the four powers were unable to agree on common policies for the conduct of the occupation, their views on the form which a future German government should take were of less practical importance. But these too were far apart. The Russians wanted a "central German government capable of bearing the responsibility for the fulfilment by Germany of her obligations to the Allies." They opposed the imposition by the Allies of a federal structure in Germany. This decision, they said, should be left to "a free vote of the German people." With a few general conditions, they were prepared to leave the drafting of a constitution to a convention of "democratic parties, free trade unions, and other anti-Nazi organizations and representatives of the Länder."* The United States and British governments opposed a strong central government because, as the American Secretary of State pointedly phrased it, "they think it could be too readily converted to the domination of a regime similar to the Nazis'."[15] They favored a division of powers between the constituent Länder and the central government, "with all powers vested in the Länder except such as are expressly delegated to the central government to secure the necessary political, legal, economic and financial unity."[16]

The French began the other way about by stipulating that the major powers of government in each field, including the power to tax, should belong to the Länder and by providing only for "coordination" at the center by councils and committees of Land ministers and officials. The national legislature was to consist only of a chamber of states.[17]

Many developments in 1947 combined to convince the French that they could not continue to administer their zone of occupation separately from the rest of Western Germany. The four foreign ministers had failed to agree on any issue in two meetings within eight months, and quadripartite government in Berlin was virtually at a standstill. The hope of the French that they could preserve four-power control in Germany by preventing consolidation of the Western zones and keeping open a way for the resumption of a working relationship appeared a forlorn one. They found their position increasingly untenable as measures were initiated in the bizonal area which urgently needed to be applied on a trizonal basis or concerning which the French especially wished to have a controlling voice. Of these, the most important were the impending reform of the banking system and the currency, the joint export-import pro-

---

* Statement and Proposal of the Soviet Member of the Council of Foreign Ministers of March 22, 1947 (CFM/47/M/46). [13] In the Weimar constitution, the German states were designated as "Länder" ("Land," singular). It has become common to use this German term in writing in English about the German states from the Weimar period on.

gram, and the proposed reorganization of the coal and iron and steel industries.

The United States and British governments had made it clear on more than one occasion that whatever the French decided, they intended to proceed with the strengthening of the bizonal economy and the return of responsibility to the German authorities. The plan for American economic aid to European countries, announced in the early summer of 1947 by the American Secretary of State, also set a premium on unification of the Western zones. Except as a temporary arrangement, it would be difficult (and the Americans took pains to make this clear) for two Western German economies to qualify for American assistance and to participate in the Organization for European Economic Cooperation. The French, themselves expecting extensive assistance under the European Recovery Program, were the less disposed to appear unco-operative so far as the program concerned their zone in Germany.

At the conclusion of the London meeting of the foreign ministers in December, 1947, the French foreign minister, M. Bidault, agreed with his British and American colleagues that a conference of representatives of the three powers should be called early in 1948 to consider trizonal fusion and the establishment of a Western German government, provided that the future status of the Ruhr and security controls were taken up concurrently.*

2. THE LONDON CONFERENCE AND ITS DECISIONS

The conference convened on February 23, 1948, at India House in London. The United States ambassador in London, Mr. Lewis Douglas, led the American delegation, which included General Lucius D. Clay and his political adviser, Mr. Robert D. Murphy, the American Assistant Secretary of State, Mr. Charles E. Saltzman, and Mr. Samuel Reber. Sir William Strang headed the British delegation, which included, besides General Sir Brian H. Robertson and his political adviser, Mr. C. E. Steel, Sir Ivone Kirkpatrick, and Mr. Patrick H. Deane. The French were led by the French ambassador in London, M. René Massigli, and the delegation included M. Mau-

---

* These two conditions were ultimately fulfilled by agreements to establish an International Authority for the Ruhr, to maintain occupation troops in Germany, and to establish an Allied Military Security Board to administer Allied laws prohibiting Western Germany's rearmament and limiting her industrial production.

rice Couve de Murville, M. Hervé Alphand, and Ambassador Tarbe de St. Hardouin. General Pierre Koenig attended from time to time. The delegation from the Benelux nations included for the Netherlands, Ambassador Jonkheer E.S.M.G. Michiels van Verduynen, for Belgium, Ambassador Vicomte Obert de Thieusies, and for Luxembourg, the Luxembourg minister, M. André Clasen.

The British and American delegations met a few days before the conference to decide how best to approach the French to obtain their agreement for the establishment of a central government in Western Germany with sufficient authority over the Länder to take the measures necessary for reconstruction in Western Germany and to play a dependable part in the co-operative effort to be made by all the Western European countries to achieve economic recovery. The protest which the French had recently made (January 24, 1948) against organizational changes in the German bizonal administration pointed the way to the position they would take on the structure of a future Western German government. Each of their objections turned on the powers to be exercised by the central or bizonal authority in relation to the Länder. They had objected to the US/UK military governors' failure to give the Länderrat (composed of Land representatives) legislative powers equal to those of the economic council; to the grant of limited powers of taxation to the bizonal administration, which, the French maintained, should be dependent for revenue upon contributions from the Länder; to the establishment of single heads of the German administrative departments, responsible to the economic council rather than to a committee representing the Länder; to the establisment of a supreme or high court for the bizonal area. These arrangements in the bizone, the French contended, prejudged a decision regarding the form which a future government for Western Germany should take.

The American and British delegations put to the French the argument that the economic unification essential for Western Germany's participation in the European Recovery Program could not be achieved and safeguarded without a central government of sufficient authority to command the respect and co-operation of the governments of the Länder. Otherwise, they contended, the economic policies of the central government might be upset at any time by the refusal of one or several of the Land governments to co-operate.

They pointed out that if a Western German government were so handicapped that it could not deal with pressing economic and social problems effectively, a situation might develop that would be ripe for exploitation by Soviet power.* The Americans stressed that, without an effective West German government, it would be difficult to include Germany in the European Recovery Program. A well-organized "Bizonia," they said, was to be preferred to a weak and poorly organized "Trizonia."

The French replied that they were alive to the dangers of the prevailing situation in Europe but that their assessment of them differed from that of their Allies. Safeguards must be provided, they said, to insure that Western Germany could not be exploited by either Russian or German aggressive power. Among these safeguards, they included continuation of the occupation of Western Germany, adequate controls for the Ruhr, and the organization of Western Germany as a loose association of the Länder. If the Soviets had set themselves up as champions of German unity, the French said, it was only because the centralization of power in Germany would afford to the Communists the easiest means of penetrating the government and seizing control.

Hence, the views initially put forward by the French on the structure of a Western German government called for sovereignty to be vested in the Länder, with the limited powers of the central government to be specifically delegated. If a bicameral legislature were to be adopted (the French preferred only a chamber of states), the upper chamber should be chosen by the Land governments and the lower by the Land legislatures. A lower chamber elected by the German people as a whole, the French contended, would be in a position to dominate the Land governments. The central government should not have the power of direct taxation, but should derive its revenues from customs and from allocations made by the individual states out of taxes levied and collected by them. Except for foreign affairs, customs, and possibly the railroads, no central administrative apparatus should be created, and civil servants from the Länder should be seconded to man this limited central administration. The Benelux proposals closely followed those of the French.

* The Communist party had seized power in Czechoslovakia on February 23, 1948.

The Americans questioned whether a central government so constituted would have sufficient power to put into effect essential policies on a national basis. For instance, in the event of an acute food shortage in Western Germany, they asked, would the central government be in a position to compel a Land with a surplus of food to share with others? In the American view, the central government must be more than an instrument for co-ordinating quasi-sovereign states. It should be intrusted with the powers it would need to cope with the political and economic problems of the day. Such powers should be clearly defined and the residual powers reserved to the Länder. In particular, central control of the police and security forces must be avoided. Cultural, educational, and religious affairs should be specifically confined to the competence of the Länder. The financial independence of the Länder should be secured, but the central government should possess authority to raise the revenues needed to discharge the functions and responsibilities assigned to it by the constitution. The democratic character of the central government could be assured by the popular election of one house of the legislature, and its federal character by a second chamber representing the governments of the various states. There should be adequate guaranties against concentration of power in the executive, whether it had an independent status or acted under responsibility to the legislature. There should be the maximum delegation of administrative responsibility from the center. The integrity and independence of the judiciary must be assured and civil rights and personal freedoms guaranteed. Finally, the American delegation desired that only the most general restrictions required by the present and long-term security interests of the Allied powers should be placed on the German constituent assembly, which should be left to determine the detailed provisions of the constitution.

The British representative said that his government's views on the future political organization in Germany had already been set out in proposals presented at both the Moscow and London conferences of the foreign ministers.[18] These should now be adapted to the present situation to create in Western Germany a governmental system strong enough to resist Communist infiltration. In general, the British views corresponded closely with those of the Americans, but they laid greater stress on the powers which a central government would need, particularly to meet the "present acute economic difficulties in Germany, relating . . . to the supply of food, the distribution of food and raw materials in short supply, the planning of industry and the control of labour, wages and prices."[19] In view of the heavy expenditures which would fall upon the central budget to cover occupation costs, repair war damage, and subsidize industries, the British could not agree to limit the central financial powers as the French wished. The chamber of states, they considered, should have only a suspensory veto over legislation adopted by the popularly elected chamber, not full powers of approval.[20]

The discussions which ensued brought the views of the delegations closer together, but important differences remained at the conclusion of the first series of conference sessions on March 6.

At Berlin, during the recess of the London conference, the military governors established a working party to negotiate the outstanding points of difference. But it soon became apparent, as the representatives of the three nations attempted to settle the distribution of powers and the nature of the institutions which the central and Land governments were to possess, that there was still a gulf between the American and British conceptions, on the one hand, and the French on the other. The French continued to think in terms of a loose confederation and insisted upon placing many detailed restrictions on the future central government which the other Allies felt they could not accept. The military governors could report little progress to the London conference.

While the discussions in Berlin were taking place, an event occurred which had a decisive influence on the French point of view, at least in Paris, and, consequently, on the course of the further deliberations in London. On March 20, the Soviet military governor withdrew from the Allied Control Council in Berlin, and quadripartite government in Germany came to a stop. The French realized that the United States and British governments would now be impatient to establish a government in Western Germany and would proceed, with or without French participation. In General Clay's words:

They [the French] knew that we were ready to proceed in the three zones, but otherwise were determined to go ahead in two. We were no longer willing to have a political and economic void in Central Europe, which would interfere with the recovery of the European countries participating in the Marshall Plan.[21]

The French now had to choose between carrying on with the project of western unification, on which they would inevitably have to make wide concessions to the majority views of their Anglo-American partners, or standing aside in helpless disapproval while the Americans and British set the pattern for future developments in Western Germany. At the renewed discussions in London in April they did not immediately give way. They again called for a national legislature elected by the Landtage of the Länder; they opposed any power of taxation for the central government; they wanted to exclude the central government entirely from any competence in the police field, and so on.

In the meantime, however, shortly after the Soviet withdrawal from the Control Council, M. Couve de Murville of the French delegation had seen General Clay in Berlin, and together they had drawn up the draft of an agreement in which only the most general guidance was to be provided the German constituent assembly:

> The constituent assembly . . . will draft a democratic constitution which will establish a federal type governmental structure for the participating states which will protect the rights of the participating states and which will contain guarantees of individual rights and freedoms.[22]

General Clay explains that he advocated this new approach in order to avoid further argument about "details which might not necessarily develop in the German draft."

> We should concentrate on establishing the broad principles to be given the German assembly for its guidance and also the principles which would be given to the military governors to guide them in determining whether the constitution conformed to these broad conditions.[23]

The agreements eventually reached by the London conference on the political organization of Western Germany did in fact take this form. The first ("Document I," as it was subsequently called) simply authorized the ministers-president of the Western German Länder to call a constituent assembly to "draft a democratic constitution which will establish for the participating states a governmental structure of federal type which is best adapted to the eventual re-establishment of German unity at present disrupted and which will protect the rights of the participating states, provide adequate central authority, and contain guarantees of individual rights and freedoms." The second ("Document II") requested the ministers-president to examine and make recommendations concerning the revision of the boundaries of the Länder. The third ("Document III") set out in general terms the powers which the Allied governments would reserve to themselves during the occupation period.

The fourth was the key agreement.* It set out the criteria which were to guide the military governors in determining whether the Germans had produced an acceptable constitution. The London conference was able to agree on the terms of this instruction, partly as the result of substantial concessions made by the French to the American and British views, and partly by omitting or postponing for future settlement points on which the delegations could not agree. For instance, provision of a bicameral legislature in which one of the houses should represent the individual states was stipulated, but nothing was said of the other chamber—either whom it should represent or how it should be elected. As for the legislative competencies of the federation and the Länder, the fields were listed in which the central government should not *in any case* be permitted to exercise power, i.e., education, cultural and religious affairs, and local government; no others were mentioned except public health and welfare, concerning which certain conditions were made, and the exercise of police powers, which was left to be settled by the military governors in Germany. On finance, the French gave way to the Anglo-American view. The federation, it was conceded, could raise revenue for purposes "for which it is responsible" and set rates on taxes "for which uniformity is essential." A federal administration, also, was to be permitted, but to be limited to fields in which state implementation was "impracticable." But these general phrases, however satisfactory they may have been to the diplomats in London, were to lead to trouble in Germany.

Read independently of the background of discussions in London, these documents conveyed the impression that a very wide latitude

* The text of this agreement (see Appendix B) was given to the Germans much later than the other three, in the form of an Aide Memoire dated November 22, 1948.

had been left to the German constituent assembly to draft its constitution as it thought fit. They were so interpreted by the Germans.

3. RECEPTION OF THE DECISIONS IN GERMANY

The agreements of the London conference were promptly approved by the American and British governments. In the French National Assembly they were received with hostility, particularly the agreement on the Ruhr. The French government had originally asked for separation of the Ruhr from Germany.[24] Its representatives had taken to London what they regarded as a compromise plan calling for full international control of the Ruhr industries, including their management. But they had won agreement only on international control of the allocation of Ruhr products—coal, coke, and steel—between domestic consumption and export, and on international supervision of trade practices in the Ruhr. Management of the industries was to remain in German hands. However, by making it known that it had reserved the right to reopen the Ruhr agreement, the French government on July 18 finally secured the National Assembly's approval of the London decisions by a majority of six. As to the proposed scope and form of the future Western German government, there was strong opposition, not only in the French Assembly, but also, as had already appeared during the London and Berlin talks, within the government itself and, above all, within the French military government in Germany. As the three military governors in Germany in the succeeding months attempted to reach agreement on an occupation statute, on a constitution, and on the economic and financial problems of the trizonal area, General Koenig and his staff offered determined and persistent opposition to courses of action to which both General Clay and General Robertson believed the French had committed themselves in principle at the London conference. General Clay writes:

. . . I believed the French position to be inconsistent with the London agreements. Although M. Schuman had endorsed this program and promised to support it, I felt that the French administration in Germany did not share his views and was determined to delay, if not to thwart, the establishment of Western German government.[25]

The military governors met the ministers-president of the Western German Länder on July 1 to inform them of the London decisions. German political leaders and the press gave them a mixed reception. To the Germans, the advantages of improved economic prospects which the promise of American aid on a large scale afforded and an increased share in the management of their own affairs were offset by the thought that establishment of a Western German government must confirm the division of Germany and indefinitely defer a peace settlement for all of Germany. The leaders of both the major Western German political parties, the Christian Democrats and the Social Democrats, were reported to be unwilling to identify themselves with any step which would set the seal on a partitioning of Germany.[26] The powers which the occupation governments proposed to reserve to themselves in an occupation statute caused much dissatisfaction. Dr. Reinhold Maier, the minister-president of Württemberg-Baden, told the Landtag on July 7:

> We would rather continue without legal status, dangerous though that may be, than accept a statute of this kind, the provisions of which might perpetuate themselves as a permanent evil. . . . We expected the basic rights of the Germans in relation to the occupying powers to be laid down. The Military Governors have turned the tables on us and formulated only the basic rights of the occupying powers toward the Germans.[27]

At this stage, before the full effect of Western countermeasures had become apparent, the Soviet blockade of Berlin was making its greatest impact on the Western German mind. In the atmosphere of anxiety which the blockade had produced in Western Germany, apprehension readily arose as to the provocation the Soviet Union might take if the establishment of a Western German government went ahead. Increasing publicity was given in the German press to a solution less ambitious than that agreed upon in London, by which a central German administration on the model of the bizonal administration would be established, acting under an administrative statute to be drawn up by representatives of the Landtage.[28]

The ministers-president conferred at Koblenz from July 8–10 on the documents they had been given by the military governors. On July 10 they forwarded their comments and counterproposals to the military governors. In these, while the ministers-president agreed that "the critical difficulties faced by the German people could best be overcome only if they were enabled to administer their affairs on the broadest territorial basis possible," they insisted that any appearance of conferring the character of a state on the governmental structure to be created must be avoided. They stipulated specifically that the calling of a German constituent assembly and the drafting of a German constitution should be deferred until the conditions for an all-German government existed and German sovereignty had been restored. They were, however, prepared to recommend that the Landtage of the three zones should elect a representative body (a "parliamentary council") whose task it would be to draft a "*Grundgesetz*," or "basic law," for the unified administration of the Western occupation zones. Ratification of such a basic law by a popular referendum was rejected as conferring an importance on it which should be reserved only for the constitution ultimately to be adopted.[29]

Allied officials in Germany, particularly the Americans, did not conceal their disappointment with this response. The German authorities, in rejecting "the character of a state" for Western Germany, were thought to be seeking the recovery of political power without responsibility for its exercise.[30] Their position was described as inconsistent with past German demands for a larger share in control of their affairs.[31] General Clay was reported as having told the ministers-president of the Länder of the American zone "at the frostiest conference of the last twelve months" that he "felt deserted in his struggle with the Russians for Berlin and for the development of Western Germany."[32]

When the military governors met on July 15 to consider the reply of the ministers-president, General Koenig expressed sympathy with their position. The London decisions, he believed, could be modified to take account of the apparent German preference for a less ambitious undertaking. If the Allies would adopt an occupation statute fixing in definite terms the powers they intended to reserve to themselves, it should then be possible to determine what functions would be left to the Germans and what kind of political organization they should have.

General Clay and General Robertson insisted that the Germans could and should be persuaded to accept the London decisions. The international situation, they considered, made it imperative that the Western Allies should put their plans into effect as rapidly as possible. To reopen the London decisions meant delay, and to delay would be a fatal mistake. If it were only the term "constitution" to which the ministers-president objected, General Robertson suggested that it should not be difficult to find another.

General Koenig doubted that the ministers-president were objecting merely to terminology. They wanted to avoid adopting a constitution, he said, and would not be satisfied to evade the difficulty by a change of name—by "calling a jacket a pair of trousers." Both of his colleagues expressed dismay at General Koenig's apparent readiness to depart from the London agreements. General Clay said that these agreements had to be regarded as a whole—that departures could not be made at one point without making them elsewhere. He reminded General Koenig that the Ruhr agreement was a part of this whole.

When the military governors met the ministers-president on July 20 and again on July 26, it was made clear to them that they must either accept the London decisions substantially as they stood or face the prospect of an indefinite delay in the return of authority to German hands.

We told them [General Clay writes] that the London decisions were governmental and that marked deviations might require further governmental consideration which would delay the whole program, and that they would have to accept responsibility for failure to return government to German hands promptly.[33]

Confronted with this prospect, the ministers-president speedily modified their position. Herr Max Brauer, the Bürgermeister of Hamburg, wanted the military governors to know that

the attitude of the Ministers-President as a whole to the London decisions was fundamentally positive. . . . In his opinion, if a solution to the outstanding problems was not reached quickly, there was a risk that the application of the Marshall plan and the economic recovery made by Germany since currency reform would be jeopardized. . . . The remaining divergencies concerned only the methods to be adopted and not the objects in view. The Ministers-President would not insist on these procedural points if there were a risk of jeopardizing the whole. . . . The Ministers-President, when translating the word "Grundgesetz" into English had chosen the term "basic law." They felt, however, that a more adequate translation would be "basic constitutional law." The term "Grundgesetz" had been chosen only in order to avoid aggravating the conflict with the East and the struggle which the Ministers-President were obliged to carry on against the propaganda of the SED* and the other parties of the Eastern zone. This struggle would be made easier if the terms chosen by the Ministers-President could be accepted by the Military Governors.[34]

The ministers-president had at first objected to the ratification of a basic law by popular referendum as conferring on it a status which they wished to withhold from it. They now raised the further objection that a popular referendum under the conditions then prevailing in Western Germany would offer the Communists the opportunity they had been seeking. Herr Brauer drew attention to the agitation for a national referendum, which the SED had already set on foot throughout Germany. Herr Arnold, the minister-president of North Rhine-Westphalia, said that if a referendum were held, the Communists could be expected to do their utmost to represent the basic law not as a German enactment, but as a statute imposed by the Allied powers.[35] If, as the result of such a campaign, a basic law were to be rejected, it would be also a repudiation of the London decisions—a development which would be a catastrophe not only for Germany but for the whole of Europe.

The military governors had already agreed to accept "parliamentary council" as the designation for the constituent assembly. Now that the ministers-president had made it clear that the basic law would be a constitution in all but name, they accepted "Basic Law (Provisional Constitution)" as the designation for this document. The new light in which the arguments of the ministers-president had placed a popular referendum on the Basic Law had also impressed the military governors, and they agreed to reopen this question with their governments.

With these understandings, the way was now clear for the ministers-president to arrange the election of the delegates to the Parliamentary Council. The British and American estimate of the considerations that would weigh most with the ministers-president had proved to be correct.

4. THE CHIEMSEE CONFERENCE

On July 25, the day before they reached their final understanding with the military governors, the ministers-president had already

---

* The Socialist Unity party, an alliance between Socialists and Communists fostered by the Soviet administration in the Eastern zone.

agreed among themselves to convene a committee of experts on constitutional law, whose task it would be to produce guiding principles for the drafting of the proposed Basic Law which could be used by the Parliamentary Council to facilitate its work when it convened on September 1. A delegate with full power of decision was appointed from each of the Länder and from Western Berlin.

The committee met at Herrenchiemsee on August 10. Its accomplishments must be unique in the history of constitutional conventions. A main committee and three subcommittees in forty-six sittings in two weeks produced not merely "guiding principles" for a basic law, but the complete draft of a constitution, together with an extensive analytical report of the considerations governing the committee's proposals and a further section of commentary on individual articles of the draft.[36] The basic nature of the work done at Chiemsee in those thirteen days is reflected in the extent to which the provisions of the "Chiemsee draft" have survived in the Basic Law. The general structure and order of the Basic Law follow the Chiemsee draft. The primary emphasis on human rights and the obligations of the Federal Republic under international law derive from the Chiemsee draft. It also foreshadows the Basic Law in avoiding constitutional innovation on any large scale. The new constitutions of the Länder and the Weimar constitution were taken as models, and their provisions, although freely adapted, are discernible in the final document. The preoccupation of the Parliamentary Council with supposed defects in the Weimar constitution already existed at Chiemsee. Even the disagreements of the Chiemsee experts concerned those provisions which later were to be the most contested in the Parliamentary Council: the form and powers of a second chamber, the division of powers between the federation and Länder, and the financial powers.

5. ORGANIZATION OF THE PARLIAMENTARY COUNCIL

The first step taken by the ministers-president after their conference with the military governors on July 26 was to agree upon the terms of a model law for the election of the Parliamentary Council, to be adopted by the Landtage of the Länder. This provided that each Landtag would elect to the Parliamentary Council a deputy for every 750,000 of the Land's population, with an additional delegate for any remainder of more than 200,000.

The delegations of the various Länder were chosen during the month of August. The political parties were represented in each in numbers proportionate to their strength in the Landtage. Altogether sixty-five were elected, with five non-voting representatives from Western Berlin. The nearly equal popular support which the two major parties, the Christian Democratic/Christian Social Union (CDU/CSU)* and the Social Democrats (SPD), had received from the electorate of Western Germany in the Land elections of 1946 and 1947 was reflected in the return of CDU/CSU and SPD delegations of exactly equal numbers, each having twenty-seven deputies from the Western Länder. The Free Democrats (FDP) were represented by five, and the German party (DP), the Center party (Z), and the Communist party (KPD) by two each. Of the five non-voting deputies from West Berlin, three were Social Democrats, one a Christian Democrat, and one a Free Democrat. Seventeen of the deputies were from North Rhine-Westphalia, thirteen from Bavaria, nine from Lower Saxony, six from Hesse, five from Württemberg-Baden, four from Rhineland-Palatinate, four from Schleswig-Holstein, two from Baden, two from Hamburg, two from Württemburg-Hohenzollern, and one from Bremen.

The Parliamentary Council convened at three o'clock in the afternoon of September 1 in the Pädagogische Akademie in Bonn. The deputies were addressed by the Hessian minister-president, Herr Christian Stock, the chairman of the conference of ministers-president. He told them:

We meet today for the first time in the new era of German history since the capitulation, not by *Diktat*, but as the result of agreements which have been reached between the military governors and the ministers-president.

The economic council was established by a military proclamation of two of the occupation powers. The Parliamentary Council has been formed and has been called together by German decision.

The Council elected Dr. Konrad Adenauer,† the Christian Democratic leader, as president, Herr Adolf Schönfelder (SPD), first

---

* The Western German political parties are identified and described in chap. iv.

† For brief biographies of the leading members of the Parliamentary Council, see Appendix C.

vice-president, and Dr. Hermann Schäfer (FDP), second vice-president. These, together with the four secretaries—Frau Dr. Helene Weber (CDU), Herr Christian Stock (SPD), Dr. Max Becker (FDP), and Frau Helene Wessel (Z)—composed the *Präsidium*. To assist the president with the conduct of the Council's business, a council of elders was formed, consisting of the president, the two vice-presidents, and ten representatives of the party factions, including the chairman of each faction.

The formal organization of the Parliamentary Council, in addition to the *Präsidium* and the council of elders, included a main committee and a group of special committees. The main committee, whose province it was to review the work of the special committees and to make major political decisions, was composed of twenty-one members—eight from the CDU/CSU, eight from the SPD, two from the FDP, and one each from the DP, Z, and KPD. The membership of the major parties in the special committees was also of equal strength, five each in the committees with twelve members and four each in those with ten. Two members from the smaller party factions were also included in each of these committees. Special committees were established for "basic rights" (twelve members); "distribution of powers" (ten members); "finance" (ten members); "governmental organization" (twelve members); "constitutional court and judiciary" (ten members); "Occupation Statute" (twelve members); and "electoral questions" (ten members). A committee on rules of procedure consisted of eleven members, three each from the CDU/CSU and SPD, one each from the FDP, DP, KPD, and Z, and one member of the *Präsidium*.

In addition to these committees, three *ad hoc* committees were established during the course of the negotiations. At the beginning of November, the council of elders formed a three-man committee to review the texts of the successive drafts of the Basic Law for editorial corrections. However, the influence of this committee, composed of three men with fertile minds and a spirit of initiative—Dr. Thomas Dehler (FDP), Herr Georg-August Zinn (SPD), and Dr. Heinrich von Brentano (CDU)—was much greater than that of an ordinary editorial body. They did not confine themselves to questions of style and uniformity of presentation, but put forward a number of substantive amendments of their own. Over the objections of the special committees, many of these were accepted by the main committee.

To further a settlement of the outstanding points of disagreement between the political parties which remained after the second reading of the Basic Law in the main committee in December, an interparty committee, composed of two CDU/CSU members, two SPD members and one FDP member, known as the "committee of five," was established. Most of the final compromise agreements between the parties were negotiated in this committee. After the Allies had made known their objections to the Basic Law in early March, 1949, this interparty committee of five was increased to seven, with a representative each from the German party and the Center, to consider what changes in the provisions of the Basic Law could be made to meet the Allied point of view.

There were three phases in the negotiations on the Basic Law and the electoral law. From the middle of September to the middle of November, the special committees held most of their sittings and completed a first revision of the Chiemsee draft. From the middle of November to the middle of December, the main committee completed its first reading of the draft Basic Law. Further sittings of some of the special committees followed. The second reading in the main committee, with a recess for Christmas, lasted from December 15 to January 20. The committee of five then negotiated compromises on the outstanding points of disagreement, which enabled the main committee to complete its third reading between February 8 and 10 and to turn to consideration of the electoral law which the Council adopted in plenary session on February 24.

The second phase began on March 2 when the military governors sent their objections to the third reading draft of the Basic Law to the Parliamentary Council and informed the Council that it had no competence to adopt an electoral law. German counterproposals were presented to the military governors and rejected. There followed a series of party, interparty and German-Allied meetings, without further progress toward agreement in March. The foreign ministers conferred in Washington early in April and agreed upon certain concessions which enabled the deadlock in Germany to be resolved. A final settlement of differences over the Basic Law was reached between the military governors and the Parliamentary Council representatives on April 25.

In the last phase, after April 25, the final readings of the Basic Law in the main committee and plenum of the Parliamentary Council took place. The text was then submitted for and received the approval of the military governors on May 12. The Parliamentary Council, on this occasion with Allied authorization, adopted an electoral law for the second time on May 10. Differences over this law were finally resolved early in August.

6. THE OCCUPATION STATUTE

The Occupation Statute, in which the three Western Allied governments set out the powers they intended to reserve to themselves after the establishment of the Federal Republic, had little effect on the deliberations over the Basic Law. At first it had been thought that the two statutes would to some extent be complementary, the provisions of the Basic Law taking into account those of the Occupation Statute. The military governors had promised the ministers-president that the Parliamentary Council would be consulted and kept informed of progress on the drafting of the Occupation Statute, which was to proceed concurrently with the drafting of the Basic Law. As it turned out, the two documents took form quite independently of each other. The Allied governments did not succeed in agreeing upon the terms of the Occupation Statute until many weeks after the Parliamentary Council had completed its third reading of the Basic Law. The military governors, in fact, saw the Parliamentary Council representatives only once (in December, 1948) concerning the Occupation Statute, and then only to tell them that the Allied governments could add nothing to what they had already said in Document III.

On the German side, there was at first, particularly among the Social Democrats, a disposition to keep the Basic Law short and confine its scope only to the provisions essential for a provisional government acting under occupation control. But the Chiemsee experts had already laid the groundwork for a comprehensive constitutional structure and, for good measure, had added in their report:

The conference is unanimously of the opinion that such a fragmentary state should be provided with all institutions and should be allowed a complete legislative and executive branch for internal affairs and the comprehensive exercise of judicial power. The fragmentary character of the state should find expression less in the shaping of the individual institutions than in the limitations placed upon them in practice by external constraint. The newly created institutions can and should be so formed that when the present sphere of freedom of action is broadened, they would be fully able to take advantage of it at once. . . .[37]

The German impulse to be thorough in all things soon took hold in the Parliamentary Council, and in its first draft the Basic Law was already, except in name, a complete constitution. Hence, apart from certain transitional provisions, including those covering occupation costs, the Basic Law reflects the existence of an occupation statute and of occupation powers only in references to the German areas not incorporated in the Federal Republic, and in the omission of any provision for the defense of the federal territory.* In all other respects, the Basic Law reads as though occupation powers had never existed.

Since the Occupation Statute had little influence on the development of the Basic Law, only a brief account of it will be given here.[38] In any case, the real interest of the Statute lies not in its formal provisions, but in the manner in which it was applied during the first three years of relations between the Allied high commission and the government of the Federal Republic. In Document III the Germans were told that the military governors would grant them legislative, executive, and judicial competence, reserving to themselves only the powers "necessary to ensure the fulfillment of the basic purposes of the occupation," such powers to include: the conduct of foreign relations; the exercise of control over foreign trade, the Ruhr, reparations, the level of industry, decartelization, disarmament, demilitarization, scientific research; the protection of the prestige and security of the occupation forces and the satisfaction of their requirements within defined limits to be agreed upon by the military governors; the enforcement of the observance of the federal and Land constitutions and the approval of amendments to these constitutions, and of laws and regulations emanating from the Ger-

* Before amendment.

man authorities. The resumption of full power of government by the military governors was provided for in the event of an emergency threatening security, or if required to secure compliance with the federal or Land constitutions or the Occupation Statute.

After the London conference, the military governors were unable to agree on the text of a statute incorporating these provisions. The French wanted to spell out the reserved powers in greater detail than the Americans and British could accept. The latter, on the other hand, against French wishes, wanted to give the German authorities power to legislate concurrently with the Allies in the reserved fields. The French held that occupation costs should be paid by the governments of the Länder, whereas the Americans and British insisted that they be charged to the federal budget. These disagreements were reported by the military governors to their governments, which did not succeed in reaching final agreement on the text of a statute until the meeting of the foreign ministers in Washington in April, 1949.

The military governors, at their July meetings with the ministers-president, had invited them to submit their observations on the provisions in Document III and had promised to keep them informed of developments in the drafting of the Occupation Statute. The military governors, however, were unable to keep this promise. Progress was so slow and the Allied positions were so far apart that the military governors decided that an interim report to the German representatives would lead only to misunderstanding.

To the Germans, naturally, the reservation of any occupation powers, with the possible exception of those relating to the immediate need for defense of Western German territory, was unwelcome. Their views were made known in comments submitted by the ministers-president on Document III, and later in a resolution adopted by the Parliamentary Council on December 10.

The ministers-president asked[39] that the exercise of the reserved powers should be limited strictly to measures for the accomplishment of the occupation objectives, which they defined as guaranteeing the security of the occupation forces, the maintenance of a democratic order in Germany, the demilitarization of Germany, and the fulfilment of German obligations abroad. They proposed direct exercise of power by the Allied authorities only in foreign affairs. In other fields (foreign trade, the Ruhr, reparations, etc.), they requested that Allied activity should be confined to the supervision of German agencies. The Allies should intervene in German legislation, the ministers-president submitted, only when the accomplishment of their objectives was endangered. The jurisdiction of the occupation courts, they proposed, should be confined to members of the occupation forces and to offenses against the security or property of the occupation powers or personnel. Lawsuits between members of the occupation forces and German citizens were to be dealt with in mixed German-Allied courts. Occupation costs and requirements would be determined jointly by the military governors for the entire federal territory on an annual basis, with due regard to the capacity of the German economy to bear this burden. They would be met as a charge on the federal budget.

The Parliamentary Council's resolution sought further curtailment of occupation controls. It reduced the list of "occupation objectives" for which reserved powers might be exercised to the security of the occupation forces, the security of Western Germany, and the promotion of democratic institutions. The Council asked for the freeing of German foreign trade from Allied supervision. Implementing provisions for the Occupation Statute, it was proposed, should be prepared by a joint Allied-German commission. The extension of the jurisdiction of German civil law courts to members of the occupation forces was stipulated, with the competence of occupation courts to be confined to criminal offenses committed by members of the occupation forces and to offenses against the security of the occupation forces or infractions of occupation law committed by Germans or other foreigners. Emergency powers were to be taken by the occupation authorities only in the event that the German authorities should prove unable to act, and then only for a limited period.

The three Western governments made few concessions to the German views in the text of the Occupation Statute finally approved. In all material points it followed the agreement already reached in London. It did, however, provide for German legislation in reserved fields after due notification by the federal government to the occupation authorities. The governments expressed their "hope and expectation that they will not have to take action in fields other than those specifically reserved." The occupation authorities were directed not to disapprove German legislation unless, in their opinion, it was "inconsistent with the Basic Law, a Land constitution, legislation or other directives of the occupation authorities themselves, or the provisions of this instrument, or unless it constitutes a grave threat to the basic purposes of the occupation."

CHAPTER II

THE FEDERAL STRUCTURE
OF THE BASIC LAW

> While federalism all over the world implies the uniting of
> what was separated, it is apparently intended to introduce
> federalism in our case to separate what had already been
> united.
>
> CARLO SCHMID

1. FEDERALISM IN GERMANY AND THE UNITED STATES

Although the German and American constitutional traditions are commonly designated as "federal," they differ in nearly every essential characteristic. This has led foreign observers, particularly those with experience of the American and British Commonwealth systems, to doubt that the Germans have now or have ever had a form of government which could properly be called "federal."[1] It also led to critical misunderstandings between the Parliamentary Council and American occupation officials over the Basic Law, each side tending to interpret the London instruction to "establish a governmental structure of federal type" in terms of its own tradition. The Parliamentary Council's approach to this task and its objections to the changes which the Allied governments wished to impose may be better understood, therefore, if they are viewed in perspective with what the Germans—and, for purposes of comparison and contrast, the Americans—consider a federal structure of government to be.

In the United States, the relation between the federation and the states is one of complete duality: dual sovereignty of the people as citizens of a state and of the federation; dual legislative, administrative, and judicial functions, with a dual legislative, administrative, and judicial apparatus of government—each center of government acting directly on persons and property within its territorial limits. The original pattern of the federation's "enumerated" powers and

27

the states' "residual" powers, although modified in the course of
time by judicial interpretation, still survives. This system has been
described as "vertical" federalism.[2]

Federalism in Germany, to the extent that it can be epitomized, is
functional or "horizontal." Legislative and policy-making power has
been concentrated at the center, with the officials of the state governments participating directly in the exercise of that power. The
states have retained legislative autonomy only in fields where—in
Germany—local differences of custom and outlook are of critical
importance: education, religion, cultural affairs, and local government. On the other hand, administration and the execution and enforcement of laws (both of the federation and of the states) have
largely been left in the hands of the state governments. Although
the Reich's (or the federation's) share of powers has greatly increased and a federal bureaucracy has since been established, the
basic federal pattern laid down in the Reich Constitution of 1871
has survived.[3] Hence, when the question of altering the federal balance arises in the United States, the American immediately thinks of
adding to or subtracting from the fields in which the federation has
legislative competence. The federation's power (or lack of it) to
implement and to enforce legislation and to finance its activities follows automatically. When the question arises in Germany, the German immediately thinks of increasing or reducing the powers of the
Bundesrat, or the number of federal field administrative agencies
permitted in the Länder, or the taxes which the federation is empowered to collect.

But even in their common points, there are differences between
the two systems—one might almost say differences of quality or of
historical "feel": those disparities which strike one instantly when
the newer states of the American Far West, even to their inhabitants
little more than geographical expressions, are contrasted with those
centers of ancient tribal and cultural affinity, the south German
Länder; when that proud banner of a word "the Union" is coupled
with "*das Reich,*" with its more subtle and ambiguous overtones of
old glory and old humiliation; when the United States Senate, whose
greatest names may be better known than those of cabinet members
and governors of states, is compared with the legislative workshop

manned by industrious and cheerfully anonymous civil servants from the Länder, the German Bundesrat.

A nation spanning a vast continent cannot be effectively governed except by combining with a central government multiple regional centers of government equipped and empowered to act on their own responsibility in a wide range of matters. The American form of federalism has endured because it has responded, however imperfectly, to this practical necessity. The need of reconciling a deeply rooted particularism in the constituent units with the national interest has played but little part in its history. In the name of "states' rights," to be sure, great social and economic issues have been contested. But the interests involved in these controversies have invariably extended far beyond the bounds of one state or locality. They were in fact conflicts on a national scale between economic and social classes and broad regional interests, which were transformed into a struggle over "states' rights" as soon as one set of partisans perceived that their opponents had mustered the votes to control the federal government. But hostility to a particular policy or measure—the establishment of a national bank, the prohibition of chattel labor in the Western territories, government support for railroad interests, or the adoption of a uniform national code of "fair employment" practices—was the true ground of feeling, not devotion to "states' rights." The cry on behalf of "states' rights" has been raised against their opponents at different times by all the parties—radicals and conservatives alike—and by all the interests, by big business and little business, by farmers and workmen, and in the North, the South, the East, and the West.

In the first years of the Republic, to be sure, owing to their differing colonial origins, social composition, and economies and to competitive interest in the frontier, a particularistic spirit was abroad in the original states. Nevertheless, they did join voluntarily to revise the weak Articles of Confederation, and subordinated themselves to a constitution providing stronger central government. As the century passed and new territories to the West were opened and settled and, in due course, advanced to statehood, the factors (barring the South's "peculiar institution") making for a common life and a common outlook in the states were always in the ascendancy. The new states established their governments on a common model, extending even to the architecture of their capitol buildings. Local pride and patriotism have always existed, but these feelings are more often attached to cities and towns and regions than to a state. Even the fabled pride of the Texan is but a pale shadow of the tenacious loyalty to homeland of the Bavarian, the Swabian, or the citizens of the Hanseatic and Rhineland cities.

The authors of the United States constitution were constructing a system of government on a continent largely unsettled except for its eastern seaboard by people of European stock, with but few ties and traditions, and these mainly of common origin. They were free to experiment, to introduce innovations, to order and adjust matters very much according to their own notions. The novel federal institutions that evolved were consciously elaborated not only because they were thought most suitable to the conditions which existed on the North American continent, but also because they were considered to be the most conducive to liberty: they provided the means of handling common affairs in common, while leaving to the states and localities the maximum freedom for self-government. Federalism, James Madison wrote, was "the best guardian . . . of the liberty, safety and the happiness of man . . . the last hope of true liberty on the face of the earth." This notion that there is somehow a direct connection between federal institutions and democratic liberty has become a fixture of the American ideology. It is in keeping with the American tendency to value freedom less as the condition of cultural variety and intellectual non-conformity than of individual and corporate self-reliance, of the spirit of enterprise, "get-up-and-go," and standing on one's own feet. The states, and under them the counties and municipalities, are equipped with the powers and the apparatus of government to enable them to look after themselves, and they are expected to do so.

Federal institutions developed in modern Germany in very different circumstances. There was no *tabula rasa*, but rather a multiplicity of kingdoms, principalities, and duchies. Although consolidation*

* Toward the end of the Holy Roman Empire, there had been 1,700 territorial units—kingdoms, archduchies, duchies, principalities, archbishoprics, bishoprics, and free cities—independent of each other, of which 300 could be classed in some sense as "states." Consolidation was accelerated by the Napoleonic Empire. The Regensburg Commission of 1803 eliminated more than 100. The Congress of

proceeded through the century and a quarter after the Congress of Vienna, the variation in the size of the states was always such as to make a balanced federal structure impossible. The twenty-five states of the Bismarckian Empire, including three free cities, ranged from Prussia with 24.7 million inhabitants and an area of 134,616 English square miles to Schaumberg-Lippe with 32,000 inhabitants and an area of 131 square miles. Most of the provinces of Prussia were larger than most of the other states of the Empire. By the time of Weimar, Prussia, with nearly 40 million inhabitants, included three-fifths of the national population, Bavaria and Saxony another fifth, and the other fourteen states made up the remaining fifth. Nor were the territories of the German states contiguous. Owing to the accidents of dynastic inheritance, parcels of the territories of the states were separated from each other. At the end of the Weimar period, it was estimated (no one in Germany knew the exact position) that two hundred such enclaves still existed.

The German Confederation (1815–66), an improvisation of the Congress of Vienna to fill the political void left by the disappearance of the Napoleonic Empire, was devised to reinstate and confirm the German princes in their powers and possessions. Separate foreign policies, armies, police, currencies, and customs barriers were retained by the states. The Federal Diet, meeting under the presidency of Austria, was in reality an assembly of diplomats representing sovereign princes. The powers of the Confederation, designed mainly for defense, were weak and used mostly to suppress political movements feared by the princes. The nationalist and liberal movements in Germany became identified as an outcome of this arrangement. German liberals and radicals embraced the national cause, because they saw the particularism of the German states with their feudal remnants standing in the way not only of German national unification, but of liberal reforms. Hence, too, liberal thought in Germany has held federalism in little esteem, at most tolerating it as a temporary expedient.

As a form of government valued for itself, federalism, in the

---

Vienna in 1815 had to deal with 39 German states. Bismarck united 25 in the German Empire. The Weimar Republic, beginning with the same 25, reduced the number to 17 by combinations. The National Socialist regime eliminated two more.

course of the century after 1848, came to be associated with its principal advocates—south German particularists, the Greater Germany "diehards," Rhineland separatists—and hence, after the founding of the Reich, was viewed by the national parties with suspicion: by the Liberals as inimical to the interests of the unified Reich they had won, by the Conservatives as inimical to the interests of Prussia, and, later, by the Social Democrats as inimical to their socialist objectives. Characteristically, in the United States the term "federalist" is taken to mean one who wishes to strengthen the central power; in Germany it is applied to one who wishes to weaken it.

However, it was Bismarck, wielding the military power of Prussia—not the Liberals—who was to deal with "petty particularism" and lay the foundation for the unification that was so fateful for the future. His Junker supporters had little sympathy for the nationalist aspirations of the Liberals—much less for the "Greater Germany" demanded by the radicals, romantic Conservatives, and the Catholics. Their sole concern was to secure the position of Prussia, the merging of which into a liberal national German state they saw as a threat not only to Prussian power, but to their class and its interests.* Bismarck's first allegiance, equally, was to Prussia, but he came in time to see that Prussia's ambitions, or at any rate his ambitions for Prussia, could be realized only in conjunction with a solution for the problem of Germany as a whole. If unification had to come, then it must come about under Prussian leadership. "The two ends coincide," he said, "the leadership of Prussia from the Prussian standpoint" and "the unification of Germany from the national standpoint."⁴ The wars with Austria (1866) and France (1871) established the requisite conditions for the exercise of this leadership. The German states north of the Main were brought into line after 1866, the remainder in 1871.

In essence, what happened in 1866 and 1871 was that the German

---

* Moritz von Blanckenburg, after a visit to Bismarck at Versailles at the end of 1870, wrote that he was "terrified by the rash entry of Hesse, Württemberg and Baden into the Confederacy" and looked upon it "as a settled matter that the majority of the new Reichstag must become National Liberal, since it is impossible to obtain other elements from such quarters. The aim of all Liberals remains to economize in military matters. Yes, an inner necessity drives them; they are bound to devote all their efforts to disarming the forces after the peace" (F. Darmstädter, *Bismarck and the Creation of the Second Reich* [London: Methuen, 1948], p. 386).

states were federated with Prussia, not Prussia with the states. The popular movement for unification was strong throughout the German states, and the Prussian initiative won much support from it. But Prussian power was the effective agent of unification, and Bismarck did not hesitate to use it against recalcitrant states. He preferred, however, to enlist the support of the German princes for the Reich and improvised a federal structure designed to transfer effective power to the center, hence into Prussian hands, while disturbing the apparatus of government in the states as little as possible. Legislative powers over a wide range of matters—wider by far than in the American federal system—were vested in the Reich. These, together with imperial prerogatives in foreign and military affairs, provided the tools for the work of consolidating the Reich under Prussian leadership.

Federal bodies, the Bundesrat and the Reichstag, exercised the legislative power. The sovereignty of the Reich was vested in the Bundesrat, the federal council of princes or their representatives—ostensibly the principal organ of Reich government. Not only was the Bundesrat's approval required for Reich legislation, but it had the power of initiating legislation and of deciding what legislation should be considered by the Reichstag, as well as the responsibility for supervising the whole administration of Reich legislation. It was both a legislative and an executive council. In practice, Prussia dominated this body. She had seventeen of fifty-eight votes and could count upon the votes of certain of the smaller states who were virtually her dependencies. The Prussian prime minister, in the person of the Reich chancellor, presided ex officio as chairman of the Bundesrat, and, as Prussia's foreign minister, cast Prussia's votes. Prussia could veto any move to alter these arrangements, for fourteen negative votes in the Bundesrat sufficed to kill any constitutional amendment. The Bundesrat in time came to count for less in his "orchestra of the Reich" than Bismarck had planned. This resulted partly from Bismarck's own practice of negotiating with the major states directly, rather than through the Bundesrat, and partly from the growing importance of the Reichstag, which, although confined by the constitution to a negative role, increasingly asserted itself as the national forum chosen by universal suffrage and representing all the people. It did so by exercising its right to refuse legislation and money in such a way as to compel the chancellor (who was responsible to the emperor and not to the Reichstag) to build temporary majority blocs in the Reichstag to support his policies.

The Bundesrat was of less importance to the states than their monopoly of administration. Outside Berlin, the apparatus of government—and hence the responsibility for administration, including the execution of Reich legislation—was almost entirely in their hands. Except for the federal postal service and the navy, none of the Reich departments of government had field agencies. Finance until the 1914–18 war was also primarily a state responsibility. Even the customs, although the tariff rates were set by the Reich, were collected by the states and remitted to the Reich treasury. Reich income from customs and excise was supplemented by periodic "matricular" contributions from the states, assessed on the basis of population. Law enforcement and administration of justice were entirely state matters. So also was the administration of the army, for, although financed by the Reich, the German army was divided into state contingents—Prussian, Bavarian, Württembergian, and Saxon. In addition to control over their military affairs in peacetime, Bavaria and Württemberg had also been able to win from Bismarck certain other "reserved rights"—to their own postal and telegraph system, to assess and retain the income from their own taxes on beer and spirits, and to certain nominal powers in foreign affairs.

The attitude of Bavaria—largest state of the Reich after Prussia and the most independent—toward the Bismarckian constitution has always been equivocal. On the one hand, Prussia was feared and distrusted. Bismarck's attack on the Catholic church (1871–78) roused a bitter animus in Bavaria, the Rhineland, and other predominantly Catholic areas. The heir to the Bavarian throne, afterward Ludwig III, told the Duke of Connaught "how much he hated Prussia." Yet the Bavarians, because of the absence of Reich agencies within their territory and the special care taken by Bismarck with Bavarian interests, were on the whole content with the federal arrangements of 1871–1918. At any rate, they have wished to return to them ever since.

This horizontal division of responsibility between the Reich and the states for policy and lawmaking on the one hand and administration on the other, besides avoiding the duplication and overlapping of administrative machinery characteristic of other federal systems, suited Germany in another respect. It left German state and local government relatively free of the inhibiting control of central departments to develop administrations of unsurpassed excellence. Even in centralized Prussia, the practice of delegated administration (*Auftragsverwaltung*) allowed the provinces, districts, and cities a high degree of autonomy in the conduct of their affairs.

The efficiency of German administration has often been attributed to a peculiarly German talent. A more plausible explanation would seem to be that men of outstanding ability, repelled by the frustrations of political life in Germany at the national level, have preferred over the years to apply themselves to administration in provincial and local government, industry, and the army, or to scientific analysis and theory in the universities—a legacy of the Bismarckian system that has been at once a boon and a disaster for Germany.

At Weimar, with the abdication of dynastic power throughout the Reich and with Prussia converted by electoral reform from a pro-monarchist Junker to a republican and democratic stronghold, the way seemed open to the Democrats, political heirs of the Liberals of 1848, in alliance with the Social Democrats, to establish the long-deferred liberal national state. Hugo Preuss, a Democrat and the author of the first draft of the Weimar constitution, proposed a governmental system on unitary lines, the states to be reorganized on the basis of social, economic, and cultural ties into units of balanced size whose administration would be subject to central supervision. But the interests of the states were too strong to be thus summarily dealt with. The leaders of the state governments of all parties, including the Social Democrats, protested. A committee of states was established, and as the result of its intervention, modifications in the Preuss plan in favor of the states were made. The trend toward centralization, however, was not reversed. Instead of the senate planned by Preuss, a "council of states," the Reichsrat, was retained as a second legislative chamber, but no longer with the right of absolute veto over either legislation or constitutional amendments. The range of central legislative powers was extended even beyond the broad catalogue of 1871. New subjects were listed. The Reich was given power to legislate so far as "uniformity" might be required or to establish "guiding principles" in fields that were traditionally the concern of the states, such as welfare, education, and religious affairs. The way was opened to the establishment of Reich administration in many new fields: defense, railroads, waterways, veterans' affairs, unemployment—above all, finance. The financial powers were of such scope as to enable the Reich government virtually to reverse the position which had hitherto existed. The Reich now fixed and collected the major taxes and returned a proportionate share to the states.*

Nevertheless, the extent to which the Weimar Republic moved toward centralization can be and has been exaggerated. The administration of justice (except for the Reich supreme court), police, education, and local government continued to be exclusively the responsibility of the Länder. Measures to impose a uniform school system throughout the Reich were repeatedly thrown out by representatives of Land interests in the Reichsrat and the Reichstag. Even though deprived of financial autonomy, the Länder and localities did not lose all independence of action in discharging their own functions, either through a direct refusal of funds or the application of indirect fiscal pressure by the Reich. They were guaranteed a fixed proportion of the proceeds of the income and turnover taxes, the whole income of certain other taxes, and, subject to an upper limit, were allowed to assess and collect the taxes on real estate.

As for Prussia, the Weimar constituent assembly, although unable to agree upon a reorganization of the state units, nevertheless provided in the constitution for a future reorganization by way of constitutional amendment. As time progressed and more Reich administration was introduced, the Prussian "state within a state," duplicating a central governmental apparatus in three-fifths of the territory of the Reich, became increasingly anomalous. This circumstance, reinforced by the inability of the smallest of the Länder to stand on their feet financially, led to the establishment of a governmental reform committee, which from 1928 to 1930 produced a plan of state reorganization calling for the elimination of Prussia, the fusion of Prussian with Reich administration, the transformation of the thirteen Prussian provinces into "new" Länder, and the combination of undersize states and enclaves with these new units.[5] There was to be a difference of status between the "new" Länder and the

* Or Länder, as they were now termed.

"old" (Bavaria, Saxony, Württemberg, and Baden), in that the former were to have their constitutions legislated for them by the Reich—presumably gaining few rights beyond those they possessed as Prussian provinces—while the latter were to retain their own constitutions, boundaries, and existing powers. This plan was accepted by the great majority of Land representatives in the committee, including Prussia's. Bavaria, paradoxically, hastened to the defense of Prussia, seeing in the plan for the dissolution of its old enemy the danger of a future movement to assimilate the position of the "old" Länder to that of the "new." Brüning, the chancellor to whom the commission reported, had participated in its work and approved the result. But he was preoccupied with the economic crisis, and deferred legislation to effect the reorganization. When, at the elections of April, 1932, the Nazi party became the largest in the Prussian Landtag, Brüning returned to the reorganization plan as a means of keeping control of Prussia out of Nazi hands.[6] But he was dismissed before he could act. Von Papen, his successor, dealt with the problem in his own airy fashion, dissolving the Prussian government by emergency decree and replacing it with a Reich government composed of the chancellor and Reich commissioners. When the unconstitutionality of this move had been established and the Social Democratic ministers were reinstated, they took up the constitutional solution for Prussia themselves, pressed the new chancellor, von Schleicher, to introduce a reform bill, and thought even of proposing it themselves in the Reichsrat. Discussions between the Prussian government and von Schleicher were to have been held on the day of the last Weimar chancellor's dismissal.

The differing circumstances in which they came into being, the differing methods by which union was achieved and strengthened, have imparted, then, a different direction to the development of the German and American federal systems. Whereas the American federation came about by agreement between states of recent origin and of similar size and status, in Germany federation was imposed by one state of vastly greater size and power on lesser states with historic rights and traditions. Federalism in North America meets the needs of a country of continental dimensions, combining common government in common matters with maximum state and local self-government. This relative independence and freedom of the localities from the interference of central government has become associated in the American mind with democratic liberties and institutions. The functional federalism of Germany, with the function of "command" or rule concentrated at the center and executive functions left to the states, was designed to reconcile the hegemonic position of the greatest of the German states with the historic particularism of the remainder. It balanced between alternatives equally unacceptable to Prussia: a "truer" federalism, in which she would have stood on an equal footing with the other states, and a fully unitary state, in which she would have been subordinated to the Reich. Liberal and socialist thought reacted against both Bismarckian federalism as the instrument of Prussian conservatism and a "truer" federalism as looking to the restoration of a reactionary particularism. Hence, federalism in Germany has never been identified to any extent with the movement for liberal reform and democratic institutions.

2. THE STATUS OF THE LÄNDER

Is the Basic Law a federal compact between free states? Although the election of the delegates to the Parliamentary Council by the Landtage of the Länder suggests that it might be, other aspects do not fit such a picture—quite apart from the fact that the Allied directive left the Parliamentary Council no choice in the matter.

The eleven western Länder of 1948, if they could be so described at all, were "states" only in the most rudimentary sense. Reduced by Hitler to administrative districts of the Reich government, the Länder in the Western zones had been restored by the occupation governments to something of their former dignity, but after a territorial reorganization which left only three—Bavaria, Bremen, and Hamburg—with any claim to continuity as historic German states. The remainder were new creations, formed in some instances with total disregard for traditional loyalties and cultural and economic ties. Dr. Theodor Heuss brightly described them as *"weniger origi-när als originell."*[7] In the south, in order to provide the French with an area of occupation and yet leave the United States Army ready access to the middle Rhine region and northern seaports, the historic states of Württemberg and Baden were arbitrarily divided* to form Württemberg-Baden, Baden (south), and Württemberg-Hohenzollern. Hesse was composed, less eight Landkreise transferred to the French zone, of the former Land Hesse, the former Prussian Hesse-Cassel and Hesse-Nassau, and the city of Frankfurt. The British raised the Prussian province, Schleswig-Holstein, to the status of a Land, combined the northern part of the former Rhine province with Westphalia and Lippe to form of the Ruhr and neighboring industrial regions a single state in Land North Rhine-Westphalia, and merged Hanover, Schaumburg-Lippe, Oldenburg, and Brunswick in Land Lower-Saxony. The French, besides South Baden and South Württemberg-Hohenzollern, had a group of territorial fragments, including the southern part of Rhine province, which they joined to make Land Rhineland-Palatinate.

These eleven Länder, although possessing new constitutions which they had been encouraged to adopt by the military government, had little independence of action, few real powers, much less, state sovereignty.† Effective power was still reserved to the occupation gov-

* Philip E. Mosely, the principal assistant of John G. Winant, the U.S. representative on the European Advisory Commission, has written: "... The boundary between the French and American zones was to be drawn so as to leave in the American zone the main highway, or Autobahn, through Ulm-Stuttgart-Karlsruhe, as well as the trunk railroad. Administrative and traditional divisions were disregarded completely. The sole concern was to assure access under American control to the Middle Rhine region and the seaports. On two occasions Mr. Winant and I wired strong protests to Washington against the breaking up of both Baden and Württemberg. We pointed out that if it was the American intention to revive and strengthen the federal states in Germany as a possible safeguard against excessive centralization of power, it was hardly logical to begin the reconstruction of Germany by breaking up two of the Länder possessing a strong sense of regional identity and a certain attachment to democratic self-government. We suggested some other device be sought for assuring freedom of movement over the highways and railways" ("The Occupation of Germany: New Light on How the Zones Were Drawn," *Foreign Affairs*, XXVIII, No. 4 [July, 1950], 600).

† Bavarian pretensions to a freedom of decision to join a "voluntary union of German states" (Art. 178, Bavarian constitution) were rejected by the American military governor in his letter of approval of the Bavarian constitution of October 24, 1946. "The expressed will to join in a federal German State," he wrote, "must be interpreted as an instruction to the representatives of Bavaria, who may later participate in a determination of the form of the future German government, and not as a right to refuse to participate in whatever form of German government may be established as an interim measure by Allied authorities or as a lasting form of government by the German people as a whole." [18]

ernments and, in the bizonal area, was exercised to a considerable extent under American and British supervision by the bizonal economic council.

The Parliamentary Council delegates bore no special mandate from the people of the individual Länder, for they were chosen by Landtage which themselves had been elected before any question of uniting the Western zones had arisen. The delegates, with few exceptions, regarded themselves as representatives of the whole people, not of the Länder in which they had been elected. In Carlo Schmid's words,

> The members of the Parliamentary Council have indeed been elected by the Landtage, but they are not deputies and representatives of the Länder. They do not represent the interests of the Länder, but the interests of the nation as a whole. That the deputies were chosen through the Landtage does not alter that fact in the least.[8]

The phrase in the preamble of the Basic Law, ". . . the German people in the Länder Baden, Bavaria, Bremen [etc.] . . . has enacted by virtue of its constituent power this Basic Law for the Federal Republic of Germany," reflects only (and not altogether exactly*) the special limitations and procedures under which the Basic Law was drafted and ratified. It cannot be taken as implying either constituent power or separate sovereignty in the Länder, derived from the people of the several Länder. Both at Chiemsee and in the basic rights committee, the majority refused to recognize the Länder in a constituent role.[9] Sovereignty is vested in the people as a whole (Article 20[2]), the Parliamentary Council having specifically rejected amendments acknowledging a joint or dual sovereignty, e.g., "*Volk und Länder sind Träger der Bundesgewalt.*"[10] The Basic Law, so far therefore from being a constitutive act of the Länder, is rather itself, as an enactment of the representatives of the whole people, the source of Land, as of federal, authority.[11]

* Neither general elections for a constituent assembly nor a referendum for ratification of the Basic Law were held, it will be recalled. In the federal elections of August, 1949, in which 78 per cent of those entitled to vote participated, the people had the first opportunity of expressing judgment on the work of the Parliamentary Council. It is significant that less than 15 per cent of the voters supported parties (the Bavarian Christian Social Union, the Bavarian party, the German party) which claimed that the Parliamentary Council "represented" the Länder and voted against the Basic Law because of dissatisfaction with its treatment of rights of the Länder.

3. PARTY ATTITUDES TO FEDERALISM

Yet a federal structure, as the Germans understood it, accorded with the wishes of the majority of the Western German people. Despite differences on particular issues, it was supported in principle by all the parties save the Communists. In the aftermath of war and defeat of an authoritarian regime, the unitary state was in disrepute, and even the parties favoring centralization felt obliged to take account of the feeling against it. Moreover, Western Germany includes most of the historic centers of local patriotism in Germany— Bavaria, Württemberg-Baden, Hanover, the Hanseatic cities, the Rhineland. Relatively, therefore, the particularist influence carried greater weight at Bonn than at Weimar. Although within the Christian parties, the trade-unionist and other left-wing elements and the Center party held centralist or moderate federalist views, the preponderant Catholic opinion was strongly federalist. This, too, counted for more in a Western German assembly than it would have done in an all-German convention. As in the Weimar period, elements hostile to a liberal social state—the most conservative business and agricultural interests and extreme nationalists—joined the federalist camp, with the hope of curtailing the powers of such a state. These currents of opinion combined to swell a tide toward federalism which flowed far stronger at Bonn than at Weimar.

That a federal structure was to be established was thus taken for granted by the great majority of the delegates when the Parliamentary Council convened. Opinion divided sharply, however, on its form and scope. The spectrum of party views appeared in the earliest debates, ranging from Communist "democratic centralism" at one extreme to the "states' rights" federalism of the Bavarian Christian Social and the German party at the other.

The *Communists* used most of their debating time to attack the establishment of a Western German state. But having thus dissociated themselves from the purpose of the assembly in which they were sitting, they went on to to demand that all power in such a state be concentrated in the hands of a "freely elected peoples' parliament" and a peoples' government commissioned by it.

The *Social Democrats* approached the task of federal construction warily and without enthusiasm. Carlo Schmid conveyed their mood of skepticism in an acid comment on the Allied directive:

We have to draft the Basic Law so that a federal structure will result from it. Obviously, this has been imposed upon us as a part of the so-called "security policy." While federalism all over the world implies the uniting of what was separated, it is apparently intended to introduce federalism in our case to separate what had already been united. . . . Does anyone seriously believe that the security of our neighbors can be guaranteed by constitutional artifice? I do not believe that federalizing Germany as such constitutes any guarantee for our neighbors, but I do think that the democratization of Germany would assure their security. . . .

And later:

The egoism of the Länder should not be allowed to endanger the vital interests of the whole . . . [but] what a Land can do without prejudice to the federation it should do on its own, for it has, after all, the advantage of being on the spot.[12]

The Socialists' notion of a federal system, as their speakers sketched its main lines, was hardly more robust than that of Weimar. The central legislative power was to be extended even further. The chamber representing the Länder was to have only a suspensive veto. Finance was to be entirely administered by the federation.[13] On the other hand, they offered a formula for that measure of decentralization which they thought compatible with, and even essential to, their Socialist program: "Planning from above, execution from below; central direction and legislation, but decentralized administration."[14]

The *Free Democrats* at the outset had little to say on the subject, but the direction of their thinking was unmistakable in Dr. Heuss's remark:

We want to avoid making a fetish of a word when we are seeking to establish a government of "federal" type. . . . I certainly do not wish to expound centralistic propaganda, but I do say this: the committee on division of powers will suddenly become aware one day that their activity is but a toying with words, unless they perceive behind it that the great centralizer of Germany's fate is Germany's distress and Germany's poverty.[15]

The *Center party* adopted an intermediate position. They desired German unity, but not a centralized state; they advocated federal institutions, but rejected separation and narrow, state particularism. The Länder should participate in the federal legislative process, but with only a suspensive veto.[16]

By the time the Parliamentary Council had finished its work, nearly every part of the Weimar constitution had been made to bear responsibility for National Socialism by one party or another. The *Christian Democrats, Christian Social Union,* and *German party* now had their day.

From an overly refined formal democracy, from a sham federalism with strong unitarian tendencies, the centralized totalitarian state of the Third Reich evolved almost organically. Everyone recognizes this danger today, but recognition alone is not enough. We must try at the outset to antici- pate this danger. Preventatives must be incorporated in our design.[17]

. . . We see in a unitary state the danger above all that such a state, even if it is democratically formed, could readily lead to the revival of the authoritarian state and to its transformation into a dictatorship.[18]

A genuine federation must, therefore, be established, they held, in which the Länder would, like the states of the American union, retain their autonomy.

Each constituent state must remain in a position to lead an independent existence of its own as a state, in such measure as will permit the free de- velopment of the vital forces of its own people. The old Reich derived its greatest strength from the autonomous statehood of the Länder. It was the Länder in confederation who made Germany great and furnished it with its riches and the varied flowering of its culture.[19]

For the CSU deputies, federalism was also necessary for a prop- erly ordered national life. For them *"das Volk"* was not an "un- organized mass," but a "well-ordered organism, built up from natural groupings—from the family, the local community, the state—in which the next highest grouping develops organically from that below. Within the whole organism, the individual members must be granted and have secured to them their due influence in decision- making for the whole."[20]

The Social Democratic slogan, "central planning and decentral- ized administration," by no means sufficed for the Christian Demo- crats. The Länder, they held, must be more than bare administrative districts owing their existence and functions to central dispensa- tion.[21] They must be genuine states, existing in their own right, with a full right to participate in making decisions for the federation. For this purpose, a legislative chamber representing the Land governments should have an equal voice with the popular national chamber in lawmaking and the decisive voice in any alteration of the federal division of powers. The federal bureaucracy must be strictly limited and the approval of the chamber of states required for the establishment of new federal administrative agencies. The Länder should collect and administer taxes, with the federation confined to a supervisory role.

In these early debates, the main lines of German thinking on the federal structure of the Basic Law are already clear. They run well within the German tradition. The most federalist-minded of the parties, it will be seen, had no thought of altering the traditional pattern along American lines. Characteristically, the main controversies were developing around the following issues:

To what extent should the Länder participate in the exercise of the central power? What should be the composition of the federal body representing the Länder? What its powers and functions? To what extent should the federation have administrative machinery of its own to execute its laws and perform other functions in the field of its legislative competence?

How far should the federation be empowered to impose uniform taxes throughout the federal territory? How should the proceeds of taxes be divided between the federation and the Länder? Which taxes (if any) should be assessed and collected by the federation and which (if any) by the Länder?

How should the compliance of the Länder with the Basic Law and federal legislation be secured and federal encroachment in the province of the Länder be prevented?

To an account of these, we now turn.

4. THE CONSTITUTION OF THE BUNDESRAT

In a functional federalism such as the German, a body participating directly in the operations of government can act to preserve the federal order more effectively than a court. The Bundesrat occupies this key position in the German federal structure. Not only is it the forum in which the Länder take part in federal law and policy-making, but it is also the guardian of the rights of the Länder —the "observation post" from which the Land representatives keep watch on the activities of the federal government and intervene if the line of demarcation of functions peculiar to the German system is overstepped.

The awareness of the Parliamentary Council deputies that the real balance of power between the federation and the Länder and, in large measure, the relative power and influence of the parties in the future federal structure turned on the form, composition, and powers of the Bundesrat, made these the most keenly contested provisions in the Basic Law. Thus the Council proceedings on these issues moved at two levels: the level of sober academic discussion of the alternatives and the more exhilarating level of party maneuver and negotiation, in which the parties, in terms of their political, economic, and social outlook, sought in the final compromises to swing the federal balance as far as possible in the direction they favored and to maximize their future influence in the second chamber.

Form of the As to the form which a second chamber should
Second take, three proposals were made: a traditional
Chamber federal council, or Bundesrat, composed of rep-
(Article 51 [1]) resentatives of the Land governments (CDU/
CSU, the Center and German parties); a senate, elected by the Land parliaments on the basis of proportional representation (SPD);* a "mixed" chamber, composed both of members of the Land governments and members elected by the Landtage (FDP).

For a Bundesrat, the case was put that the Länder, as constituent powers (*Machtfaktoren*) in the federation, could be represented effectively and exercise their rights in the making of decisions for the federation only through their governments.[22] In a federal system in which the Land governments would be called upon to admin-

---

* The Communists proposed direct popular election of the second chamber (Paul [KPD], Plen. 3s. 9/9/48, p. 53), the sole function of which would be to "review" the legislation of the lower chamber. Since Land and federal parliaments and governments alike were elected by and responsible to the people, if all behaved "democratically" there should be no real divergence of interest between the federation and the Länder, they contended (Renner [KPD], HA 1R, pp. 137–38).

ister the laws of the federation, they would discharge this task more willingly and intelligently if they had actually taken part in making the laws. A Bundesrat, whose members would be sitting concurrently in the Land cabinets, could be an effective mediator between the federal and Land governments. The sanction of tradition was invoked: from the earliest times of the old Reich, a "federal council" had proved peculiarly suited to German needs. The Bismarckian and Weimar "federal councils," it was claimed, had been distinguished for the high quality of their work. The different political complexions of the Land governments, even the local preoccupations of Land governments led by the party or parties nationally in the majority, would insure an "objectivity" of attitude in the Bundesrat toward the prevailing political majority in the Bundestag. On the other hand, a senate chosen by the Landtage would be but a replica of the party-dominated Bundestag and not truly representative of the interests of the Länder. In the smaller, poorer Länder it would be difficult to find qualified persons to serve as senators, because they would not be able to afford absences from their businesses and professions or the expense of a personal staff needed to assist them in their legislative work. A Bundesrat could draw upon the services of the expert, higher permanent officials of the Länder.

A *senate*, its supporters argued, would at last enable Germany to do what to her detriment she had so far failed to do: utilize in the legislature the abilities and experience of her distinguished senior citizens, the "elder statesmen" with achievements in government, the professions, industry, the trades unions, the universities. These, while considering political problems from a "higher level," could maintain close contact with the Land governments and represent the Land interests, but without losing independence of decision. A senate chosen by the people's elected representatives in the Länder would be more responsive to public opinion than a bureaucratic Bundesrat. Senatorial independence of party organizations and the Landtage could be strengthened by providing a longer than normal term of office (six years) and by renewing only a part of the membership at each election. In the concept of a Bundesrat, with its "instruction bound" delegations and responsibilities shifted to the shoulders of civil servants, there still survived too much of the bureaucratic inflexibility and undemocratic attitudes of the monarchical states of the last century.

In a *"mixed"* *second chamber*—a precedent for which was found in the Staatenhaus proposed in the Frankfurt convention of 1848–49 —the advantages of both a Bundesrat and a senate could be realized and their disadvantages neutralized, the Free Democrats urged.

But behind the façade of debate, party policy and interest weighed heaviest in determining the final decision.

The CSU members were confident of continuing to head their own or a coalition government in Bavaria, and therefore of controlling a Bavarian delegation to a Bundesrat. In a senate, in which opportunity would be opened to the national parties to obtain representatives in the Bavarian delegation, Bavarian influence would only be attenuated.

The Christian Democrats were drawn in two directions. For the sake of harmony with their fellow CSU deputies, they had to take account of Christian Social preoccupation with Bavarian interests. On the other hand, as a national party they were concerned to maximize in a second chamber the CDU/CSU representation from the country as a whole. From any method of representation related to population they stood to gain, owing to their leading position in the most populous Länder, North Rhine–Westphalia and Bavaria. But the Christian Democrats were less interested in the second chamber's composition than in obtaining for it full equality of power (*Gleichberechtigung*) with the Bundestag. If a compromise on composition could gain them *Gleichberechtigung* and representation weighted for population, they were ready to move in that direction.

The Free Democrats' preference for the "mixed" solution reflected at once their nationalist dislike of state particularism, their conservatism, and their position as a minority party. They wanted a strong second chamber as a brake on a popularly elected legislature,* but they were not prepared to give full powers, on the one

* Thus Dr. Thomas Dehler (FDP), citing the precedent of 1848 in support of a "mixed" chamber: "We have perhaps the last chance . . . of creating a healthy democracy, and I have an appalled feeling that we are going to spoil that chance. Our grandfathers were much more clever than the authors of the Weimar constitution. They hadn't such Jacobinical notions as the twentieth century. . . . Here

hand, to a Bundesrat "tied by instructions of the Land governments," or, on the other, to a senate "merely duplicating a party-dominated Bundestag." At the same time, the Free Democrats knew that as a small party—in opposition, or at best as a minority partner in Land coalition governments—they would have little influence in Land governments sending delegations to a "pure" Bundesrat. With the election of a part of these delegations by the Landtage in proportion to the strength of parties, they stood to gain representation of their own in the second chamber.

The Social Democrats sought to maximize popular influence in the legislature by preserving the dominant role for the popularly elected Bundestag and by making the second chamber as broadly representative as possible. It soon became apparent, however, that these objectives were tactically incompatible; for the nearer the composition of the second chamber was brought to accord with Social Democratic views, the weaker became the case for not giving it powers equal to those of the Bundestag. Indeed, at first the Social Democrats seemed ready to agree to *Gleichberechtigung* for a senate and a Bundestag,[23] but they soon retracted. Dr. Rudolf Katz told the committee on organization that his party would in no circumstances agree to equality between the two chambers. If a senate were adopted, they would concede a requirement for a two-thirds majority in the Bundestag to override a senate veto; with a Bundesrat, they insisted, a majority of the Bundestag must suffice to override a veto.[24] Thereafter Socialist strategy was ruled exclusively by the objective of maintaining the dominance of the Bundestag in legislation. Dr. Walter Menzel, one of the Socialist leaders in the Parliamentary Council, writes:

In the Parliamentary Council, the SPD made every effort to preserve sole sovereignty for the future Bundestag. We wanted above all to avoid a sharing of this sovereignty in legislation and would not have succeeded in doing so had the second chamber been composed of members directly

---

we have a solution that I can support wholeheartedly: a second chamber to which full powers equal with those of the lower house of parliament can be given, which can act as a counterbalance to any—as we think, deplorable—tendency toward an overweening parliamentarism. . . . We strongly favor the incorporation of a check against one of the chief maladies of our time—'hypertrophy' of legislation—against this deluded belief that everything in life can be regulated, that by regulation one can accomplish any miracle" (Plen. 7s. 21/10/48, pp. 88, 89).

elected in the Länder. Such a second chamber in all probability would soon have attained the upper hand, as in the United States.[25]

Meanwhile, Dr. Hermann von Mangoldt,[26] Dr. Robert Lehr, and others had convinced the majority of the CDU/CSU faction of the advantages of a "mixed" chamber. The conversion, announced by Dr. Lehr at the seventh plenary session, was cordially welcomed by the Free Democrats. The Bundesrat, so constituted, would have consisted of two panels or "courts." In one, the delegates of the Land governments and senators chosen by the Landtage were to be associated in exercising the Bundesrat's legislative powers; in the other, on administrative and other matters more directly affecting Land interests, the Land-instructed delegates were to sit alone. The CDU/CSU agreement to the "mixed" solution, however, carried the condition that the senators should not be freely elected by the Landtage, but chosen by them from lists prepared by the Land governments.

The Social Democrats could not be won to this "hybrid" form of second chamber in which, they argued, the political responsibility for exercise of its legislative powers would be confused between the diverse elements participating.[27]

The Social Democrats now faced the imminent prospect of a majority which could carry against them a "mixed" Bundesrat, possessing legislative powers equal to those of the Bundestag. If the CDU/CSU bloc held together, with the FDP votes, the "mixed" solution needed only support (or abstention) of either the German or the Center parties, who still clung to a "pure" Bundesrat, for a clear majority over the SPD and KPD opposition. There were signs that the German party would come round.[28]

The Social Democrats responded with a bold maneuver. They made common cause with the most federalist of their opponents, the Christian Social faction. Dr. Walter Menzel, as spokesman for the SPD, met Dr. Hans Ehard, the minister-president of Bavaria and leader of the Christian Socialists, and found that although Ehard still strongly desired a Bundesrat representing the Land governments, he feared that he would not be able to carry it. Menzel was now able to offer Ehard his party's support for such a Bundesrat. Ehard in turn was prepared to go a considerable way to meet the Social Democrats' desire for a federal instead of a Land administration of finance. It was agreed that a Bundesrat so constituted would have only a veto, not full powers, in legislation.[29]

Dr. Adenauer, the Christian Democratic leader, in a last effort to retrieve *Gleichberechtigung*, proposed a three-chamber legislature— a Bundestag and senate with equal powers, and a further special chamber in which the Land interests would be represented. This found favor with no other party. The Christian Democrats, to preserve a united front with the Christian Social Union, therefore had no alternative but to return to support of a "pure" Bundesrat.[30] With this retreat, the possibility of a majority for *Gleichberechtigung* altogether disappeared, for the Free Democrats had repeatedly made it clear[31] that they would never support full powers for a Bundesrat in the traditional form. In the voting, a Bundesrat of members of the Land governments was adopted with only one dissent (KPD).[32] *Gleichberechtigung* was defeated by twelve votes to nine, with the Social Democrats, Free Democrats, Center, and Communists forming a majority against the CDU/CSU and the German party.[33]

Thus, although the majority of the members of the Parliamentary Council wanted to reform the second chamber, they failed because they could not agree upon both its composition and powers. The Bavarian federalists were the beneficiaries of this disagreement, winning a Bundesrat in the traditional Bismarckian form. Dr. Heuss expressed the widespread disappointment over this outcome in a wry comment during the closing days of the Parliamentary Council:

> I believe actually the most interesting event which occurred during our labors was that by now legendary breakfast which Herr Abgeordneter Menzel took with Herr Minister-President Ehard of Munich; for through their conversation over breakfast, the Bundesrat came into being. . . . It will be an amusing anecdote for the historian to recount some day how the Rhenish Socialist and the *weiss-blau* statesman found themselves in the company of Bismarck. . . . These two latter day "Bismarcks" have forgotten one thing, however—that Bismarck's edifice, as the essential feature of its federalism, had Prussia in the background. Without Prussia, that whole historical structure can not be understood. And now in place of this Bismarckian federalism, something else has emerged. . . . Now we face the very great probability of getting a federalism of bureaucracies and, with it, the trouble of having uniform conditions of life for the whole community upset.[34]

Size of
Representation
of the Länder
(*Article*
51 [2] [3])

The Parliamentary Council had next to decide in what strength the Länder should be represented in the Bundesrat. In both the Bismarckian Bundesrat and the Weimar Reichsrat, it will be recalled, the states had been represented relative to their size. In the Reichsrat, all states had one vote, but the larger had additional votes for each 700,000 of their population. Under the census of 1925, this gave Prussia twenty-six, Bavaria eleven, Saxony seven, Württemberg four, Baden three, Thüringen, Hesse, and Bremen two votes each, and the remaining states one vote each.

On this issue, the parties reversed roles: the Social Democrats became ardent federalists, defending the rights of the Länder as *"gleichberechtigte Staatspersönlichkeiten,"* while the Christian Democrats, Christian Social, Center, and German parties took up the cry for democratic principles and representation proportionate to population.

In proposing equal votes for the Länder, Dr. Katz suavely suggested,[35] the Social Democrats were only basing themselves on sound federalist principles. If, as his opponents had so often maintained, the Länder possessed *"gleiche Staatspersönlichkeit,"* then, surely, they deserved equality of treatment. He had the feeling that, on this issue, the north German Länder were more federalist-minded than the south German Länder, Bavaria particularly. The differences of population of the Länder were not, after all, so great as in America, where the states had equal senatorial representation. In any case, among the Länder of least population, Bremen and Hamburg had an importance as centers of trade and shipbuilding more than compensating for their lack of numbers.

For Dr. Adolf Süsterhenn, the Christian Democrat, it was unthinkable that Land Bremen, with half a million inhabitants, should have the same number of votes and the same influence as Land North Rhine-Westphalia, with twelve millions.

Such a leveling of the states would be to ignore realities and the real factors of power. Without wishing to disparage the importance of the Hanseatic cities, we are of the opinion that in a democracy the law of numbers must rule.

Anyone with a taste for political irony, Dr. Heuss said, would find this paradoxical shift in the positions of the major parties an amusing development. For him, it was a case of "plague on both houses." If the CDU proposal for representation strictly according to population were adopted, the Bundesrat would lose altogether its character as a chamber representative of the interests of all the states, because the instructed delegations of the largest Länder would dominate it. The Germans, he said, had had bitter experience in their history with the struggle for mastery between Prussia and Austria, and they did not want another such contest between North Rhine-Westphalia and Bavaria. On the other hand, he could not support the Social Democratic view that in a genuine federal council the states must be equally represented. The American Senate was not a relevant example, he contended, because at the time of its establishment the American states had been of corresponding size and population. He therefore urged a compromise which would give *some*, but not proportionate, weight to size of population.

The fortunes of the major parties in elections in the Länder during 1947 and early 1948 suggest an explanation for Dr. Heuss's "paradox." The Social Democrats had led in six Länder, Hesse, Württemberg-Baden, Bremen, Hamburg, Lower Saxony, and Schleswig-Holstein, while the Christian Democratic / Christian Social Union led in five, North Rhine-Westphalia, Bavaria, Baden, Rhineland-Palatinate, and Württemberg-Hohenzollern. Of the most populous Länder, the CDU/CSU led in two, North Rhine-Westphalia (13.6 millions) and Bavaria (9.1 millions), while the SPD led in one, Lower Saxony (6.7 millions). With this distribution of party strength, the Social Democrats under their scheme of representation (three delegates for each of the Länder) could expect to head Land governments sending eighteen representatives to the future Bundesrat, as against the CDU/CSU's fifteen. With the system of representation which it favored (one representative for each million of the population or for each fraction over 500,000), the CDU/CSU bloc could hope to control between twenty-five and twenty-eight delegates in the Bundesrat against the SPD's nineteen. On this issue, therefore, the two major parties were acting only prudently in departing from strict consistency in their views on the rights of the Länder.

Under the compromise finally adopted—a little more liberal to the smaller Länder than that originally proposed by the Free Democrats—each Land has three votes, but Länder with more than 2 million inhabitants have four, and those with more than 6 million inhabitants, five votes. In the first Bundesrat, there were twenty-four delegates from CDU-led Land governments and nineteen from SPD-led Land governments. When the new Southwest State was established in 1951, combining Baden, Württemberg-Baden, and Württemberg-Hohenzollern, the balance between the parties in the Bundesrat shifted for the time being in favor of the Social Democrats.

Civil Servants in the Bundesrat There were also differences of opinion about the part which senior civil servants of the Land governments should be permitted to play in the Bundesrat. In the Reichsrat it had been the custom for the Land governments to be represented a great part of the time by their higher permanent officials, with the Land ministers attending only on rare occasions for important matters with which they were particularly concerned. The Social Democrats were highly critical of this practice, claiming that it had served to make the Reichsrat an inflexible and bureaucratic body, unresponsive to democratic pressures. On the other hand, it was obviously impractical to insist that a sufficient number of Land ministers should be present at every session of the Bundesrat to make up the full complement of the Land delegations.

Senior officials could of course attend the Bundesrat as expert assistants, Dr. Katz (SPD) said, but the votes of each Land should be cast by a responsible Land minister.[36]

Dr. Hermann Höpker-Aschoff (FDP) doubted, on the basis of his experience of the Reichsrat, that a requirement for attendance of the Land ministers would be practical. The Reichsrat had had many tedious agendas and in future one could expect equally tedious discussions in the Bundesrat over trifling matters. It was impossible to expect ministers from all the Land capitals to attend all sittings of the Bundesrat, which might meet as often as twice a week. It should be left to the Land governments to decide whether ministers or deputies would attend.

Dr. Schmid (SPD) replied that the Bundesrat was a federal body and that its membership could be determined only by federal decision. He would remind the delegates that when the opposing cases for a senate and a Bundesrat were argued, the supporters of the Bundesrat had insisted that it would not become an assembly of civil servants (*Beamtenparlament*).

In the end, the understanding that a Land's constitutional obligations could be satisfied by authorizing one minister to act for it seems to have satisfied the majority of the Council. In a definitive interpretation, the main committee chairman, Dr. Schmid, made it clear that the effect of Article 51(3) would be to insure that the votes of a Land were cast not by a civil servant nor by telephone or telegraph, but by a member of the Land government present and empowered for that purpose.[37]

5. POWERS OF THE BUNDESRAT

On paper, the Bundesrat's powers are less than those of the Bundesrat of 1871–1918 and greater than those of the Weimar Reichsrat, although, in practice, the Bundesrat looks as though it is becoming a more effective representative of Land interests than either. Like both its predecessors, the Bundesrat has both legislative and administrative functions. Its legislative powers extend to constitutional amendments, federal laws in general (over which it has a suspensory veto), and federal laws particularly affecting Land interests (over which it has an absolute veto).

Over Constitutional Amendments (Article 79)   Under the Weimar constitution, the Reichsrat had no final veto on constitutional amendments. If it did not approve an amendment adopted by the Reichstag, it could ask for a national referendum.[38] If it did not ask for a referendum, the Reichstag could again pass the amendment by a two-thirds majority. It then became the Reich president's decision whether to submit the amendment to referendum or promulgate it. In the Parliamentary Council, there was nearly unanimous agreement that the Bundesrat should share equally with the Bundestag the power over constitutional amendments, two-thirds of the membership of each to be required for adoption of amendments. Controversy centered on a further provision stipulating the Bundesrat's approval of "any law altering the essential character of the federal structure." This was repeatedly approved in committee over the protests of the Social Democrats, who argued that, without definition of "essential character," every adjustment of the functions of federal and Land administrative agencies might become a cause of litigation in the constitutional court.[39] The provision was finally dropped in the fourth reading, because its purpose had been accomplished by agreement to forbid altogether[40] any constitutional amendment altering the division of the Federal Republic into Länder or abolishing the right of the Länder to participate in the federal legislative process.

Over Legislation (Article 77) With the defeat of *Gleichberechtigung*, the parties advanced competing proposals regarding the size of the Bundestag majority to be required to override a Bundesrat veto[41] of legislation approved in the Bundestag. The fraction in each case exactly measured the degree of party attachment to federalist principles:

Three-fourths of all the members of the Bundestag.....CDU/CSU, DP
or, failing this,
Two-thirds of all the members ....DP
Two-thirds of the members present, including at least a majority
of all the members ....FDP, Z
Absolute majority of all the members ....SPD
Simple majority of the members present ....KPD

In the final compromise negotiated by the committee of five, there is the wisdom of Solomon. If a Bundesrat veto is adopted by an absolute majority of all the members, it can be overridden by an absolute majority of all the members of the Bundestag. If the veto is adopted by a two-thirds majority of all the members of the Bundesrat, it can be overridden by a two-thirds majority of the members of the Bundestag present, which must include at least an absolute majority of all its members.

But the Bundesrat's real power in the legislative field consists less in this suspensory veto than in its special powers over legislation particularly affecting Land interests—the so-called *Zustimmungsgesetze*.

The Chiemsee experts had already recommended that in legislation on a limited number of subjects vital to the Länder special approval of the Bundesrat should be required.[42] With the defeat of *Gleichberechtigung*, this provision acquired a key importance in the negotiations. It became, so to speak, the "elastic clause" of the Basic Law, facilitating compromises in other controversies over the division of powers, administration, and finance. By additions to the list of *Zustimmungsgesetze*, the federalists were reconciled to grants of powers to the federation desired by the centralists. For example, the right was conceded to the federation to enact legislation on taxes to establish uniform rates for the whole federal territory, but on the condition that all legislation on taxes accruing to the Länder and Gemeinden* must be approved by the Bundesrat. It was agreed that the federal government might establish new federal administrative agencies additional to those specified in the Basic Law, but only with the Bundesrat's approval. Or, again, the inevitable controversy over nationalization of industries was reconciled by an agreement that federal legislation on the transfer of resources and industries to national ownership would require Bundesrat concurrence. The list of *Zustimmungsgesetze* thus grew in the course of negotiations from three subjects in the Chiemsee draft to eleven in the draft approved in third reading.

The elasticity which this clause afforded for negotiations was useful in reverse when the Allied demand for a greater measure of federalism in the Basic Law had upset the complex of compromises between the parties. By striking subjects from the list of *Zustimmungsgesetze*, the committee of seven partly compensated the Social Democrats for their reluctant agreement to modify the legislative and financial powers of the federation along lines desired by the Allied authorities.

In the Basic Law in its final form, the listing of *Zustimmungsgesetze* in a separate article was abandoned. They are now to be found in their appropriate chapters. The most important of these matters upon which the Bundestag can legislate only with concurrence of the Bundesrat are: changes in the territory of the Länder (Article 29 [7]); the establishment of new federal administrative agencies *in the field* (Article 87 [3]); federal regulation of procedures and of the establishment of agencies for administration *by the Länder* of federal legislation (Article 84 [1], [2], [5] and Article 85); taxes the proceeds of which accrue in whole or part to the Länder and Gemeinden (Article 105 [3]); the division of the revenue from the income and corporation taxes between the federation and the Länder (Article 106 [3]); measures to equalize financial burdens between the Länder (Article 106 [4]); the "final" distribu-

* Local communities.

tion of taxes between the federation and the Länder (Article 107); regulation of the administration of federal taxes by the Länder (Article 108 [3]).

The German federalists have the intervention of the military governors to thank for the fact that this list no longer includes the transfer of industry and resources to public ownership, the regulation of the supply of power, federal co-ordination of the criminal police, federal provisions regarding the employees of the Länder, the Gemeinden, and public law corporations, and—most important of all—the establishment of new federal administrative agencies at the *national level* and of public corporations subject to federal control.

Over
Administration
The extensive control which the Bundesrat exercises over federal administration—a function uncommon in a second chamber*—is a logical safeguard in a federal system in which the chief business of the states is administration. The Basic Law defines in great detail the constitutional relationship of the federal and Land administrations. To preserve this relationship, the Bundesrat is empowered to intervene directly in federal decisions at several vital points.

The most important of these are ministerial ordinances implementing federal legislation (Article 80), which the Bundesrat has the power to approve or to reject in a majority of fields. Since it is a common German practice to establish broad provisions in legislation and to leave to ministers the promulgation of detailed procedures and provisions in ordinances with the effect of law (*Rechtsverordnungen*), the Bundesrat is thus closely involved in decisions of the federal ministers affecting not only the application but the substantive content of much federal legislation. The Bundesrat's approval is also required for the creation of new federal administrative offices and agencies in the field (Article 87 [3]), individual instructions by the federal ministers to the Land authorities (Article 84 [5]), measures to compel a recalcitrant Land to fulfil its federal obligations (Article 37), and the use by the federal government of police forces of the Länder to avert a threat to the "free democratic order" (Article 91 [2]). It is for the Bundesrat to decide, after

* Apart from powers of investigation and review and control of appointments, such as the United States Senate possesses.

representations by the federal government, whether a Land is executing federal laws and ordinances satisfactorily (Article 84 [4]).

6. LEGISLATIVE POWERS OF THE FEDERATION AND THE LÄNDER[43]

To speak of a "division" of legislative powers between the federation and the Länder in the Basic Law is more convenient than it is accurate. Only the powers of the federation are defined, and these, with the exception of a few matters, pre-empt the field. The federation possesses only a third of these as matters of "exclusive" jurisdiction, but, as we shall see, in the exercise of the remainder— the "concurrent" powers* which it shares with the Länder—the federation is so far pre-eminent that these too must as a practical matter be reckoned as federal powers. The Basic Law's division of powers is thus formally similar to that of the American constitution: it is one of enumerated or delegated federal powers and residual state powers. "The Länder have the power to legislate insofar as the Basic Law does not confer legislative powers on the federation," Article 70 reads. But even this provision, definite though it may seem, does not finally secure all residual powers to the Länder; it merely establishes a presumption in their favor. According to prevailing German legal[44] and judicial[45] opinion, the lengthy constitutional enumeration does not exhaust the federation's powers. It also possesses unwritten "inherent" (*aus der Natur der Sache*) and "implied" (*kraft Sachzusammenhangs*) powers.

On the proposition that the main competence in legislation should belong to the federation, German opinion of all shades, of all parties and interests, united from the beginning. On marginal issues, particularly powers closely related to the residual competence of the Länder in education, religious and cultural affairs, police, welfare, and local administration, there were disagreements. On the grant of broad powers to the federation over the economy—industry, the land, labor—communications, transport, the legal system, and the postwar problems of reparations, war benefits, and care of refugees and expellees, harmony prevailed from left to right, between cen-

---

* The so-called third type of federal legislation—the enactment of general rules (*Rahmenvorschriften*) on the matters listed in Article 75—is but a special case of the federation's "concurrent" powers, such legislation being addressed to the Land legislatures rather than to the citizen.

tralists and federalists alike. Few discordant notes were sounded until the Allied military governors entered the proceedings.

The strength of the German constitutional tradition, the German preference for order and uniformity in the basic conditions of industrial, commercial, and professional life, and the ambitions of the Socialists and other reformers with plans for national betterment all helped to produce this unanimity of view. More telling even than these were the conditions of life in Western Germany which daily confronted the Parliamentary Council deputies. The Council met in the autumn following currency reform when Allied and German officials were still grappling with the economic problems arising from the war and the sealing off of the zones of occupation. It was the season of compulsory measures for the collection of food from the farms, of a fuel and power famine which produced crises throughout the whole of German industry, of a chronic deficiency of exports and foreign exchange with which to pay for vital imports. All parties were ready to equip the central government with powers adequate to deal with these problems.

Dr. Walter Strauss said of himself and his fellow Christian Democrats:

> In the committee stage, we have very deliberately . . . made the federation strong when it came to . . . the division of powers, because we are convinced that under present conditions which will face the country for some time, it is impossible . . . to confine the federation to a narrow competence. . . . Those members who originally began their work with quite a different point of view have been convinced by the weight of the facts and the views of the experts.[46]

Federal Supremacy in Legislation   The federation's supremacy in legislation is founded upon its "exclusive" powers (Article 73) and the long list of so-called "concurrent" powers (Articles 74, 75). The latter can be exercised by the federation, however, only if a *need* for federal legislation exists because:

a matter cannot be effectively dealt with by the legislation of individual Länder, *or*

dealing with a matter by a Land law might prejudice the interests of other Länder or of the entire community, *or*

the maintenance of legal or economic unity, especially the maintenance of uniformity of living conditions beyond the territory of a Land, necessitates it [Article 72].

At first glance, a reader accustomed to American constitutional usages might think that, by a restrictive interpretation of these conditions, the constitutional court could reserve a substantial sphere of legislative power for the Länder, or at least deny it to the federation. There is little likelihood that this could happen.

The Germans from the start[46a] regarded these first and foremost as federal powers. They emphasized this in three ways:[47] (1) by naming them "priority" (not "concurrent") powers of the federation; (2) by specifying as the sole condition for their exercise by the federation that they must be used to "regulate only what must be uniformly regulated"; (3) by stipulating that they should be available to the Länder only to the extent that no use of them was made by the federation. On the principle of all this, there was no disagreement, scarcely any debate, in the Parliamentary Council.

The Allied military governors, however, took strong exception to federal powers in legislation on this scale. They set about redressing the balance in favor of the Länder not by proposing a clear reallocation of powers to the federation and to the Länder,* but by asking the Parliamentary Council to define the circumstances in which the federation would be entitled to exercise the "concurrent" powers, as those

where it is clearly impossible for a single Land to enact effective legislation, or where the legislation if enacted would be detrimental to the rights or interests of the Länder; ... and provided that the interests of the Länder are clearly, directly and integrally affected.[48]

The Parliamentary Council unanimously opposed this demand, not only for the change it sought to make in the federal balance, but for the manner of bringing it about. The introduction of such language into the Basic Law, they feared, would invite constitutional contro-

* A doctrine of American federalist theory holds that it is more "federalistic" for the central government alone to have powers delegated to it. The central government thus becomes one of "limited" powers as compared with the state governments, which retain sovereignty in all residual fields. For the irrelevance of this notion to conditions in Western Germany, cf. C. J. Friedrich and H. J. Spiro, "The Constitution of the German Federal Republic," in E. H. Litchfield and Associates, Governing Post-War Germany (Ithaca, N.Y.: Cornell University Press, 1953), chap. v, p. 127.

versy and open the way for the judiciary, after the American example, to become the arbiter of the federation's legislative powers. The Germans succeeded in carrying their point. Any *one* of the three conditions finally incorporated in Article 72 suffices as a ground upon which the federation may legislate in the concurrent fields. The last—"for the maintenance of legal or economic uniformity"[49]—affords an authorization of powers as broad as any possessed by previous Reich parliaments.[50]

As to the right of the judiciary to examine and decide whether a "need for federal legislation" in the sense of Article 72 exists, Dr. Strauss, the Christian Democratic leader, leaves no doubt of the Parliamentary Council's attitude in his frank account:

> We discussed the formula with the military governors in our last meeting with them, then retired to a corner and made several alterations. I recall that we discussed among ourselves in quite a small circle the question of review by the courts of decisions as to the need for federal legislation [*Bedürfnisfrage*] ... how we could prevent the federal constitutional court from interfering in these matters. . . . We were being compelled here by the occupation powers to a course of action which was unacceptable to each of us, but which we had to tolerate in the interests of a higher cause. . . . We were unanimous in this small circle that the constitutional court could examine only an abuse of discretion [*Ermessensmissbrauch*] by the federal legislature, but not the question of the need for legislation [*Bedürfnisfrage*], the decision as to which must be confined exclusively to the Bundestag and Bundesrat.[51]

To minimize the effect of possible future interference by the Allied authorities or the constitutional court in federal legislation, the Parliamentary Council contrived to insert—unnoticed by the military governors—a provision[52] in the Basic Law to the effect that all *existing* legislation in the concurrent fields would take effect as federal law. If the Allies persisted in their attitude, it was reckoned that the extensive zonal and amended Reich legislation already in force in Western Germany would go a long way to bring central regulation in the controversial fields.[53]

However, as it turned out, the Allied high commission did not interfere, and the constitutional court itself has taken the position that the decision regarding the need for federal exercise of the concurrent powers under Article 72 is solely within the discretion of the federal parliament and "not by its nature a justiciable question."[54]

We may conclude that, as matters stand, the legislative supremacy of the federation is assured. It must be borne in mind, however, that the first government of the Federal Republic—moderate in its social policy, opposed to governmental controls and intervention in the economic sphere, and comprising in its coalition two of the most federalist-minded of the political parties—has subjected the federal division of powers to no very severe strain. A Social Democratic government, relying upon the concurrent powers to carry through an extensive program of economic and social measures, might put the constitutional court's restraint in this field to a greater test.

Inherent and   Although Bavarian "strict constructionists"[55]
Implied Powers   contest it, the federation is generally conceded
to possess powers not specified in the Basic Law. Such powers are of two kinds: "inherent" (*aus der Natur der Sache*) and "implied" (*kraft Sachzusammenhangs*). The inherent powers govern matters which by their nature require to be regulated by the federation: e.g., the location of the federal capital and the relationships between the Federal Republic and the occupation powers. In the Weimar period, many important Reich powers were thus adduced, including those to establish a Reich financial administration and to equalize financial burdens between the Länder.

The implied powers are those thought essential to the complete exercise of powers within the federal competence, or as means to the exercise of such powers. In the Weimar period, the competence of the Reich to legislate on the administrative courts in the Länder was declared by various authorities[56] to be implied in the constitutional provision for the establishment of a Reich administrative court. In the Basic Law, the absence of a federal power to declare general amnesties has been remedied by deducing one from the concurrent power (Article 74 [1]) over criminal law and the execution of sentences and the procedure of courts.[57] It cannot be thought, however, that these concepts will play such a part in the future in Germany as they have played in American constitutional history. It would be surprising indeed if many more federal powers could be found to "inhere" in or be "implied" by the Basic Law than it plainly states.

Controversial
Issues

Few matters in the catalogues of exclusive and concurrent powers became the subject of controversy between the parties, except those closely affecting the residual powers of the Länder: e.g., federal intervention in the criminal police field; the promotion of scientific research; regulation of administrative courts and of the legal and notarial professions in the Länder; road traffic and highways; the promotion of agricultural and forest production; and regulation of the trade in food, stimulants, fodder, and agricultural and forest seeds.

Of these, the debates on the police power (Article 73 [10]) and on promotion of scientific research (Article 74 [13]) may be taken both as typical and of particular interest.

It is well known that the Allied governments opposed placing any considerable police power in the hands of a central government. The military governors had already made it clear in their *aide memoire* to the Parliamentary Council of November 22, 1948, that the powers of the federal government in the police field would be limited to those especially approved by them during the occupation period. Nevertheless, many in the Parliamentary Council, having in mind the failure of certain of the Weimar Länder to take effective measures against Nazi and other antidemocratic elements, felt strongly that there should be some federal control and co-ordination of police activities in the Länder. The Social Democrats and Bavarian federalists soon fell afoul of each other. In the first reading of a provision for a federal criminal police to "combat offenses dangerous to the community as a whole," the debate[58] ran: ˙

Dr. Paul de Chapeaurouge (CDU): "I propose the striking of this clause. It is both unnecessary and objectionable. Criminal matters are a part of the police jurisdiction and the police is basically a Land subject. . . . We had no Reich police in the Weimar state. That was a development in the era of Heinrich Himmler. In the Weimar time, after the assassination of Rathenau and Erzberger, the adoption of a Reich criminal police law was discussed but turned down because all the Länder expressed themselves against it. . . ."

Herr Stock (SPD): "Had the Weimar constitution provided for this, much later misfortune might perhaps have been avoided. At that time, police jurisdiction was confined to the Länder. It was therefore possible for the Pöhner police in Bavaria to fail to find the assassins of Rathenau and Erzberger, although . . . we saw those assassins daily. If you do not adopt this provision and such gangs of murderers spring up again, we run the danger that again some Land—it might not even be Bavaria—might acquire a reactionary government, might get a police president who in his own administration—I can offer proof—employed assassins and provocateurs. . . ."

Dr. Wilhelm Laforet (CSU): "What Herr Colleague Stock has brought out is certainly very true. But there are other considerations to be taken into account. Through individual defects of the police—"

Dr. Menzel (SPD): "It was intentional!"

Dr. Schmid (SPD): "That was no defect. What was done in that case was entirely intentional!"

Dr. Laforet: "I regard it as a defect."

Herr Stock: "Then it was a 'defect' that Pöhner was made police president."

Dr. Laforet: "We agree about that."

Herr Stock: "But the Bavarian government did not agree about it in those days —"

Dr. Josef Schwalber: "It agreed —"

Herr Stock: "— that he be given office and that the assassins be protected."

Dr. Laforet: "The real issue at stake is whether we are to go so far as to infringe a constitutional principle upon which the Basic Law is based, namely, that legislation on police is essentially a matter for the Länder. Actually, everything necessary for the apprehension of offenders has been achieved by agreement between the Länder. All these questions: the criminal police searching system, the apprehension of international pocket thieves, information on missing and unidentified dead persons, a central agency for gypsies, a central agency for fingerprinting are already regulated by means of agreements between the Länder. . . . The only question is whether there is not a danger here that a Himmler-like federal criminal police office will be created."

Dr. Schmid: "The Presidency of Herr Pöhner preceded Himmler."

Herr Stock: "Quite right! He was Himmler No. 1."

Dr. Schmid: "What we have here is a technical and political question. On the technical side, I must say that unfortunately it is no more the case that offenders confine themselves to a limited territory, as did the old bandit gangs, but conduct operations on a wide scale. We can combat them only by having a criminal police operating on a correspondingly large scale. . . . As for the political aspect, we hope our concern for the future will prove to be unfounded. But we don't know the future. Conditions may possibly develop in a Land where the Land government will no longer be master of its police executive and where the police president will not arrest an offender on political grounds. Then it must be possible for police under orders of the federation to intervene. If we have to proceed by way of federal compulsion and the constitutional court, the culprit will long since have disappeared."

Deletion of the federal police provision was defeated, but a compromise taking account of the CDU/CSU point of view was reached by adopting as the definition of federal competence in this field: "Co-operation of the federation and the Länder in matters of criminal police."

The Social Democrats proposed[59] as an entirely new concurrent power of the federation the "promotion of scientific research" (Article 74 [13]). They read into the record a letter from the German scientists, Professors Heisenberg, Regener, Rein, and Zenneck, pointing out that the scope of scientific research had long since outgrown the power of individual Länder to finance it and urging that scientific research should be made a matter of federal legislative competence.

In debate,

Dr. Laforet (CSU), while agreeing that the promotion of scientific research was of the first importance, could not see the necessity for a federal power to "organize" it. This would only be a foot in the door for government interference with the freedom of scientific research. Why indeed was legislation on scientific research needed? He could not imagine what it would concern. It was not necessary to "compel" the conduct of research—all that was needed was a budgetary grant.

Herr Stock (SPD) could not understand Dr. Laforet's position. It had already been admitted in the American zone and in the Bavarian Landtag, of which Dr. Laforet was a member, that the individual Länder could not meet the costs of these institutes. If a zonal-wide uniform law for these institutes could be adopted in the American zone, one would have thought that without more ado the responsibility could be made federal-wide.

Dr. Höpker-Aschoff (FDP) called attention to the fact that both the *"Notgemeinschaft deutscher Wissenschaft"* and the Kaiser Wilhelm Institute, now continuing as the Max Planck Institute, had been established as national institutions on the basis of private law and had been supported by both Reich and Länder contributions. There was nothing to prevent the federation from contributing to the support of such institutions. The question was: should the federation itself be allowed to establish institutes and, beyond that, university institutions that would soon lead to the necessity of federal as well as Land cultural administration.

Dr. Schmid (SPD) pointed out that the federation would be precluded, under the terms of its financial powers, even from devoting money to this purpose unless it had been given a specific competence in the field. Nor, he said, could federal funds be appropriated for this purpose without any conditions being laid down regarding their use. On this basis, Dr. Laforet and his colleagues accepted the clause at a later sitting.

7. ADMINISTRATION

As a counterpart to the federation's supremacy in legislation, the Basic Law gives the Länder primary responsibility for administration (Article 83). A constitutional enumeration, hence a limitation, of the federation's powers—absurdly elaborate though it may be as a method of securing a half-dozen residual legislative powers to the Länder—is therefore appropriate, indeed, essential, in the field of administration.

As the Germans see it, this was the precise point at which the federal structure broke down in the Weimar time.[60] The Weimar constitution recognized (in Article 14) the competence of the Länder to administer the laws of the Reich, but at the same time opened the way, without limit, to the establishment by simple enactment of Reich administrative agencies at all levels. The clarity of the German administrative system, with the Reich administration confined to the central departments in Berlin and field administration in the hands of the states, soon gave way to a confusion and overlapping of jurisdictions, particularly in Prussia, as Reich authorities with administrative staffs reaching down to the Gemeinden were added for an ever broadening range of functions, some new, some taken over from the Länder.

The federalists in the Parliamentary Council were determined this time to pin the federation down in the administrative field. Dr. Josef Schwalber, one of the CSU leaders, told the delegates:

As regards administration, the principle, already laid down in Article 14 of the Weimar constitution will be indisputably acknowledged today: that the execution of federal legislation is a matter for the Länder, to be carried out by their own authorities. A right of supervision and of inspection will be conceded to the federation, limited to insuring that this execution has been carried out in conformity with the law. Whereas under Article 14 of the Weimar constitution an exception to the principle referred to could be made by simple Reich law, Article 30 of the Chiemsee draft stipulates that the Basic Law itself will regulate the assignment of administrative competence to the federation. That must be firmly established to prevent the undermining of the competency of the Länder, a deviation from the principle of federalism, and dislocation of the federal equilibrium.[61]

The Basic Law fixes bounds for the administrative activity of the federation in two ways: by limiting the scope of federal administration proper and by specifying how far and under what conditions the federal government may intervene to enforce, direct, or supervise administration of federal legislation by the Länder.

For this purpose, five types of administration are distinguished in the Basic Law:*

a) Federal administration of federal laws (*Bundeseigene Verwaltung*)— Articles 86–90, 108(1);

b) Land administration of Land laws (*Landeseigene Verwaltung*)—Article 30;

c) Administration of federal laws by the Länder "as a matter of their own concern" (*Landeseigene Verwaltung*)—Articles 83, 84, 108(3);

d) Administration of federal laws by the Länder under delegation from the federation (*Bundesauftragsverwaltung*)—Article 85, 108(4);

e) As a special case of (*a*), administration of federal laws by federal corporations chartered under public law (*Bundesunmittelbare Körperschaften des öffentlichen Rechtes*)—Article 87 (2)(3).

Restriction of Federal Administrative Agencies (Bundeseigene Verwaltung)— Articles 86, 87

The Basic Law makes no provision as to the number, kind, and size of federal ministerial departments. The federal government and parliament are free to establish as many ministries as they please if they concern matters for which the federation is competent.[62] Neither the Parliamentary Council, nor the Chiemsee conference before it, occupied themselves with federal administration in this sense—with policy-making and administrative direction at the high-

---

* Examples of each: Under (*a*), the federal foreign, postal, and railway services have their own subordinate administrative structures and carry out as a matter of federal responsibility all legislation in these fields. The Land authorities under (*b*) administer legislation on the police and local government. Under (*c*), they administer federal labor law and federal legislation on public relief. Under (*d*), to the extent that administration has been delegated to them, the Länder carry out legislation on waterways, the *Autobahnen,* and federal highways used by long-distance traffic. Under (*e*), federal corporations have been established for unemployment insurance (10/3/52), for air insurance (23/3/53) and insurance for public employees (7/8/53).

est level. The level at which they wished to apply a brake was somewhat lower: at the point where administrative decisions and actions begin directly to impinge on the life of the community. Thus they were concerned with restricting the number of federal departments *with subordinate administrative structures*, as well as federal administrative agencies and federal public corporations established for special tasks.

The Chiemsee conference proposed that only three ministerial departments with "subordinate administrative structure" should be authorized—for foreign affairs, posts, and railroads. The Parliamentary Council added federal finance and federal waterways administration.

German ministers commonly rely to a great extent upon federal agencies (*Bundesoberbehörden*), responsible to them but relatively independent of their departments, to carry out particular administrative tasks for which these agencies are especially established.* The Chiemsee conference recommended that constitutional authorization for such agencies be confined to "cases of need" for matters *within the federal legislative competence*, that a list of authorized types of agencies be annexed to the Basic Law, and that Bundesrat approval be required for the establishment of all new agencies. Federally supervised public corporations were to be chartered only for social insurance functions and only with Bundesrat approval.

As the federal legislative competence grew ever more broad in the course of negotiations, the limiting of federal agencies to matters within the federal competence increasingly appeared to be no limit at all. The Parliamentary Council therefore fell back on the second device, strengthening it by stipulating the approval of two-thirds of the Bundesrat for new federal "intermediate" and "lower"† agencies, while retaining the requirement of a simple Bundesrat majority for new "superior"† federal agencies. At the same time, the Bundesrat majority required for approval of new public corporations was raised to two-thirds.

* In a twelve-month period in 1951–52, the following were established: *Bundesstelle für den Warenverkehr der Gewerblichen Wirtschaft*, 29/3/51; *Aussenhandelsstelle für Erzeugnisse der Ernährung und Landwirtschaft*, 17/12/51; *Bundesaufsichtsamt für das Versicherungs- und Bausparwesen*, 31/7/51; *Kraftfahrt-Bundesamt*, 4/8/51; *Bundesgesundheitsamt*, 27/2/52; *Bundesamt für Auswanderung*, 8/5/52.

† Broadly speaking, these terms distinguish between field agencies in the Länder and agencies at federal level.

Under Socialist pressure, the Council made the administrative device of the public corporation available for use by the federal government in fields other than social insurance. The Socialists pointed out that the federation was to have power to transfer industries and resources to public ownership. Was it wise, they asked, by leaving it no choice, to compel a future federal government to administer such public undertakings through the regular departments rather than by the less bureaucratic method of the public corporation? In the industry of the Ruhr, particularly, they foresaw an opportunity for the use of such corporations.[63] The Socialists also asked whether constitutional authorization could not be given to a type of administration intermediate between that of departments and agencies of the federal government proper and the federally supervised independent public corporations—administration which Carlo Schmid[64] likened to the "Anglo-Saxon boards" and the *Reichsstellen* of the Third Reich. This suggestion, however, was unfavorably received on all sides. Dr. von Brentano objected:

. . . There were agencies of this kind under the Third Reich and we all had experience of what they meant then. In my opinion, we have every reason to establish in the constitution clear and unambiguous lines of responsibility; we must therefore take special care lest any of these anonymous bodies, who escape responsibility to either the federation or the Länder or any parliamentary control, are able to celebrate a joyous resurrection. One ought to be clear as to the legal position of any institution and to whom it is responsible. . . . In my view, it would be a desirable objective in the constitution to prevent the establishment of institutions of a nature intermediate between these two familiar forms and about whose activities and development we would not be at all clear when we set them up.[65]

The Bundesrat's control over the size of the federal bureaucracy was a casualty of the Allied intervention. After this intervention, a majority could no longer be found in the Parliamentary Council for Bundesrat control over the establishment of "superior" federal administrative agencies and of public corporations.[66] Only legislation to create new "intermediate" and "lower" federal agencies remains among the *Zustimmungsgesetze*. Important for the Länder as this remaining check on the expansion of federal agencies into the field may be, the loss of the other two controls was a severe blow to the German federalists. As Dr. Süsterhenn (CDU) said:

The principle laid down in the constitution is that administration, particularly that requiring a subordinate administrative structure, is a matter belonging to the Länder. . . . If, as here, one leaves it open to the federation, by simple federal law in any form it pleases, to establish independent corporations under federal supervision and with their own subordinate administration in the Länder, the right of the Länder to conduct administration at that level will be undermined.[67]

To the members of the Land governments in the Bundesrat, these two controls over the size of federal administration could have been far more useful in preserving the federal equilibrium of the Basic Law than are the obscure conditions with which the Allied military governors insisted upon qualifying the concurrent legislative powers.

Limits of Federal Intervention in Land Administration (Landeseigene Verwaltung) —Article 84; (*Auftragsverwaltung*)—*Article 85* The Basic Law presumes that the greater part of federal legislation will be administered by the authorities of the Länder on their own responsibility—or, as the Germans phrase it, as "matters of their own concern" (*als eigene Angelegenheit*). Administration which the Länder undertake under delegation from the federation (*Auftragsverwaltung*), hence for which they are *directly responsible* to the federal government, is confined to the limited purposes in the Basic Law (the federal *Autobahnen*, long-distance federal highways, federal taxes, etc.) and cannot be enlarged without constitutional amendment.[68]

Hence an inducement existed in the Parliamentary Council both for centralists and federalists to define with precision the relation between federal authority and the Land administrations—for the centralists, to prevent frustration of the federation's legislative intentions by an obstructive or incompetent administration in the Länder; for the federalists, to preserve the autonomy of the Land administrations from erosion through the constant intervention of the federal departments.

Accordingly, the Basic Law prescribes in some detail what the federation may do (and, by implication, what it may not do) to overcome obstruction in the Länder, to correct deficient administration, and to insure, by provisions of its own, the implementation of federal legislation by the Länder according to its wishes.

If a Land is obstructive and fails to carry out its federal obligation under the Basic Law or a federal law, the federal government (i.e., the federal cabinet) may, with the consent of the Bundesrat, take the necessary measures to compel it to do so (Article 37). For this purpose, the federal government may give instructions to all the Länder and their authorities. The Land against which such measures are applied may appeal against them in the constitutional court, but no prior determination by the court on the issues is required before the federal government can act,[69] nor does the filing of a suit have the effect of suspending the compulsory measures.[70] This is the *"Reichsexekution"* of the Weimar constitution, with the powers taken from the president and put into the hands of responsible ministers, whose use of them can be restrained by the Bundestag and, on behalf of Land interests, by the Bundesrat as well. There was general agreement in the Parliamentary Council on this provision.

As a safeguard against deficient or incompetent administration, the federal government may exercise supervision to insure that the Länder execute federal laws "in accordance with applicable law." For this purpose, it may send commissioners to the highest Land authorities to observe and obtain information on their operations (Article 84). With the consent of the higher Land authorities or, failing this, with the consent of the Bundesrat, federal commissioners may also be sent to subordinate Land authorities. If the federal government finds "shortcomings" in the execution of federal laws which the Land authorities do not correct, the Bundesrat decides whether the Land has "infringed the law." The Bundesrat's decision may be challenged in the constitutional court.

The test which the federal government is entitled here to apply to Land administration of federal law is a purely legal one: does it conform to the provisions of the legislation in question and any other pertinent laws or regulations?—not a test as to the "fitness" (*Zweckmässigkeit*) of the means chosen to accomplish the task. The second test may be applied to delegated administration (Article 85 [4]), but not to administration which the Länder undertake on their own responsibility. By means of this distinction, the federalists[71] sought to preserve the principle that in *Landeseigene Verwaltung*, the Länder (unless an exception is authorized by the Bundesrat) are fully autonomous in establishing their own administrative organizations and procedures (Article 84 [1]). How useful such a distinction may be in practice is questionable, particularly where general standards for the provision of services or the performance of obligations have to be laid down.

On the other hand, the Social Democrats feared that an obstructive Land government might deny to a federal minister access to information to "prove" deficiencies in administration to the Bundesrat or the constitutional court. They therefore demanded for a minister the right, with the approval of the Bundesrat, to send his investigators to Land authorities at all levels, if necessary over the objections of a Land government.[72] As Dr. Heinrich von Brentano (CDU) pointed out, such a right would gain the federal minister nothing if the Land government then instructed its subordinates to refuse information to his representatives.

The mutual distrust of the supporters of the federation and of the Länder thus led to a series of provisions aimed at forestalling hypothetical "abuses," which are of doubtful practicability and would be likely to magnify rather than ameliorate differences between the federal government and the Länder.

Dr. von Brentano made the point forcefully:

We ought to try to get away from this intolerable distrust we are introducing into the constitution. We are assuming from the start that each Land will necessarily either refuse to implement federal legislation or fail to do it properly, that it will evade control, that the federal commissioners will be refused the information they require by the Land authorities. Equally, the Länder assume that the federation will abuse absolutely every power with which is has been provided. In fitting out the constitution with all these checks and dams to prevent abuse on both sides, we are, in my opinion, burdening it with a mass of provisions that will probably work out disastrously in practice.[73]

What can the federal government do by way of prior regulation or instruction to insure that the Land authorities administer laws according to its wishes? We have already noted that federal ministers are commonly authorized in federal legislation to supplement its broad provisions by detailed ordinances which have the effect of law (*Rechtsverordnungen*) and that these must be approved by the Bundesrat where the legislation concerned affects Land interests. Distinct from these ordinances, which like their parent laws are addressed to the citizens, the federal government is also entitled to issue "general administrative regulations" (*Allgemeine Verwaltungsvorschriften*) which are addressed to and binding upon the officials of the public service. In connection with *Landeseigene Verwaltung*, federal ministers, with the approval of the Bundesrat, may issue such general regulations for the Land administrations. It is easier to state concretely what may *not* than what *may* be regulated in this manner. Federal ministers may not regulate the establishment of Land administrative organizations, their procedures, or the recruitment or training of staffs.[74] Nor may they, by way of regulation, "instruct" the administrative authorities in the Länder in particular matters. Nor may regulations be addressed to the administrative authorities of a single Land, except where the conditions to be regulated are confined to that Land.[75] Within these limits, federal ministers may set guiding lines and standards for administration in the Länder.

The Social Democrats were unwilling to leave the federal ministers with no power of issuing direct instructions to the Land authorities on particular matters. The need for such a power, they argued, had been amply demonstrated in the bizone, where the authorities dealing with the problems of the economic emergency would have been helpless without it. They were thankful that the British in their zone of occupation had established central administrative offices equipped with such powers; for through them, disaster in the Ruhr had been staved off in the winter of crisis of 1946.[76] The Socialists therefore proposed that in special fields—regulation of the economy, labor, refugees, securing the food supply, currency, customs, and shipping—the federal government should be empowered to instruct the Land authorities directly on individual problems.

For the federalists, who maintained that the federal government could accomplish everything necessary to its purpose by a law or by administrative regulation, such a right meant a foot in the door for the totalitarian state.

Here a decisive question faces us: are we to restore the position which existed until 1933 or are we to adopt the procedures of the Nazi state, the unitary state? First, to clear up a mistake. Some take it for granted that a "right of instruction" must be expressly provided for the federation in the Basic Law in cases where a federal minister, under powers conferred by law, wishes to effect certain arrangements with the Land authorities. That is not right. There is nothing to prevent the federal government, as circumstances may require, from prescribing certain obligations or procedures for the Länder. . . . It may, for instance, by a federal law on refugee matters, stipulate that refugees from one Land will be settled in another. Or so long as the food position continues as it is now, a federal law may authorize a federal ministry to specify quotas of agricultural products to be made available by a Land. For these purposes, no instruction is necessary; the obligations of a Land have already been laid down by law. The federal government can go even further and, with Bundesrat concurrence, adopt general administrative regulations limiting—or even excluding—any discretionary judgment on the part of the Land authorities. . . . On the other hand, it must be stressed that by infringing the fundamental autonomy of Land administration—in a limited number of matters to be sure, but those the most important—there is a serious danger of recreating a Nazi-type uniform administration.[77]

The issue was settled by a compromise which provides (Article 84 [5]) that federal ministers may issue direct instructions in individual cases to the Länder, but only under the authority of a federal law approved by the Bundesrat. This in effect confines the exercise of this power to circumstances in which the federal government can convince the Bundesrat that a case for its use exists.

On the other hand, where the Länder administer federal law under delegation (*Auftragsverwaltung*), they are fully subject to the supervision, direction, and instruction of the competent federal minister (Article 85).

8.   FINANCE

The problem of deciding where to locate in the federal structure the power to levy and collect taxes raised for the Parliamentary Council a dilemma that confronts every federal nation. How are financial resources to be secured to the states and their local communities, freeing them of dependence on, and hence control by, the central government, without creating conditions for the growth and perpetuation of inequalities between the states injurious to the welfare of the citizens of the several states, to economic enterprise, and, ultimately, to the national interest itself?

In the strictest sense, states in a federation can be financially independent of the central government only if, as in the United States, they possess power of their own to tax and spend within their area of jurisdiction, subject only to the limits of the tax burden the people will bear and the resources available. But from this arrangement, serious economic and social disadvantages may result. Even if the several states individually conduct their fiscal policies with maximum care for the effect on economic activity both within the state and the nation at large, adventitious differences in taxes, rate scales, and principles of assessment and collection within the several state systems will inevitably diminish uniformity of competitive conditions and the national market.

But, further, the states may deliberately pursue a policy of self-interest, manipulating taxes to attract new industries or to win industries from other states in an interstate competition, or to penalize or exclude the products of industries competing with home industries, or to discourage the entry of "foreigners" into protected trades, professions, or businesses. Heavy state expenditures in good times and correspondingly severe reductions in depression, combined with regressive tax structures concentrating the tax burden on consumption, may frustrate national efforts to avoid or mitigate the effects of a trade cycle. If the distribution of industries and other sources of wealth throughout the federal territory is not a balanced one (and it seldom is), the revenue resources of the states will be unequal. If, further, the states and communities are largely responsible, as they commonly are, for furnishing basic services to the public, the provisions for education, health and medical care, social security and welfare, transport facilities, and so on, will vary from state to state according to the scale of financial resources available to support them. The accident of place of birth and residence will thus determine the kind, amount, and quality of public services provided the citizen and his family. The purpose behind these services—to provide a basic equality of opportunity and a basic minimum of protection against the accidents of life for all—will be frustrated.

Such, in fact, have been the consequences of state financial autonomy in America, and such has been the price the people of the United States have paid for it.[78] The American federal government, to be sure, may do and has done something by grants-in-aid to the states to mitigate the worst inequalities. Unfortunately, this method of offsetting deficiencies, while correcting some anomalies, only intensifies others. Apart from the fact that federal grants have been made piecemeal on an *ad hoc*, unco-ordinated basis for a wide variety of purposes of unequal merit, they are available to the states and communities usually on the condition that they contribute a share to the cost of the project or service for which the funds are allocated. This has two consequences. Local services (e.g., the public schools) which do not qualify for federal assistance are doubly penalized, for they must then compete at a disadvantage with those that do qualify for local funds. But, further, federal grants for which "matching" contributions are stipulated do little to correct disparities between the public services of the states, since the better-off states are in a position to qualify for a larger share of federal appropriations than the less well off.

The Parliamentary Council delegates did not choose to follow the American example and give both the federation and the Länder autonomy in finance, because they thought Western Germany could not afford it. As Dr. Höpker-Aschoff* said:

> Our poverty and the high level of our tax rates will not permit us the luxury of an entirely unregulated scramble for tax sources between two competitors. In the United States it may be possible for the federation to levy and collect its own income tax and the states to levy and collect their income taxes—the same with inheritance taxes and so on. For us, it would be entirely unworkable.[79]

As the Germans saw it, they had only these alternatives: to vest responsibility for finance either in the federation or in the Länder. As between national fiscal uniformity and financial autonomy for the Länder, the majority of the Council came down on the side of the first. At the same time, they were ready to guarantee constitutionally to the Länder the revenues of specific taxes adequate to enable them all to carry out their functions. The Council therefore

concentrated the legislative power to establish taxes and fix rates in the hands of the federation, with the exception of a few taxes of purely local application;

proposed a federal financial administration to assess and collect all taxes, with the exception of the taxes of local application;

provided for a constitutional division of the revenues of specific taxes between the federation and the Länder, with the proceeds of the largest revenue-producing taxes—the income, corporation, and turnover (sales) taxes—to be shared between them;

provided for a redistribution of part of the revenues of the financially "strong" Länder to the financially "weak" Länder.

---

* Höpker-Aschoff, a former Prussian minister of finance, was the most influential member of the Parliamentary Council's finance committee.

The Allied authorities opposed this solution as insufficiently federalistic. By stipulating that federal legislation must be confined to taxes used to finance federal activities, they sought to enforce a dual exercise of the tax power by the federation and the Länder. Similarly, they proposed a dual tax administration, the federation to collect taxes the whole revenue of which accrued to it and its share of the income and corporation taxes, the Länder to collect the remainder of the shared taxes and revenues of taxes accruing in full to them. They asked that the revenues of additional taxes be assigned to the Länder. They rejected any scheme for equalization of revenues between the Länder.

To the extent that the Allied authorities hoped to persuade the Germans to adopt such a decentralization of public finance in their own interests and as a democratic safeguard, the Germans found the arguments offered them doctrinaire and the methods proposed ill-suited to the conditions of their country and its problems: —

Was such decentralization an essential of democratic government? Had the concentration of these powers under the Weimar constitution any real connection with the totalitarian methods of the Third Reich? The Germans thought the point was at least debatable. No doubt the National Socialists had found the Weimar financial system easier to adapt to their purposes than others might have been, but did this prove that the system itself was essentially undemocratic or more prone to exploitation for undemocratic purposes than any other? How could central financial control in Great Britain and France be reconciled with such an argument?

Must the division of financial powers and responsibilities between the central and state governments in other federal systems be taken as a model for Western Germany? To the Germans, it seemed self-evident that methods satisfactory to peoples living in other conditions might not necessarily be appropriate for them. They saw no intrinsic merit, for example, in turning the tax system into a competition between rival taxing authorities and patching up the results by piecemeal subsidies from the central government. Given a federal structure of government, they agreed that a way had to be found to secure the financial position of the Länder. But they believed that they could best judge, in the light of their own experience and the problems they faced, how this was to be done.

Earlier German   The Parliamentary Council's approach to public
Public Finance   finance can be better understood in the light of
German practice in the past. The foundations of
the German federal tax structure were laid in 1834, when most of
the German states united in a customs union. Uniform customs and
excise taxes were established by parallel laws in the states, and the
proceeds were collected and distributed to the states according to
the size of their populations. Upon its establishment in 1871, the
Reich government assumed sole legislative competence over customs and excise. Henceforth until 1918, the Reich fixed and received
the proceeds from customs and excise and some transactions taxes,
which were collected for it by the state administrations. To the extent that these revenues of the Reich were not adequate to meet its
needs, periodic contributions were assessed to the states according to
population. The Reich had the power to impose direct taxes, but
made no use of it until capital levies and a property tax were introduced to finance the 1914–18 war. Until 1914, direct taxes were thus
left entirely to the states, which set and collected the income, property, and inheritance taxes and some transactions taxes. Taxes on real
estate and businesses and lesser indirect taxes were commonly left to
the Gemeinden (municipalities). The Prussian provincial and Land-
kreis (county) administrations were supported from state funds.

Under the Weimar constitution, the Reich legislated on[80] and,
through its own administration,[81] collected most of the taxes. To the
customs and excise taxes, it added a new turnover (sales) tax and
new transactions taxes (capital transactions, transportation of pas-
sengers and freight, motor vehicles, etc.). It took over from the
Länder the fixing and collection of the income, property, and inheritance taxes. To the Länder were left only legislation on and (if
they chose) administration of the real estate, business, and house-
rent taxes and certain transactions taxes. The Reich transferred to
the Länder 75 per cent of the proceeds of the income and corporations taxes, 30 per cent of the proceeds of the turnover tax, and the
whole of the proceeds of the motor vehicles, race-betting, and acquisition of real estate taxes, less costs of administration. To the Gemeinden were normally left certain business taxes, surtaxes on real
estate, and their traditional small indirect taxes. The Prussian provinces and Landkreise continued to be supported by state appropriations.

The National Socialist regime, in keeping with its general policy of reducing the Länder to administrative districts of the Reich, converted the remaining Land taxes to Reich taxes and assigned real estate and business taxes again to the Gemeinden for collection. The Land and local administrations were financed by the Reich government according to its own conception of their needs.

Thus, when the Allied military governments took control in 1945, all but a few local taxes had been established by Reich legislation. Military government preserved this tax structure. Under military government, taxes continued to be exclusively subject to the legislation of central authority—military government itself or, in certain cases, the bizonal economic council. From the capitulation, Land administrations in the United States and French zones had collected all except the local taxes. In the British zone until April 1, 1948, taxes were collected through a central finance office, and the proceeds were remitted to the Länder. Thereafter, they were collected by Land administrations.

TAXES IN WESTERN GERMANY[82]
(1945–1949)

Taxes established by Reich legislation, as amended or supplemented by military government and bizonal economic council legislation, and collected by the Länder in the U.S. and French zones and by a central finance office in the British zone:

INDIRECT		DIRECT
Customs	Turnover	Income and corpora-
Excise	Transactions	tion
Tobacco	Acquisition of real	Property
Sugar	estate	Inheritance
Sweets	Capital transactions	Capital levies for non-
Salt	Exchange	recurrent purposes
Coffee	Transportation of	(e.g., equalization of
Beer	passengers and	war burdens)
Vinegar	freight	
Ignitors	Motor vehicles	
[*Zündwaren*]	Race-betting and lot-	
Illuminants	teries	
[*Leuchtmittel*]	Insurance	
Playing cards	Fire protection	
Mineral oil		
Spirits and		
Match monopolies		

Taxes established by Reich or former Land legislation and collected by the Gemeinden:

INDIRECT	DIRECT
Surtax on acquisitions of real estate	Real estate and business
Increments of value	
Entertainments	
Victualers' licenses	
Local spirits tax	
Hunting licenses	
Dog licenses	

As to the relative importance of the major taxes, of a total revenue in the bizonal area of approximately DM. 14.5 milliard in 1948–49, customs and excise taxes accounted for DM. 2.6 milliard; the turnover tax, DM. 3.35 milliard; the income and corporation taxes, DM. 6.41 milliard; and the remainder, DM. 2.1 milliard.

Legislation on Taxes (Article 105)   The Parliamentary Council delegates took up the slogan of the Chiemsee conference: "The Länder shan't be boarders of the federation, nor the federation a boarder of the Länder." ("*Länder nicht Kostgänger des Bundes; Bund nicht Kostgänger der Länder.*") But the two assemblies did not entirely agree on the way to attain this objective.

The majority of the Chiemsee experts held not only that adequate and secure sources of revenue should be available both for the federation and the Länder, but that the levying of certain indirect taxes, taxes of local application, and the fixing of the direct taxes on income, corporations, and property within the framework of general federal legislation should be left to the Länder.[83]

The finance committee of the Parliamentary Council did not accept this view.[84] If legislation on *indirect* taxes were left to the Länder, they argued, some Länder would benefit at the expense of others. Although, through the passing on of the taxes in prices to the ultimate consumer, the burden would fall upon the people of all the Länder, the border states would benefit extensively from customs, the centers of production from excise taxes, and the Länder with the largest financial and trade operations from transactions taxes. Since both excise and transactions taxes entered into the costs of production, these could not be regulated by the Länder without introducing variations in competitive conditions throughout the economy. In the interests of the country's foreign trade, the committee held, the central government must be in a position to make uniform adjustments in customs and excise and sales taxes to preserve both fair competitive conditions in the internal market and a favorable competitive position for German exports in foreign markets.[85]

As for *direct taxes*, Dr. Höpker-Aschoff told the Council[86] that varying state income and property taxes had been practicable in the time of the Empire, because rates were low. The highest Prussian rate on an income of RM. 100,000 had been 4 per cent, and on property 0.5 per thousand. Today, he pointed out, the rates were 95 per cent and 0.75 per cent respectively. Variations in these taxes, he went on, would lead not only to injustices between taxpayers in the several Länder, but to different levels of investment in the Länder and costly shifts of industries from place to place to avoid the higher rates of the financially hard-pressed Länder—moves which the economy could ill afford. If, as the Allied authorities insisted, there was to be a division of taxing powers between the federation and the Länder, it would have to take into account their respective revenue requirements—which, for the Länder, amounted to more than half the total available sum. All of the direct taxes would therefore have to be assigned to the Länder, for, whatever happened, the finance committee had no doubt that customs, excise, and most transactions taxes must be reserved for uniform central legislation. But powers over direct taxes were also essential to a government aspiring to carry out an enlightened social policy and a financial policy aimed at promoting national production and full employment. "Were the means of doing this to be afforded the Länder, yet denied the federal government?" Höpker-Aschoff asked.

We have the teaching of the great English thinker, Keynes, to thank for recognition of the fact that government through its financial policy can influence the course of economic development. The government ought in times of depression to promote investments through credits and cover its current expenditures with credits and then, naturally, in good times must accumulate the necessary funds to cover these credits. We know, moreover, how the government through its financial policy can influence the relation of supply and demand and thereby the level of prices and purchasing power—that is to say, the value of money—so that in monetary policy, public finance can not be ignored. All of these tasks can be carried out for a homogeneous economic area only by a central legislative authority, that is, by the federation. It follows that it is altogether impossible to leave an extensive field of tax legislation to the Länder, irrespective of what revenues from the federally regulated taxes may be assigned to the Länder to cover their functions.[87]

With the exception of a few taxes of local application, the finance committee therefore proposed, and the Parliamentary Council agreed, that the federation should have "exclusive" legislative competence over customs and "priority" legislative competence over all the remaining taxes, both direct and indirect. There was little dissent. The Bavarians at first held out for their traditional right to fix their own taxes on beer, but later gave this up on the understanding that they would be allowed to retain the greater part of revenue from the tax. The CDU/CSU also pressed for a constitutional right for the Länder to add their own surtaxes to the federally established income and corporation taxes. This was rejected by the majority, who agreed, however, that the right could be extended to the Länder by federal legislation at any time in the future.

The military governors, when the final German draft came before them, took the position that the tax power should be shared—that the federation should legislate only on the taxes which it might claim either in whole or in part to cover its own responsibilities.[88] In so stipulating, the military governors went beyond their first advice to the Council. On October 20, through their liaison officers, and again in their November 22 aide memoire, they had told the Parliamentary Council that, while they disapproved of other financial provisions as they were developing in the finance committee, they agreed that the federation might legislate to set rates and principles of assessment on taxes "for which uniformity is essential." The military governors had not specified the taxes for which such uniformity might be essential. The Germans supposed that the decision had been left to them.

The Germans closed ranks at an interparty meeting on March 3 and 4, 1949, and resolved to stand firm. At a meeting on March 9, their experts reproached the military governors' finance advisers for the inconsistency of the Allied position. Not only had the military governors departed from their own directive, they were now compelling the future German government to forego that uniform tax structure which the military governors themselves had inherited and had not seen fit in four years of occupation government to discard.

The finance advisers did not attempt to justify the Allied position. Later, however, the military governors gave way and agreed that *either* their own criterion *or* the need for uniformity (as defined in the qualifying conditions for federal exercise of the concurrent legislative powers [Article 72]) could serve as a ground for federal exercise of the tax power. Since, as we have seen,[88a] the constitutional court considers the federal parliament alone competent to decide whether a need for legislation under Article 72 exists, federal supremacy in legislation on taxes may be taken as established.

Administration of Taxes (Article 108) On the question of tax administration—how taxes were to be assessed and collected—opinion in the Parliamentary Council was as divided as it had been united on tax legislation. The delegates considered that they had only two practicable alternatives: administration by the federation *or* by the Länder. The experts who were called by the finance committee to give their views,[89] the centralists,[90] and the federalists[91] all agreed upon one thing: Western Germany had neither the funds nor the trained personnel to afford the luxury of duplicate federal and Land finance administrations.

The Free Democrats and Socialists put the case for a federal administration in the finance and main committees.[92] Without a single administration for the whole federal territory, they argued, the purpose of establishing fiscal uniformity by federal legislation would be defeated. Through the varying practices of eleven Land administrations in assessing taxes and granting tax postponements, exemptions, remissions, and cancellations, the inequities and anomalies which it was the object of federal legislation to eliminate would be introduced into the fiscal system by another door. They denied that a sufficiently uniform administrative practice could be secured either by consultation and agreement between the Länder or by making the Land finance authorities subject to the supervision and instruction of the federal finance minister. Nothing, they maintained, could take the place of a single homogeneous service, whose officials had received the same training, were subject to the same discipline, and were thoroughly versed in operating uniform procedures. The postwar administration by the Länder of the Allied Control Council taxes showed this. Eleven separate tax administrations would be both more costly and less efficient than a single service. No matter how carefully the legislation might be thought out, they held, the administration of the forthcoming equalization of war burdens, with all its complex assessments, would require a continuous stream of instructions and individual decisions from the center. How was it possible to carry out such a task with eleven separate finance administrations?

The federalists (CDU/CSU and DP) contended that the assessment and collection of taxes should be made the responsibility of the Länder, to balance federal predominance in tax legislation. The broad principle of allocating in the Basic Law legislative functions to the federation and administration to the Länder should be adhered to in finance. They did not deny the need for uniformity of practice in the assessment of taxes and granting of tax reliefs, but held that this could be accomplished by giving the federal finance minister, in connection with federal taxes, the right to issue regulations and instructions on the procedures to be followed in the Länder; to provide uniform training for young tax officers of the Länder; to participate in the selection of the higher finance officials of the Länder; and to audit the accounts of the Land finance officers.[93] A Land administration, staffed with local people, would be in a better position than a remote central bureaucracy to take account of local needs and sensitivities.[94] How, for instance, could a Bavarian farmer be expected to be co-operative and forthcoming with a tax officer who was not his own countryman? Possessing the advantage of local knowledge and experience, a Land administration could be counted upon to collect the taxes more efficiently and with as many as a third fewer officials than a federal bureaucracy.[95] Most important, the Länder could be sure of prompt receipt of their revenues if they collected them themselves. When the Weimar Länder had turned their taxes over to the Reich finance offices for collection, they found that they got second-best service.

We had the famous Paragraph 19 of the Reich Tax Ordinance [*Abgabenordnung*], which provided that the Reich finance administration could take charge of the Land taxes upon the request of the Länder. In Bavaria, unfortunately, we had some very sad experiences. The Land taxes were treated like stepchildren. The finance offices looked above them and thought to themselves: "We shan't get into so much trouble if we fall behind with these as we shall if we delay the Reich taxes."[96]

Of the financial experts who appeared before the finance committee, the majority favored a federal administration. So also did the majority of the Land finance ministers who gave their views to the committee or whose views were known.* The finance committee recommended to the main committee that a federal administration should be established for all taxes but those of local application, with the proviso that the heads of the federal finance and customs offices in the Länder should be appointed by agreement with the Land governments. This was adopted by a narrow majority, eleven to nine—the Social Democrats, Free Democrats, Center, and Communists joining against the CDU/CSU and the German party.

In terms of the Allied directives, the Parliamentary Council was not on such firm ground in establishing a federal tax administration as it was in providing for uniform tax legislation. As early as October 20, the military governors' liaison officers had called on Herr Schönfelder, the deputy chairman of the Parliamentary Council, to draw his attention to the military governors' concern over the decisions taken in the finance committee. The military governors agreed, Herr Schönfelder was told, that the federation might fix the rates and principles of assessment for non-federal taxes for which uniformity was necessary, "but the collection of these taxes and the disposition of their revenues must be left to each state individually." When Herr Schönfelder demurred and said that, whatever might be possible for such prosperous countries as Switzerland and the United States, Germany could not afford finance administrations for both the federation and the Länder, he was treated to a characteristic Allied homily on democratic salvation through federalism. The military governors reaffirmed their position on November

* For a federal administration: the ministers of North Rhine-Westphalia, Rhineland-Palatinate, Württemberg-Baden, Schleswig-Holstein, Hamburg; for a Land administration: the ministers of Bavaria, Hesse, Württemberg-Hohenzollern, Lower Saxony.

22.[97] On March 2, they informed the Parliamentary Council that the assessment and collection of taxes must be left to the Länder, except those to be used *in their entirety* to support authorized federal activities and the income tax "to the extent that such a tax is for federal purposes."[98]

The Parliamentary Council therefore had no choice but, as Dr. Höpker-Aschoff expressed it, "to bite into the sour apple of divided finance administration."[99] To avoid the cost and confusion of introducing at that stage in Western Germany entirely new administrative machinery and procedures at federal and Land level, the German finance experts redistributed the sources of tax revenue between the federation and the Länder as nearly as possible on traditional lines (indirect taxes to the federation, direct taxes to the Länder), so that the existing apparatus could be adjusted to a dual responsibility for administration with as little difficulty as possible.[100] Since, in practice, the federation has either made use of Länder staffs to administer its taxes or delegated their administration to the Länder, by far the greater part of tax administration today is in the hands of the Länder. For the administration of the equalization of burdens legislation, a hybrid federal-Land administration under federal direction had to be established.

There has been much discontent with these arrangements. In 1953, 214 deputies in the Bundestag, opposed by 151, voted to amend the Basic Law to permit the establishment of a unified federal financial administration (267 votes were required to carry the amendment in the Bundestag). The Free Democrats who introduced the measure, with the support of the Social Democrats, held that it was essential to increase efficiency in tax collections and to combat tax evasion and could be expected to raise tax receipts throughout the federation by as much as DM. 1 milliard. The federal finance minister, Dr. Fritz Schäffer,* has so far opposed the establishment of a federal finance administration. Its supporters believe, however, that he, as well as his senior officials, have been converted by experience to the necessity of a unified administration, and that Dr. Schäffer is restrained only by political considerations from throwing his support behind it.[101] He is a leader of the Christian Social Union and represents the parliamentary constituency of Passau *in Bavaria!*

* Dr. Schäffer has since been replaced as finance minister.

Division of Tax Sources between the Federation and the Länder (Article 106)

Two provisions are made in the Basic Law to secure the financial position of the Länder. In the first, the revenues of specific taxes are assigned respectively to the federation and the Länder. In the second, a part of the funds accruing to the Länder may be reapportioned to strengthen the financial capacity of Länder with low tax revenues and to equalize among the Länder a differing burden of expenditure.

A specific division of tax sources between the federation and the Länder was inserted in the Basic Law at the request of the federalist parties. They wanted to establish for the Länder a constitutional claim to the revenues of definite taxes, thereby giving the Land finance ministers a measure of certainty as to the basic sources of revenue which would be available to finance Land services.[102] The finance committee had accepted the principle of this from the start, but had hesitated to include a specific division of revenues in the constitution because of the then-prevailing uncertainty about the scale of burdens which the federation and Länder would respectively be called upon to bear, as well as about the size of revenues which would be available to meet them. When the CDU/CSU delegates suggested that the first apportionment should be only a provisional one, subject to replacement by a final act within a period of years, Höpker-Aschoff quickly came to an agreement with them.[103] The agreement called for the provisional assignment to the Länder and the Gemeinden of the proceeds of the beer tax, the transactions taxes on race-betting and motor vehicles, and the taxes on property, inheritances, and real estate. The federation was to receive the proceeds from customs and the remaining excise and transactions taxes. The proceeds of taxes producing the largest revenues—the income, corporation, and turnover taxes—were to be shared between the federation and the Länder, according to federal legislation requiring the approval of the Bundesrat.

A dissenting voice came from Bavaria. Ministerialdirektor Ringelmann[104] said he had been instructed by his government to insist that the whole of the revenue of the income and corporation taxes should be retained by the Länder. According to his estimate, the excise taxes and the turnover tax should suffice to cover burdens arising out of the war, as well as occupation costs which the federation was to take over from the Länder. In case of special need, the federation could call upon the Länder for a share of the income and corporation taxes. Of the distribution of the revenues to the Länder by former Reich governments, he said:

Then, each Land had to see from year to year how many crumbs would fall to it from the master's table. We want no more of that in the future. We want to know with certainty that the revenue of such and such taxes will accrue to the Länder, that the Länder have a legal claim to these revenues. We want to be able to count upon having something definite, so that we don't have to live from hand to mouth, and can conduct our finances in an orderly and planned manner.[105]

Dr. Höpker-Aschoff replied that, on the distribution now proposed, and assuming that the Länder received at least as large a share of the proceeds of the shared taxes as they had received in the Weimar period, the Länder revenues should amount to DM. 8.2 milliards as against DM. 5.5 milliards for the federation.* He would scarcely describe this as "feeding off crumbs." As for the sharing of the proceeds of the turnover, as well as the income and corporation taxes between the federation and Länder, this decision had been taken to provide the Länder with a reasonably stable income in good times and bad, because the return from direct taxes was more sensitive to the rise and fall of production than the revenue of indirect taxes.[106]

The provisional distribution was adopted by a large majority. The Länder are thus afforded greater financial security than under the Weimar constitution in two ways. They have a *constitutional* claim on the revenues of definite taxes. The Land governments, through the Bundesrat, must approve any change in the basic distribution, as well as, respectively, the federal and Land portions of the shared revenues.

However, the actual apportionment of revenues had to be recast when it became clear that the Allied authorities could not be moved from their demand for a joint administration of taxes.[107] From the administrative point of view, the Parliamentary Council found it necessary to make the federation responsible for the major indirect taxes and the Länder for direct taxes and the transactions taxes. The

* This distribution of revenue—60 per cent to the Länder and 40 per cent to the federation—compares with a distribution in the United States in the last year before the war (fiscal year 1941) of 55 per cent to the states and 45 per cent to the federal government.

whole of the proceeds of the turnover tax thus passed to the federation, and of the income and corporation taxes, to the Länder. The federation may, however, with the approval of the Bundesrat, "claim a part of the income and corporation taxes to cover its expenditures not covered by other revenues, in particular to cover grants which are to be made to the Länder to meet expenditures in the fields of education, public health, and welfare."[108]

The Länder got very much the better of this exchange. Each year since 1951, the federal minister of finance has been compelled to ask the Bundesrat for an increasing share of the income and corporation taxes. The revision of these taxes and the economic recovery of the Federal Republic brought a revenue windfall to the Länder. With rising expenditures to cover new social commitments and occupation and defense costs, the federation found its constitutional revenues from indirect taxes (which government and parliament alike were reluctant to increase) perennially inadequate.[109] For 1951–52, the federal minister asked the Bundesrat for 32 per cent of the income and corporation tax revenue and was given 27 per cent; for 1952–53, he asked 40 per cent and got 37 per cent; for 1953–54 he asked 44 per cent and got 38 per cent; for 1954–55 he asked 40 per cent and again got 38 per cent; for 1955–56, the minister again asked for 40 per cent.

In the "final" apportionment of tax sources between the federation and the Länder, envisaged in Article 107, the finance minister proposed in 1955 that the federation be given a permanent right to a 40 per cent share of the income and corporation taxes. The Bundesrat vetoed this proposal. The apportionment agreed upon later and fixed by constitutional amendment is, subject to certain arrangements for review, 35 per cent from April 1, 1958.*

Financial Equalization between the Länder (Article 106) The finance committee's second division of revenues called for a horizontal redistribution of funds among the Länder to strengthen the position of the financially less well-off—the so-called "tax weak" Länder. By this procedure, a portion of the proceeds of certain of the taxes accruing to the Länder (e.g., 25 per cent of the income and corporation taxes, 50 per cent of the

* See Amendments to the Basic Law for the Federal Republic of Germany, Appendix A, p. 256 below.

beer tax, and the whole of the motor vehicle tax) was to be redistributed among the poorer Länder—according to the size of Land population and number of refugees in the case of the income and beer taxes, and according to highway mileage in the case of the vehicle tax.[109a]

The condition which this provision was designed to relieve is shown in the following figures of per capita tax revenues of the Länder of the bizonal area in 1947–48:[110]

Hamburg	DM. 1,078.1
Bremen	679.7
Württemberg-Baden	400.3
North Rhine-Westphalia	302.7
Bavaria	301.1
Hesse	285.0
Lower Saxony	255.7
Schleswig-Holstein	223.1

In succeeding years, per capita revenues of the Länder have varied as follows:[111]

(Federal Average = 100)

	1950	1951	1952
Württemberg-Baden	113.1	110.6	120.2
Hamburg	130.8	130.2	104.5
North Rhine-Westphalia	120.4	116.2	117.2
Hesse	116.0	112.1	106.4
Bremen	103.1	108.5	100.5
Bavaria	87.0	85.3	89.3
Lower Saxony	71.2	80.8	77.5
Rhineland-Palatinate	71.2	77.5	80.9
Schleswig-Holstein	34.2	48.7	52.8

The provision was unopposed in the Parliamentary Council. The federalists raised no objection, possibly because Bavaria was reckoned to be among the "tax weak" Länder.

The military governors, however, would hear of no scheme for a direct reapportionment of Land revenues by federal legislation. They feared that it would give the federation undue influence over the revenue available for the Land budgets, thereby enabling the federation to exercise control over the activities of the Länder to the detriment of their independence. On the other hand, the governors did not object to the assumption by the federation of certain of the costs of the Länder, for instance, aid to refugees. Höpker-Aschoff told the Allied finance advisers that, in his view, the taking over by the federation of particular burdens from the Länder was likely to lead to more interference in their affairs than an equalization measure. The latter, he explained, would operate automatically, certain portions of the Land revenues coming into a "common pool" and being redistributed on a different "key" from that on which they were collected. The funds would remain Land funds from first to last. In any case, through the Bundesrat, the Land governments would have full control over the terms of the equalization legislation. Such a procedure, he said, was entirely different from National Socialist practice, by which the finance minister had complete latitude to allocate funds to the Länder as he pleased. He concluded by pointing out the wide differences in tax income between the Länder. The Allied advisers did not comment on these arguments, but confined themselves to restating the military governors' views and warning the German delegates that they would run considerable risk if they did not take these views into account.

The issue of financial equalization between the Länder was the rock upon which the negotiations between the Allies and the Parliamentary Council nearly foundered. In the next month and a half, no further advance toward agreement was made. Finally, on April 28, the military governors informed the Parliamentary Council of a concession which the three foreign ministers had agreed upon at their meeting in Washington on April 5. According to its terms, the federal government might "supplement from its own revenue appropriations made by the Länder from revenues from their own taxes levied and collected by them, by grants for education, health and welfare purposes, subject in each case to specific approval of the Bundesrat."[112] The Germans interpreted this, or chose to interpret it, as an authorization for their equalization procedure. Negotiations were resumed in a hopeful spirit. In fact, what the foreign ministers had authorized were federal grants-in-aid to the Länder on the American model.

That a misunderstanding existed became obvious when the military governors met the Parliamentary Council representatives on April 25. The German draft of the financial articles still called for an equalization procedure. General Clay attempted to persuade the

German delegates that the object of their procedure could as well be attained if the federation raised special taxes and utilized their revenues to make grants to the financially weak Länder. Dr. Höpker-Aschoff replied that the division of tax sources between the federation and the Länder left very few resources upon which the federation could draw for this purpose. Large variations in the revenues of the Länder could not be diminished by federal grants without disruption of the proposed division of tax sources. He felt, in any case, that the federation would acquire greater powers over the Länder by the system of grants-in-aid than through the equalization procedure, which could largely operate without federal intervention.

The German delegation then made it clear that this was a point of principle upon which they could make no concession. After an interval for consideration, the military governors gave way, and with a minor change of drafting, financial equalization between the Länder was approved.

9. THE MILITARY GOVERNORS' INTERVENTION

The military governors have so far been represented as united in their views on the federal structure of the Basic Law. In fact, the united front presented to the Germans was the result of compromise between three different approaches. We have seen how these differences arose at the London conference and how many of them were evaded rather than resolved in the general formulations agreed upon at that time. This evasion had two consequences. The military governors were left to compose these differences under trying circumstances in Germany. Until after it had completed its work, the Parliamentary Council was given no specific guidance as to what the Allied governments considered essential in a federal structure.

Lack of Definition in Allied Directives   The Chiemsee conference produced the first draft of the Basic Law, and the Parliamentary Council began its work on September 1, 1948, guided only by the general directive which, it will be recalled, the military governors had given the ministers-president in Document I: that there should be established a "governmental structure of federal type which is best adapted to the eventual re-establishment of German unity, at present disrupted, and which will protect the rights of the participating states, provide adequate central authority, and contain guaranties of individual rights and freedom." The "letter of advice" by which the military governors were to be guided in judging the merits of the Basic Law was not published. On October 20, as we have seen,[113] the Allied liaison officers transmitted that part of the letter of advice dealing with financial matters to the Parliamentary Council. On November 22, prompted by General Koenig's[114] dissatisfaction with the course which the Parliamentary Council's negotiations were taking, the military governors communicated the terms of the letter of advice in full to the Parliamentary Council in the form of an *aide memoire*.[115] Certain of these points were reaffirmed by the military governors at a meeting with Parliamentary Council representatives on December 16. No further official amplification or definition* of these terms was given the German delegates until they received the military governors' memorandum of March 2 on the complete text of the draft Basic Law. Only the provisions of the draft Basic Law on education and family affairs,† state and local government employees, a federal finance administration, the eligibility of professional civil servants for elective public office, and (more doubtfully) those on public welfare and health plainly conflicted with the *aide memoire*. For the rest, such broad language as "to the maximum extent possible," "for which uniformity is essential," "in which it is clear that state implementation is impracticable," left ground for the Germans to assume that they had been given a wide discretion.

As soon as the Allied objections to the Basic Law became public, the military governors were widely criticized for delaying so long in making their exact position known.[116] Carlo Schmid, writing in *Die Welt* on March 17, said that the Allied governments might have proceeded in any of three ways: by combining the three zones, on the model of the bizone, into one area of occupation under an occupation statute; by leaving the Germans entirely free to determine their own constitution; by leaving the constitution to the Germans,

---

* There were frequent informal "unilateral" contacts between Allied officials and the German delegates. The Germans, of course, were entitled to give as much or as little weight to these "briefings" on Allied views as they pleased.

† For the Basic Law's provisions on education and family matters, see chap. v, "Basic Rights." The military governors did not choose to raise objections to these provisions.

subject to detailed stipulations laid down in advance on certain points.

Instead of these [he continued], a fourth way was chosen. We were authorized to establish a Basic Law on the condition that a few very general stipulations were met. Among other things, it was stipulated that a government of federal type should be established. But what on the Allied side one understood in detail by such a system we were not told. We were rather given to understand that we had a free hand to determine its concrete character ourselves—without prejudice, of course, to the right of the occupation powers to review the final draft produced by the Parliamentary Council. . . . The Parliamentary Council is now faced with the alternatives of having its draft Basic Law deprived of its character as a democratically adopted constitution or of continuing to regard the Basic Law as entirely a German affair, thereby jeopardizing approval by the Generals. . . . Would it not have been better to tell the Parliamentary Council at the very start—before the parties were involved in conflicts of view between themselves and before they had won on some points and lost on others—what exactly was meant on the Allied side by a federal structure of government?

Since the direction which the Parliamentary Council had taken was obvious by November, if not earlier, the question arises why the military governors failed to define their views precisely at that time. At the outset, they had hoped to be able to leave the Parliamentary Council as free a hand as possible, and to avoid direct interference in its deliberations. They counted upon informal contacts between their representatives and the German delegations to guide the proceedings to a conclusion in harmony with Allied objectives. By the time it became obvious that this method was not producing the results hoped for, the military governors were involved in disagreements among themselves over the terms of the Occupation Statute,[117] the basis upon which the French zone of occupation was to be fused with the bizone, and a host of problems arising out of the association of the French in the hitherto bipartite control of affairs in Frankfurt. There was more than a suspicion that similar disagreements would arise over the Basic Law, but the hard-pressed military governors were reluctant to face fresh difficulties at that stage. In these months, it must be recalled, the time and energies of the military governors and their staffs were stretched to the limit in dealing both with the regular regimen of postwar occupation problems and with special tasks arising out of the operation of the airlift to Berlin, then reaching its peak, as well as the introduction of Western Germany into the Organization for European Economic Cooperation. It is also worth recalling the demands which the complex Allied and German organization existing at that phase of the occupation made on the time and attention of the military governors. For obvious political reasons, they felt obliged to maintain their headquarters and the offices of their principal advisers in Berlin. In their own zones of occupation, the military governors had Allied and German government officials to deal with, as well as the military forces under their command. General Clay and General Robertson (and, later, General Koenig) also had a large staff of Allied officials in Frankfurt to act for them in the administration of the combined zones and to maintain liaison with the German officials of the economic council and the German administrative departments for the combined zones. At this stage, General Clay and General Robertson were conferring together and with their officials in Frankfurt each fortnight, and, on alternate fortnights, with the executive committee of the economic council and the ministers-president of the bizonal area. Monthly, or more often, they met tripartitely with General Koenig in Frankfurt or Berlin. Attention to the Parliamentary Council and its affairs had to be fitted in with all this.

If the military governors had little inclination in the last months of 1948 to probe into the generalities of the *aide memoire*, the majority of the Parliamentary Council had less. The federalists might have welcomed an intervention by the military governors, but they could not openly invite it. As for the other parties, the last thing they wanted was to provoke rulings from the military governors by raising individual points with them. Their avowed strategy was to complete the draft in the form they wished it to take and then lay it before the military governors, who, they surmised, would find it difficult to do anything but accept or reject the document as a whole.[118] At the December 16 meeting with the military governors—ostensibly arranged so that the German delegates could inquire about progress on the Occupation Statute—Dr. Adenauer referred to conflicts in the Parliamentary Council over the composition and powers of the Bundesrat and over the financial provisions and asked for the views of the military governors. He was severely criticized by the Socialist, Free Democratic, and Center delegations for giving the game away.[119] Dr. Adenauer protested that he had misunderstood discussions between the parties in the council of elders prior to the meeting. But some of the delegates suspected that he had acted from the motive of wishing to induce the military governors to give rulings favorable to the Christian Democrats on disputed issues in which they were in the minority. At Socialist headquarters in Hanover there was talk of a motion of censure, but nothing came of it. A Communist motion to replace Dr. Adenauer as chairman of the Council was refused a hearing.[120]

As it turned out, the military governors felt unable to add anything to their *aide memoire*. They were therefore in a weak position three months later to insist upon fundamental changes in the federal structure of the Basic Law, for which they had prepared neither the Parliamentary Council nor public opinion. On the other hand, the Socialists, Free Democrats, and others sharing the majority opinion on federalism in the Parliamentary Council could scarcely complain of this fact with any grace, since they had roundly condemned their chairman for attempting to draw out the military governors in December.

Discussions between the Military Governors The military governors began their review of the Basic Law on February 16 and continued it on March 1 and 2. In the interval, their political and financial advisers produced proposals for amendments to the Basic Law, eventually incorporated in the memorandum to the Parliamentary Council of March 2. General Koenig and General Clay sharply criticized centralization of powers in the federation. If anything, General Clay expressed himself more emphatically than his French colleague:

He said he was greatly disappointed in the Basic Law in its present form. Powers were largely centralized in the federal government, with only limited provisions for the Bundesrat to protect the rights of the Länder. Disregarding the November 22 *aide memoire*, the Parliamentary Council had given the federation substantial powers in the fields of public welfare, finance and public health. If his colleagues believed that an informal conference with the Parliamentary Council would persuade them to change their minds, he was ready to adopt this course, but, in his opinion, the stage had been reached at which the Parliamentary Council should be told that they must amend the Basic Law as desired by the military governors or it would not be approved.

General Robertson argued that the military governors might jeopardize the attainment of their objective for Western Germany by trying to compel the Parliamentary Council to make major changes in the Basic Law at that late stage. For his part, he found the provisions on the civil service unacceptable, but believed that the Allies could remedy this deficiency by legislation of their own.

He agreed with General Clay that, in respect of finance, public health, and other matters, the Basic Law exceeded the terms of the *aide memoire*. However, he did think that an attempt had been made to balance this concentration of powers in the federal government by giving the Bundesrat a wide power of control. Admitting that the Basic Law had imperfections, he asked if these imperfections were so serious as to warrant taking a step which might lead to rejection of the Basic Law, and hence to the interruption of their whole program for Western Germany. He reminded his colleagues that the Basic Law as it stood represented a compromise between the German political parties which had been reached with great difficulty and might be destroyed if basic amendments were insisted upon.

However, as General Robertson was in the minority, discussion of the changes to be required went ahead.

The apparent similarity of French and American views on federalism in the Basic Law did not run deep. General Koenig and General Clay approached the question from quite different premises. The French had little interest in the merits of federal institutions as such. For them, the decentralization of the powers of government in Germany was but one of a complex of checks upon German power —a substantial reservation of Allied powers in the Occupation Statute, military security controls, restriction of German industrial potential, control of the resources of the Ruhr and the Saar—which they believed essential to the security of France. They attached only a relative importance to federal decentralization. But French security depended, no less, upon the state of France's alliances and, above all, on the recovery of France itself. The policies and interests of France's allies had a vital bearing here which had to be taken into account. Hence, to the extent that French policy-makers found the pursuit of security by some means incompatible with others, there were differences of opinion about where the greater interest of France lay. Broadly speaking, those nearest the German problem— certainly General Koenig and his advisers—tended to see it in securing France against German power; M. Schuman and certain of his advisers saw it in strengthening France's ties with the other Western Allies and in promoting French recovery.

As a consequence, the French position on federalism was alternately rigid and flexible. Initially, the French stipulated for a far greater degree of decentralization than the other powers, but they were not dogmatic about the means of achieving it and were quite ready to abandon one device for another if it showed greater promise of obtaining the support of their allies. In some respects, the French showed that they understood the German approach to federal constitution-making better than their colleagues. Had the military governors, for instance, taken up a French suggestion to strengthen the Länder by expanding the list of *Zustimmungsgesetze*, they might have encountered less German resistance then by attempting to restrict the exercise of all the concurrent powers. Again, General Koenig's interest in protecting the Land administrations from federal interference accorded closely with German federalist views. On the other hand, the provisions on the administration of taxes, including the impracticable division of responsibility for collection of the income tax, resulted directly from French insistence that the size and influence of the federal bureaucracy should be kept to a minimum, and were conceded in order to induce the French to give up a patently unreasonable demand that responsibility for meeting occupation costs should be retained by the Länder. Ultimately, when M. Schuman's policy gained ascendancy, the French position on both the Occupation Statute and the Basic Law altered markedly. General Clay, as he reports, found himself alone at the end in deciding whether to persevere with the Allied objections to the Basic Law.

In a sense that applied neither to General Koenig nor to General Robertson, General Clay made his own policy. This had come about because, in the first days of the occupation, the American commander, separated by three thousand miles from his own government, needed authority to make prompt decisions for himself on urgent matters. The continuing division of responsibility for Germany between the American departments of the army and state contributed to prolong the practice. But the most important factor by far was the extraordinary confidence which General Clay himself had won from his government by the manner in which he had discharged responsibilities of unprecedented variety and difficulty.

This is not to say that Clay did not require governmental approval for his major decisions and policies. He did. But it was seldom withheld. On the Basic Law, Clay was able to tell his colleagues that he had full discretion to negotiate a compromise.

The common American belief in the power of federal institutions to afford protection to certain liberties and interests had a reverse implication in the German situation. The Germans, more than once overcome by their own folly, had thrown away their liberties and turned upon their neighbors. Their institutions, so the American reasoning ran, must be defective and ought to be replaced by others of—so it was thought—proved effectiveness. There was a certain justice in this point of view, enough to convince most Americans and even many Germans. Unfortunately, partial truth became dogma, and American solutions were sometimes applied in circumstances where they had little relevance. The desire of the Americans to see their form of federalism imported into Germany might well be thought the most doctrinaire of these reforms, ignoring as it did the history, geography, and economy of Germany and the preference of all the Germans, with the possible exception of the Bavarians. By this standard, Clay found the Basic Law deficient in provisions for dual citizenship in the federation and the Länder, for a clearly defined reservation of legislative powers for the Länder, and for financial autonomy for the Länder. By the same standard, he advocated the right of the federation—as well as of the Länder—to have a court system and administrative agencies of its own.

Were the Americans, as many Social Democrats believed, moved to press for more decentralization in the Basic Law by their aversion to socialism? The question is not whether a Western German Social Democratic government pledged to a program of nationalization and economic controls would have been unwelcome to General Clay and his government—so much may be taken for granted[121]—but whether the American authorities deliberately promoted federal decentralization with the aim of restricting the freedom of action of a possible socialist government. There is no evidence[122] to show that they did, nor is there any reason to suppose that there would be. A federal structure had been decreed by the Allied governments as the *sine qua non* for the return of power to the Germans. There was no need for any of the Allies to appear to press for it on any other ground and, with two exceptions to be mentioned later, they do not appear to have departed from a position of neutrality between the German parties. The Social Democrats, it is true, complained of the "pressure" to which they had been subjected by American and French officials[123] in the final stages of the Allied-German negotiations. It may be thought, however, that fruitless as such efforts might have seemed, the Allied officials were entitled to argue their case with the Social Democrats and that the latter were well able to hold their own against such "lobbying."

The British were relatively free of the preoccupations which exercised their allies. They had fewer preconceptions about the merits of various forms of federal organization, or indeed of many Allied reforms in Germany, and believed that security should be sought in other directions. Their primary interest lay in putting the Germans at the earliest moment in a position to assume responsibility for their own affairs, so that the strained British economy might be relieved of the costs of occupation government and assistance to Germany which it could ill afford to bear. The British feared that an attempt to impose changes of substance in the Basic Law would delay this development. They were also aware that, on their part, it would be an injustice to ask the German authorities to assume full responsibility for the many intractable postwar economic and social problems, while denying to them methods of government which they believed essential to enable them to deal with these problems—the more so since these same methods were British methods. Moreover, the British Labour government was sympathetic to a point with the aims of the Social Democratic party and the liberal Christian Democrats. While there was no question of direct British intervention on their behalf in Germany (if anything, Mr. Ernest Bevin leaned in the other direction), neither was there any disposition to override the majority decisions of the Parliamentary Council, in so many of which the Social Democrats had figured.

The Allied-German Controversy   The federalist amendments which the military governors agreed to propose have been described in detail elsewhere.[124] The Parliamentary Council responded to these proposals by enlarging its interparty committee of five to seven, to include representatives of the Center and German parties, and commissioning that body to see what changes could be agreed upon to meet the military governors' wishes. These turned out to be very few. The committee of seven's first counterproposals of March 10 were rejected out of hand by the Allied liaison officers.

Meanwhile, with but few exceptions, German opinion had united in condemning the military governors for intervening in matters thought proper for German decision. The Allies, particularly the Americans and French, were having the worst press of the occupation.

The *Allgemeine Zeitung* of Mainz, conservative, independent, and authoritative, said in a leading article of March 10:

... It has been one of the principal objectives of the occupation to win the German people spiritually from the authoritarian state of the past and to attract them to the concepts of freedom for which the Western policy stands. But to achieve this objective, it is of little use to say to the Germans: you are not to be governed as you yourselves wish, but as the occupation powers wish. It is impossible for a constitution which from the start bears in the eyes of the people the stigma that it exists in virtue of the will of the victors to win the nation's loyalty. That is not nationalism ... but the most natural thing in the world. No other people on earth would behave otherwise, would regard such a constitution with other feelings than those of the utmost reserve....

On the same day, *Die Zeit*, published in Hamburg, wrote:

The Americans have a system of federalism at home and therefore prescribe for us the strongest possible dose of this beneficial medicine. The French do not have federalism in their country, but in the interests of their security demand not merely a federal state, but a loose confederation for Germany. The English also do not have federalism at home and they sympathize with us who, while wanting a federal state ourselves, would rather not be compelled by American missionary zeal and French preoccupation with security to adopt an excessively federalistic system.

Dr. Adenauer, addressing a congress of the Western German Catholic Workers' Movement in Düsseldorf on March 15, was reported as having pleaded with the Allies to give up their demands for "an exaggerated federalism, particularly on financial matters, as a consequence of which the federation would be condemned to a shadowy existence."[125]

Some of the Social Democrats were insisting that negotiations should be broken off altogether, but after a party conference on

March 12 at Cologne, the party secretary, Herr Heine, announced that the Socialist members of the committee of seven had been authorized to continue discussions with Allied representatives.[126] It particularly infuriated the Socialists that Dr. Ehard, the Bavarian Christian Social leader, seemed disposed to use the military governors' memorandum to reopen the controversy over federalist issues on the German side. On March 6 he had described the Allied memorandum to the press[127] as a "positive basis for solving the constitutional problem," and added his hope that "the Parliamentary Council will now find its way out of the dead end to which it has come through having paid so little attention to the London directive to establish a constitution of federal character."

On March 17 the committee of seven submitted further counterproposals, but from the Allied point of view they represented little advance on those of March 10. A few legislative powers were transferred from one list to another. Federal lawmaking in the concurrent field was to be restricted to defined conditions, but one of these —"to preserve legal or economic unity"—was broad enough to cover almost any legislation which the federation might want to undertake. A similar qualification was introduced for federal legislation on the concurrent taxes. The procedure for equalization of revenues between Länder was spelled out in some detail. The provisions on financial administration were unchanged.

Both Allies and Germans now settled down to what became a two-week trial of nerve. The two positions were still far apart. Both were the result of hard-won compromises which neither side wanted to disturb. Rumors flew about. It was reported (and denied) that "if the Social Democrats in Bonn disrupted the Parliamentary Council," the Allies were preparing alternative plans for a Western German government, taking into account that "the Christian Democrats, who supported the Western memorandum rejected by the Socialists represented a majority of the voters in Western Germany."[128] According to another rumor, Mr. Bevin, at the forthcoming meeting of the foreign ministers in Washington, would seek support from his colleagues for the Social Democratic position.[129]

The German parties had agreed that the counterproposals of March 17 were to be put forward as a whole and could not be departed from in any particular without upsetting the basis of their agreement. The Christian Democrats were the first to give way. On March 30, although the military governors had not yet formally rejected the March 17 proposals, the CDU/CSU announced that it would offer fresh proposals on the financial issues.[130] "German politicians," their resolution ran, "are not warranted in wrecking the Basic Law over this problem. . . . A continuation of the present dismemberment of Germany can not be justified." Simultaneously, the Social Democrats announced that they could make no concessions beyond those agreed upon by the committee of seven and that they "stood for" immediate final adoption of the Basic Law by the Parliamentary Council. "As before," their resolution concluded, "the party believes it to be possible to adopt the Basic Law speedily and with the largest possible measure of support, provided that the parties adhere to decisions which they have heretofore regarded as right. . . ."[131]

The Free Democrats, who held the balance, did not declare themselves.

On April 5 the Parliamentary Council received this message from the foreign ministers in Washington:

The Foreign Secretaries of the United States, United Kingdom and France, who during their current meetings in Washington are studying the problems of Western Germany, are gratified to learn that the competent committees of the Parliamentary Council are pressing forward with the work of completing the draft of the Basic Law. The Foreign Secretaries understand that decisions will be taken in Bonn during the next few days on several important issues connected with the Basic Law. They trust that the Parliamentary Council and the responsible German party leaders will give due consideration to the recommendations of the Military Governors, which conform with the provisions of the London Agreement authorizing the establishment of a German democratic federal government. The Foreign Secretaries desire that the decisions of the Parliamentary Council will be taken in a spirit of facilitating a mutually co-operative attitude between the future German federal authorities and the occupying powers, which is one of the important objectives being sought in the current talks in Washington regarding Germany. [14]

Knowledge of important concessions to the German point of view, agreed upon by the foreign ministers at the same time, and which the military governors were given discretion to withhold "for a few

days,"[132] was in fact withheld from the Parliamentary Council*
until April 23.

The foreign ministers' message therefore appeared as straight
backing for the military governors—powerful reinforcements in the
war of nerve. The Free Democrats were the next to give way.
When the main committee met to consider the foreign ministers'
message on April 6, Dr. Heuss moved for consideration of the new
financial proposals of the CDU in a joint meeting of the finance
committee and the committee of seven.[133] The Social Democrats de-
clined to take part. For them, the interparty compromises of March
17 stood as a whole, and if other parties now wished to depart from
them, the Socialists said, the whole basis of agreement would have
to be reconsidered.[134] A few days later, Der Kurier[135] reported Dr.
Höpker-Aschoff, "until now, together with the Social Democrats,
one of the most zealous champions of a strong federal finance administration," as stating on behalf of the Free Democrats that the
new CDU financial proposals were "unattractive, but tenable."

The Social Democrats were now isolated. If they stood their
ground on the financial issues and refused to participate further in
the Parliamentary Council, they risked having the onus put upon

* The text ultimately released to the Germans on April 23 read:
"Acting under instructions of their Governments, the Military Governors
transmit herewith the views of the Foreign Ministers of their countries on the
Basic Law.
"These views are as follows:
. . . .
"(b) In the financial field any provisions put forward by the Parliamentary
Council in the direction of securing financial independence and adequate
strength for both the Laender and Federal Governments in operating in their
respective fields will receive sympathetic consideration.
"(c) On the question of Article 36 (Article 95[c]) they will also give sympathetic consideration to any formula which:
    (i) eliminates from the Federal powers those matters definitely excluded by
        the London Agreement;
   (ii) assures to the Laender sufficient powers to enable them to be independent
        and vigorous governmental bodies;
  (iii) assures to the Federal Government sufficient powers in the important
        fields of government to enable it to deal effectively with those fields
        in which the interests of more than one Land are substantially and neces-
        sarily involved.
"(d) Finally the Foreign Ministers are ready to contemplate a suggestion
for the right of the Federal state to supplement from its own revenues appropriations made by the Laender from revenues from their own taxes levied and
collected by them, by grants for education, health and welfare purposes, subject in each case to specific approval of the Bundesrat." [14]

them for obstructing the return of power to a German government. Dr. Schumacher told the press[136] that he found no encouragement for his point of view in the foreign ministers' message, and spoke with bitterness of the "sacrifices" which the Germans had been called upon to make to maintain good relations with the Allies. But he did not close the door to further negotiations. Instead, the Socialist leaders set about redrafting the Basic Law in a form which gave the Länder a larger share of taxes to collect and restricted the legislative power of the federation over concurrent taxes, but retained financial equalization measures and eliminated most of the compromise agreements reached with the federalist parties in other parts of the Basic Law—many of the *Zustimmungsgesetze*, a Bundesrat veto of constitutional amendments, provisions on marriage, the family, and the churches, and so on.

This draft was laid before the Socialist Party Congress at Hanover on April 20 and approved by sixty-three votes to four, with eight abstentions. On this basis, the Social Democratic delegates were authorized to resume negotiations at Bonn. A resolution was adopted which referred to the earlier agreement reached in the Parliamentary Council and deplored that:

. . . This agreement was destroyed by the repeated and detailed interventions of the occupying powers. This result was furthered by the far reaching identity of the concepts of the ruling clique of the CDU/CSU and of the occupying powers regarding the structure of a German state. This is bound to result in democracy being compromised, democratic forces becoming discredited and disrespected, German youth losing confidence in a free future, and German unification being made more difficult.

In the face of the approaching great decisions, the National Socialist and Communist attack can be broken only through the German people's own political will—not, however, through mere constitutional devices which rest on foreign orders. . . .

The Christian Democrats had already made it clear that the Socialist revision of the Basic Law was entirely unacceptable to them. Reproaches streamed from Bonn to Hanover. Herr Herbert Blankenhorn, secretary-general of the Christian Democratic party, told the correspondent of the *Manchester Guardian*[137] that the new draft constituted "a defeat of those reasonable elements of the SPD with whom we might have arrived at an agreement." "We believed," he went on, "that the outstanding differences between the right- and left-wing parties were small and capable of settlement and that our duty was still to find a compromise within the limits defined by the Occupation Powers. We are ashamed to offer the world such a picture of divided German counsels." In the Hanover resolution, Dr. Adenauer saw "with shame and sadness, a tendency, as after 1918, to incite nationalistic feeling against the policy of fulfilment" and warned against "this poisoning of political life."[138]

The breakdown of agreement between the German parties seemed complete.

What, meanwhile, had become of the foreign ministers' concessions? While General Robertson, under governmental instructions, pressed for their release to the Germans, General Clay, supported by General Koenig, held them up. Shortly before the Socialist Congress on April 20, Clay's government instructed him to deliver the message. But still he temporized.[139] Finally, on April 23 the Parliamentary Council was informed of the remaining decisions taken by the foreign ministers on April 5.

On the German side, the atmosphere instantly improved. Two days later, when the representatives of the Parliamentary Council met the military governors in what turned out to be their final conference, they were ready with agreed compromise proposals. These in effect conceded an administration of major taxes by the Länder to the Allies and a reduction of the powers of the Bundesrat to the Social Democrats, but retained for the federation power to legislate in the concurrent fields "to maintain economic and legal unity," as well as provision for financial equalization between the Länder.

In the course of this meeting, it became clear that neither General Robertson nor General Koenig would any longer oppose German wishes on the latter points. Clay writes:[140] "This placed me in a difficult position as the extent of federalization rested in my hands, and if my decision was one which could not be accepted by the Germans I would be responsible for delaying the formation of the West German Government." After the Germans had accepted certain changes of phrasing to his liking, Clay at length gave way. The German delegation retired and speedily came to an agreement between themselves to restore to the Basic Law provisions on the family, education, and the church. The major controversies were thus settled, and the Basic Law was ready for final reading in the Parliamentary Council on May 8 and approval by the military governors on May 12.

It may be thought that all this might have been accomplished some weeks earlier and much ill feeling avoided had the Germans been informed promptly of the foreign ministers' concessions. It might well seem, too, that the information was withheld in the expectation that the Social Democrats would, in the last resort and as the other parties had done, defer to Allied wishes. This is not General Clay's explanation of the motive for his action. He writes:[141]

> . . . Dr. Schumacher, in firm control of the party, had publicly announced his intent to resist the changes in the Basic Law urged by the Military Governors and to force its adoption without amendment. . . . If he and his party could defy the Occupying Powers and get away with it, they could go to the polls triumphantly proclaiming their success as defenders of the German people against the Allies.
>
> This resulted in disagreement among the Military Governors on the delivery of a second letter from the Foreign Ministers. Their first letter had called upon the Parliamentary Council to resolve its difficulties in the spirit of the London decisions. The second letter, which was sent to the Military Governors for delivery when they believed it timely, did not change this position. It did suggest that financial measures designed to equalize relief burdens among the states, thus permitting the Federal Government to supplement its own revenues from revenues levied and collected by the states to make funds available for grants for education and welfare purposes, would be approved. I was unwilling to present this letter in view of Schumacher's position that he was opposed to any changes in the Basic Law necessary to meet the views of the Occupying Powers. Our position of political neutrality had not changed. However, in this instance the CDU favored federal government, which was also tripartite policy. The letter was certain to be interpreted by the SPD as a moral victory. My British colleague, under instructions from his government, pressed hard for its delivery. General Koenig stood with me.

The explanation can be regarded only as a lame one. Apart from its tendentious imputation of motives and its depiction of Schumacher as intending to do what neither he nor any other German party leader could do, namely, force the adoption of the Basic Law in the Parliamentary Council, it reveals the author's own partisan bias. The military governors were pledged to neutrality? It could not be helped that Allied policy on federalism had favored the Christian

Democrats? Well and good. By the same token, any concessions agreed upon by the Allied governments should have been extended in a like spirit of neutrality—letting advantages and disadvantages for the German parties, or the Allies themselves, fall as they might.

The mistake of judgment was repaired in time to save the negotiations and bring them to a successful conclusion. It was a tribute to General Clay's considerable services to the German people in their worst adversity that Germans of all persuasions, very justly, bore no ill will over the matter, and, a few weeks later, joined in general demonstrations of popular feeling upon his departure from Germany.

10. CONCLUSION

The federal order of the Basic Law, as it finally took form, is essentially a German construction. It follows the German tradition, with adaptations to take account of contemporary conditions and to accommodate varying interests and political views in Western Germany today. In the result, the Allied influence on the Basic Law was comparatively slight, with the exception of the change imposed in the financial sphere to give the Länder control of the assessment and collection of major taxes. But since this arrangement suited a substantial minority of the Germans and is in keeping with earlier German practice, it cannot be described as unduly arbitrary or as having altered the fundamentally German character of the Basic Law. A more significant effect of Allied intervention was the quite unintended one of weakening the powers of the Bundesrat.

That the Allied governments had so little success in influencing the federal provisions of the Basic Law is not to be regretted, for they approached the matter from highly debatable premises: that some federal systems are intrinsically better than others and that federalism can appropriately be made to serve such purposes as the promotion of democracy and international security.

Any federal system, or any similar arrangement for decentralization of powers, is a practical solution to the problem of government in conditions where unity and diversity are to be combined, whether the diversity is geographical, racial and cultural, economic, or some combination of all. Any one arrangement might be successful in meeting needs in one place, without there being a likelihood of its succeeding in doing so elsewhere. Apart from the fact that the practicality of the American federal system in its own environment is in many respects open to question, there was no reason to suppose that it would suit the very different conditions of Western Germany. In any event, the Germans were bound to consider themselves the best judges of the matter. To attempt to impose arrangements on them which from the start they believed to be impractical was only to make doubly certain that such arrangements would fail. At the same time, the preoccupation of the Americans with introducing features of their own federal system prevented them and their allies from exploiting the better opportunity to strengthen the Basic Law's own federal provisions, particularly the powers of the Bundesrat.

The extent to which a federal decentralization of powers may be a condition for healthy democracy is questionable. Local government certainly develops responsible citizenship and provides training and experience in representative government. But autonomy in local affairs is compatible with any system of regional decentralization, or with none, under a unitary organization of the state. The existence of centralized democracies supports what common sense suggests: that federalism as such has little to do with the democratic character of a state and its institutions. It may meet the desires of the constituent peoples of a state for a greater or less degree of self-determination in their affairs and, to that extent, may be a more democratic solution than some other. But the degree or kind of self-determination settled upon for a federal state does not measure the strength of its democracy, must less secure it. Other factors are the decisive ones.

As for the security of the Allied nations and Germany's other neighbors, federal decentralization *if carried far enough* would no doubt have served that purpose. But it would have been an elaborate and costly method of attaining security, for such a solution could have been imposed and maintained only by Allied compulsion, entailing continuous intervention by Allied officials in German affairs. The objective of transferring responsibility for government to German hands would have been frustrated. The opposition of nearly all Germans would have been aroused by a forced revival of the Confederation, whereas the majority of them accepted and some even saw the justice of direct military controls.

From more than one point of view, there is a good deal to be said for the contention that the decision to form a full-fledged government in Western Germany in 1948 was premature. But once the decision had been taken, the Western Germans should have been left to make their own constitutional choices within very wide limits. The Allies were entitled to insist upon guaranties for their security, but many of the *constitutional* safeguards which would have been appropriate in terms of Germany as a whole had much less or no relevance to a Western Germany under the exclusive occupation control of the Western Allies. Allied intervention on points of detail in the federal organization achieved little, except to raise doubts in German minds as to the sincerity of Allied professions of neutrality in issues of internal German politics, to discredit the representative character of the Parliamentary Council and its work, and to embitter relations between the German parties at the start of parliamentary life under the Basic Law.

In this review of the Basic Law, the Bundesrat has emerged as the keystone of German federal structure. It is more important for the defense of the rights and interests of the Länder than even the constitutional court, because the administrative province of the Länder can be more effectively safeguarded by political than by judicial control, and because the Germans do not accord a broad right of review of the federal legislative competence to the judiciary. The constitutional court, to be sure, is the arbiter in any dispute over the Bundesrat's powers. But even here, it is the Bundesrat's constitutionally established control of the appointment of half the members of the court which, in the last resort, would save it from being swamped by a majority in the Bundestag bent upon centralization. With this exception, the composition and procedures of the court are alterable by simple federal law.

In the first five years of the Federal Republic, the Bundesrat established itself as a more effective representative of Land interests than either of its predecessors. One unexpected development, which the Parliamentary Council certainly did not foresee, was the extent to which the *Zustimmungsgesetze* would give the Bundesrat parity with the Bundestag in legislation. The Parliamentary Council expected the *Zustimmungsgesetze* to be the exception rather than the rule. In fact, of the 545 measures adopted by the Bundestag in the first four years, 200 required approval by the Bundesrat, and by the end of the first term of the Bundestag the ratio of *Zustimmungsgesetze* to other laws had increased to half.[142] When it is taken into account that the most important measures of this period were among that number* and that the Bundesrat's approval was required in an even wider field for ministerial ordinances, it would not be wide of the mark to say that, in practice, the Bundesrat has achieved *Gleichberechtigung*. In the all-important financial field, the Bundesrat has effectively defended Land interests in the sharing of revenues of the major taxes and, with the support of the constitutional court, has successfully asserted its right to have a controlling voice in any provisions for a federal financial administration.

The heavy reliance placed upon the Bundesrat in the federal system has led to the criticism in Germany[143] that a national party controlling the Bundestag and a sufficient number of the Land governments represented in the Bundesrat could in practice extensively modify or even abolish the federal provisions of the Basic Law. This is true, but it is also true of other federal systems. If a national party in the United States should gain control of the federal Congress and three-fourths of the state legislatures—by no means an improbability —it could, if it had the requisite purpose and party discipline, amend the federal structure freely. A particular federal order of government cannot be imposed for all time and against the wishes of the overwhelming majority of a country's inhabitants. At the same time, as a matter of contractual good faith, particularist minorities are entitled to a long run of constitutional protection against arbitrary assimilation. In the Bundesrat, the votes of Bavaria and Lower Saxony, the Länder in which particularism is strongest, together with those of any one of the other seven states, will always suffice to defeat constitutional amendment of the federal order. Amendments of the Basic Law to abolish the Länder as constituent units of the federation or their right to participate in the federal legislative process are not even admissible. Whether this protection goes as far as it should is a matter of opinion, but it is certainly very considerable.

If the view is taken that a federal system should be a means of meeting real needs—not preserved as an end in itself, as an anachronism behind which special interests that have nothing to do with the

---

* E.g., the Bonn conventions and defense legislation.

purpose of a federal order of government can shelter—there is much in the German federal system that an American can study with profit. It has two outstanding merits: (1) the principles have been recognized and applied in the assignment of functions to the federation and the states that creation of the minimum basic conditions for the welfare of all the people comes before the particular rights of some of them and that at each level of government should be done what can best be done; (2) the controls provided for protection of the federal order and adjustments which may be required are primarily political and only secondarily and to a limited extent judicial. This balance of elements of flexibility with safeguards suggests that, after much trial and error, the Germans may well have found a federal solution that will endure for them.

CHAPTER III

FEDERAL GOVERNMENT–PARLIAMENT– PRESIDENT

Such a flight from political responsibility we must never allow to occur again.

WALTER MENZEL

1. IMPACT OF THE EVENTS OF MARCH 1930 TO MARCH 1933

In devising the provisions of the Basic Law for the election and powers of the president, chancellor, and ministers and their relations to each other and to parliament, the Parliamentary Council had foremost in mind the circumstances which enabled Hitler first to exploit and then subvert the Weimar constitution to become master of Germany. This is not to suggest that the Parliamentary Council thought constitutional defects were solely, or even mainly, responsible for Hitler's rise to power, or that constitutional devices alone could be counted upon to forestall another breakdown of parliamentary government. Dr. Heuss was one of the first to warn the Parliamentary Council against such thinking:

The Weimar constitutional order was not such a bad one. It has become fashionable today—there have been echoes of it here in this assembly—to speak disparagingly of the Weimar constitution. That reflects just a little Hitler's propaganda, by which even many of us are still influenced. From the beginning, the German Nationalist opposition and, later, Nazi propaganda created a moral atmosphere in which it was almost impossible for the infant constitution to survive. . . . It is unquestionable that the Weimar constitution fell a victim to a stupendous error: overconfidence in the "fairness" of the German people. It is indeed characteristic of the tragic condition of our people that we possess in German no word for this concept of "fairness." Thus it came about that the development of the young democracy took place in the atmosphere of nationalistic fantasies, of attempts to restore the monarchy, and of the criminal fairy tale of having been stabbed in the back. These things were far, far more decisive

113

for the operation of the Weimar constitution than the formulation of this or that article which may not accord with present-day notions.[1]

Nevertheless, constitution-making was the business of the Parliamentary Council delegates. They could not fail to reckon with the fact that Hitler, who never won the votes of a majority of the German people in a free election nor, before power was in his hands, the support of a majority in the Reichstag, had yet managed to master the state through the processes of the constitution itself—on the face of it, a damaging indictment of that constitution and those who had played a part in its operation.

The focusing of the Parliamentary Council's attention on the events of March, 1930, to March, 1933, also had a basis in the fact that many of the delegates, as former members of the Reich and Prussian parliaments, former officials of the Reich and Land governments and the parliamentary parties, had experienced these events at first hand. As one follows debates in which speaker after speaker retraces the course of Weimar history in a search for the critical weaknesses and false turns, an impression grows of minds, as though in the grip of some quite personal tragedy, restlessly exploring the past in a search for an understanding which might bring both relief and the restoration of confidence necessary to make a fresh start. Whereas the Weimar assembly's provisions for a parliamentary government were the product of an outward-looking optimistic ambition to combine in its own the best from the parliamentary traditions of other countries, those of the Basic Law are the outcome of an introspective and disillusioned preoccupation with Germany's own recent experience. As reflection on these events played such a large part in the Parliamentary Council's deliberations, they must be held in mind in examining this part of the Basic Law.

On March 29, 1930, the last of the Weimar "great coalition" governments fell. It was led by the Social Democratic chancellor Hermann Müller, and included ministers from the Social Democratic, Center, Democratic, People's and Bavarian parties. In the two-year life of the coalition, the faults of Weimar parliamentary government were exhibited in their quintessence. No party of the coalition, not even the leading party, would permit itself to be committed by its ministers to a common policy in the cabinet. Hence it was possible, in the case of the Reichstag vote of November, 1928, on the construction of an armored cruiser, for the Social Democratic ministers to join in one decision in the cabinet and vote the opposite way with their party in the Reichstag. In the composition of his cabinet, the chancellor was confronted by demands from the party organizations not only for particular posts and for representation proportionate to party strength, but for changes as well in the cabinet of the Prussian government, also led by a Social Democratic minister-president. If their claims were not satisfied, the party factions could and did summarily withdraw their ministers from the coalition. In the midst of a cabinet crisis on February 26, 1929, Stresemann, the foreign minister, bitterly complained to his party's central committee:

> Let us not deceive ourselves: we are faced by a crisis in the parliamentary system which is more than a crisis of confidence. There are two causes of this crisis: first, that the parliamentary system in Germany has become a caricature of itself, and secondly, the completely false view of Parliament in relation to its responsibility towards the nation. What is meant by the "parliamentary system"? It means the responsibility of a Minister of the Reich to Parliament, which can, by a majority, withdraw its confidence from that Minister and compel him to resign his office. There is nowhere a condition that the Minister must be a party man; nor that the Ministerial offices shall be distributed in accordance with the strength of the fractions, nor that control shall pass from the Cabinet to the fractions. . . . I personally always refrain from using the expression that a fraction "withdraws" its Ministers. Ministers must ask themselves whether they shall assume office, or lay it down. The Reichstag can withdraw its confidence from them. The fraction can expel them. But the "withdrawal" of a Minister means that in reality he no longer has any status except as the nominee of a certain organization. This view is the final end of liberalism. If we are no longer to have any parties that can accommodate the principle of personality, they will cease to embody the liberal creed. . . . In regard to every crisis, people have predicted that it must end in a few days, whereas it has in fact dragged on like a creeping poison over many weeks. It saps our strength, fills the country with a genuine disgust for such negotiations, and is, in the present situation, intolerable. Is it not positively grotesque that at a time when all the energies of our minds and hearts should be set upon the negotiations in Paris, the Chancellor and the Foreign Minister should for days together have to be making hopeless efforts to bring the parties together?[2]

The Müller coalition broke up over the issue of raising unemployment insurance contributions to meet heavy demands on the insurance funds resulting from the onset of mass unemployment. The Social Democrats and trade unions wanted to insure the financial means of maintaining unemployment benefits at the existing level. They feared that a lowering of the scale of benefits would provide an opening for employers to demand a reduction of wage rates. Under trade-union pressure and against the judgment of the majority of the Socialist ministers, the Social Democrats rejected a Center compromise proposal to leave the insurance levy as it stood, with the Reich treasury to make up the difference in the insurance funds, subject to later review of the whole question of unemployment insurance finance. Although the terms upon which the coalition had been formed did not require the cabinet to go to the Reichstag with an agreed policy, the ministers of the Center and People's parties nevertheless resigned when the Socialists announced that they could not accept the compromise. Müller's resignation followed.

His successor, Heinrich Brüning, whose government of the Center and "bourgeois" parties was no more secure because it could not rely upon support from the parties of the extreme right, took a firm line with the Reichstag from the start. He announced that the government would "make use of all the constitutional resources at its disposal to insure that the deficit of the Reich budget was covered." When some of his tax proposals were rejected by the Reichstag, Brüning had his financial program promulgated by presidential decree under the terms of Article 48 of the constitution. The Reichstag in its turn voted for repeal of these decrees and Brüning responded by dissolving the chamber and fixing new elections. At these elections on September 14, 1930, the National Socialist and Communist delegations became the second and third largest in the Reichstag. The Nazi delegation rose from 12 to 107.

From these elections until his resignation on May 31, 1932, Brüning governed by the promulgation of emergency decrees. For this he required the support of the President, whose agreement to the use of these powers was necessary, and the toleration of the Social Democrats, whose votes, as the largest single bloc in the Reichstag, were needed to forestall any move in the Reichstag to nullify the decrees. The Social Democrats extended this toleration because they feared that the antiparliamentary forces would be strengthened if the government were overturned and elections precipitated in the deepening economic crisis.

To Hitler, these routes to power presented themselves: first, to try to take it by force; second, to win a majority in the Reichstag; third, to enter a parliamentary coalition; fourth, to persuade the President to appoint him chancellor with emergency powers. He rejected the first because experience had shown him that he would risk having the full power of the state, including the army, ranged against him. Exploration of the third course did not at first interest him except for tactical purposes. The successful pursuit of his preferred route, the fourth, as well as the third, depended upon the withdrawal of the President's confidence from Brüning. Until this occurred, Hitler concentrated on the second course, pressing for Reichstag elections and enlarging his popular support in the succession of Land and presidential elections, culminating in the election for the Prussian Landtag in April, 1932, in the course of which his share of the popular vote rose from 18.3 to 36.3 per cent. In the Prussian Landtag, the National Socialists and Communists between them won a majority and brought government in Prussia to a standstill, although of course they could not combine to replace it.

Hindenburg was averse to relying on the powers of Article 48 for an indefinite term and wanted the Reich government put on a footing which would enable it to legislate with Reichstag support. His advisers, of whom the most active was Major General Kurt von Schleicher, the defense minister's officer of liaison with other departments of government, reached the conclusion that Hitler's support should be enlisted to broaden the popular base for the government and, if possible, to secure a stable majority for it in the Reichstag. An attempt to bring Brüning and Hitler to an agreement failed. Hindenburg was then persuaded to withdraw his confidence from Brüning in favor of Franz von Papen, who had no standing in the Reichstag and who, by supplanting Brüning, alienated his own party, the Center. But support of the army and Hitler was claimed for him. Hitler's "support" was a temporary tolerance extended on the condition that elections for the Reichstag should be held forthwith and that the Brüning government's ban of the SA and SS formations be lifted. At these elections the Nazis more than doubled their representation in the Reichstag (107 to 230). With the Communists, they could combine in a majority, as in the Prussian Landtag, to prevent the normal working of parliamentary government.

Because he did not possess a majority of his own and would not enter a coalition, the chancellorship on his terms was refused Hitler by the President. Papen continued in office, met the Reichstag in November, and dissolved it. The second Reichstag election of the year brought a decrease of Nazi and an increase of Communist strength. Papen resumed his efforts to bring Hitler into a "coalition of nationally-minded parties," but did not succeed. When Schleicher and others in the cabinet, frightened by the Communist increases, expressed dissatisfaction with these efforts, Papen resigned to enable Hindenburg to see Hitler again. But Hindenburg would offer him the chancellorship only on the condition which Hitler could not and did not want to meet: that he show himself capable of producing a working majority in the Reichstag. He wanted to be appointed a presidential chancellor, like Brüning and Papen. Papen now proposed to resume office and, until he could prepare a reform of the constitution, proclaim a state of emergency and govern by decree without the Reichstag. Schleicher, claiming to speak for the army, objected that this course would risk civil war and that the army did not believe itself strong enough simultaneously to suppress uprisings from within and defend the country against possible aggression from abroad. He argued that it was unnecessary to take this risk, as he believed he was capable of securing a majority in the Reichstag.

Hindenburg gave him the opportunity to prove his contention, and Schleicher set about trying to construct a broad front from right to left. In the course of these negotiations he roused Hitler's enmity by dividing the National Socialists in an effort to win participation of the Gregor Strasser wing of the party in the government. He failed to placate the Social Democrats and trade unions, while provoking the antagonism of industrial and agricultural interests by his conciliatory attitude to the trade unions, reduction of agricultural tariffs, and plans for land settlement in East Prussia. When, at the end of January, 1933, Schleicher had to meet the Reichstag, he found he had failed to enlist support from any quarter and asked the President for a dissolution, which was refused. In the meantime, Papen had again been trying his hand at negotiation with Hitler. This time, with the decline of party strength in the elections, the defection of Strasser, the growing restlessness and tension among his followers, and an empty party treasury, Hitler was disposed to listen to proposals for a coalition. Agreement was finally reached upon a coalition to include the National Socialists, the Nationalists, and possibly the Center, in which Hitler would be chancellor and Papen vice-chancellor and Reich commissioner for Prussia, with ministers in whom Hindenburg had confidence for foreign affairs and defense. One other post—as it turned out, of key importance—the Prussian ministry of the interior, went to the National Socialists and was given to Göring.

The President agreed to appoint Hitler chancellor on the understanding that he would obtain a majority in the Reichstag, thus relieving Hindenburg of the responsibility of government by decree. As soon as he took office, Hitler opened negotiations with the leader of the Center party, but broke them off at once on the pretext that unacceptable conditions had been made. He persuaded Papen to advise Hindenburg to dissolve the Reichstag once more. In the election campaign which followed, full use was made of Göring's control of the police in the Prussian two-thirds of Germany to intimidate and suppress the opposition. A bare majority of Nazi and Nationalist deputies was returned to the Reichstag. With the Communist deputies under arrest or driven underground, in any case banned from the Reichstag, Hitler, opposed only by the Social Democrats, secured the two-thirds majority necessary to pass the enabling act concentrating full control of the state in his hands.

The assessment of responsibility for these events is disputed—at least as it concerns those participants on whom rested and who acknowledged an obligation to defend the constitution and to cooperate in making it work. For instance, the Social Democrats may be charged with a short-sighted and partisan irresponsibility in allowing themselves to be maneuvered from office in 1930 through their inflexibility on the unemployment insurance question; Brüning, with a too hasty resort to emergency powers to the neglect of efforts to come to an agreement with the Social Democrats on a program for dealing with the economic crisis; Hindenburg, with "unconstitutional" conduct in dismissing a chancellor against whom the Reichstag had passed no adverse vote since the election of September, 1930.

For the Social Democrats, it can be argued that in the spring of 1930 they could foresee neither the proportions which the depression would assume nor the radical spirit which would grip the German masses as it reached its full depth. In the opposition parties' objection to raising the insurance levy, the Socialists read signs of a threat to wage rates, a matter of as vital concern to the trade unions as taxes and tariffs were to the interests ranged behind the opposition. If the Social Democrats here pursued sectional, to the detriment of national interests, they could be accused of doing nothing of which every party was not equally to blame. The Social Democrats felt, with some justification, that over the years they more than any other party had sacrificed allegiance to their objectives in the interest of defending the Republic from its enemies. They had returned to opposition with a considerable sense of self-righteousness.

For Brüning it can be said that the economic crisis was bound to absorb his attention and that—whatever may be thought of his measures for dealing with it—it was his duty to furnish leadership to the nation in an effort to master it. If he concluded that there was little hope of obtaining agreement on a program through bargaining with the parties and that a show of resolution on his part might better serve to induce a sense of responsibility in the Reichstag and win public confidence for the government, he had ample ground for thinking it. Nor was he acting without precedent. No chancellor, not even Stresemann, had been able to deal with an internal political or economic crisis in the Weimar period without resort to special powers, whether under Article 48 or by means of an enabling act.[3]

As for Hindenburg—leaving aside the question of his political judgment and the motives of those that influenced him—it can be said that he acted "unconstitutionally" only if it is assumed that the presidential powers under the Weimar constitution were to be exercised as the powers of the crown are under the British constitution. The point is at best a doubtful one. It is true that Preuss, the author of the Weimar constitution, believed that he was establishing in the presidency an office which would function in relation to parliament like the British monarchy, but it is equally clear that he did not understand the operation of the British constitution.[4] Preuss and others in the Weimar assembly were strongly influenced by Professor Redslob, an authority of the time on parliamentary government and an admirer of the British system. Redslob believed that the British monarch could, on his own initiative, appoint and dismiss a prime minister and dissolve parliament.[5] Preuss considered that the president should have like powers. He did provide as well that presidential decrees would require the counter-signature of a responsible minister, but he also made it clear that the president would be entitled to dismiss a chancellor who resisted a dissolution and to choose one from the minority of the Reichstag for the purpose of carrying it through.[6] Such powers fitted with Preuss's conception of a president directly elected by the people and serving as a balance to the Reichstag, with the right to appeal to the people against decisions of the Reichstag—for example, by submitting its legislation to referendum. That the president could dismiss a chancellor or dissolve the Reichstag against the will of a majority of the Reichstag was disputed on both sides in the public law literature of the Weimar period.[7] The point remained a debatable one. On the other hand, there was no question that, under the constitution, the president had full discretion whether to grant a chancellor the use of emergency powers (or a dissolution). In the circumstances of 1932–33, the refusal of such a request inevitably led to the chancellor's resignation.

These controversies cannot be settled here, if they can be settled at all. They show the difficulty of singling out in the complex of events one or another individual, group, or institution on which to fix responsibility for the failure of the Weimar system. They do point the way to the Parliamentary Council's broad conclusion that polarization of power in the Reichstag and the presidency had had two bad consequences: first, that the parties in the Reichstag, in whom recognition of the need to compromise and the larger sense of obligation to the country as a whole had not developed,* were all the less constrained to take the responsibility of forming and supporting a government capable of carrying out a policy and providing national leadership, particularly in time of crisis; and second, that extensive presidential powers in a prolonged parliamentary crisis could be misused and exploited to destroy constitutional government. Dr. Menzel told the Council:

I may recall the period before 1933, when it was very easy for the parties to evade political responsibility, often even for legislative measures which they themselves held to be necessary, because in the wings stood the

---

* The principle of the Reich government's responsibility to the Reichstag had been firmly established only late in the war of 1914–18.

Reich president with his power to issue emergency decrees. Such a flight from political responsibility we must never allow to occur again.[8]

Dr. von Mangoldt writes:

The use to which the second Reich president had put his powers under the Weimar constitution to form and dismiss governments in the years 1932 and 1933 made the authors of the Basic Law deeply apprehensive of such powers.[9]

The Parliamentary Council therefore concentrated its attention on the problem how to secure effective government with a multi-party parliament and without extensive presidential powers in reserve. As they went about this task, the majority of the members of the Council squarely faced two facts: first, that for the foreseeable future it was unlikely that there would emerge two major parties in Western Germany consistently capable of achieving a parliamentary majority by themselves and governing through a homogeneous cabinet executive drawn exclusively from one party,* and second, that the parliamentary system where there are several parties will not function and cannot be expected to function as it does where there are two.

One radical solution of the difficulty—provision for an executive elected for a fixed term—was rejected. Instead, the Parliamentary Council has tried in the Basic Law to devise constitutional inducements to the parties to come together and stay together in majority coalition governments. The parties cannot shirk responsibility for government by letting it pass to cabinets of "experts" or to any other type of government chosen by and owing its existence primarily to the president rather than the Bundestag. In all circumstances, the choice of a chancellor depends upon an election in the Bundestag. The parties must come to a prompt agreement on a chancellor to whom they are prepared to give a working majority, or face the prospect either of a dissolution or the appointment of the candidate with the largest, though minority, support. Nor can the parties remove a chancellor from office unless they are prepared to join in furnishing a working majority to replace him.

Where it proves impossible to bring a majority coalition together

* This assumption and reasons for thinking it valid, despite opinion and some evidence to the contrary, are discussed in the next chapter. The popular support for the parties in the 1946–47 Land elections was: SPD, 35 per cent; CDU, 28.6 per cent; CSU (Bavaria), 9 per cent; FDP, 9.8 per cent; KPD, 9.5 per cent; remainder, 8.4 per cent.

either to support a new chancellor or to replace one who has lost
his majority, the Parliamentary Council has faced realities and "regu-
larized" the position of the "minority" chancellor. If an absolute
majority does not exist for any candidate, the man with the largest
support in the Bundestag is to be named chancellor unless the president considers that further effort to produce a majority through
dissolution of the Bundestag and new elections would be preferable.
If, once in office, a "minority" chancellor finds that the Bundestag
will not adopt his legislation, he may, with the president's agreement, dissolve the Bundestag. Or, if an election would be untimely,
the chancellor may ask the president to declare a "state of legislative
emergency" and may propose legislation for the approval of the
Bundesrat alone for a six-months period. The Bundestag can, of
course, regain control of the government at any time by producing
a majority to replace it.

The stature and powers of the presidential office are considerably
reduced. The president is elected by a representative national assembly instead of by the people at large. In his own right he disposes
of no special powers, whether to enforce the compliance of the
Länder with their federal obligations or to legislate by decree in
conditions of emergency. He has no decisive voice in the naming
of a chancellor, nor can he dismiss a chancellor or dissolve the
Bundestag (except in one case) on his own initiative. He has no
veto or right of appeal to the electorate in connection with federal
legislation. But discretion rests with him in three important cases
to prevent what, in his judgment, may be a too hasty resort to
minority government, untimely or too frequent general elections,
and an unwarranted declaration of "legislative emergency."

Such, in summary, are the relationships between chancellor, parliament, and president established in the Basic Law. We have now
to see by what route the Parliamentary Council arrived at this result.

2. FORM OF THE EXECUTIVE

Parliamentary   As it came to grips with the problem of securing
vs. Presidential   stable government with a multiparty legislature,
Executive   the Parliamentary Council had first to decide
                     whether to retain a parliamentary executive or
to break with the past altogether and provide for an executive
elected for a fixed term.

The Social Democrats wanted to keep a parliamentary executive but strengthen it. The Christian Democrats also held this view, but looked mainly to a reform of the electoral system to produce greater stability of government:

> To my mind, the question of the form of government we are to adopt—a presidential system or an elected chancellor—is of less moment than an electoral law which will produce clear majorities and enable a chancellor to be named by a large majority upon whose support he can rely to govern for the whole term of the legislature.[10]

The Free Democrats, of whom Dr. Dehler and Dr. Becker were the most active, were the principal champions of an executive elected for a fixed term. Various proposals for an executive of this type were made. Here we shall refer only to that of the Free Democrats for a president elected by a national assembly for a four-year term, with the responsibility of setting policy, leading the administration, and appointing ministers, but without emergency legislative powers, a right of veto, or power to dissolve the Bundestag.

Dehler and Becker argued that by providing that a "minority" chancellor could remain in office when a majority to replace him did not exist, the Council had already gone far along the way to an executive with fixed tenure and would do better to go the whole way, since a chancellor who held his place only because the Bundestag could not agree upon his successor would be in a weak position.[11] They doubted that the "constructive vote of no-confidence" would remedy the weaknesses of Weimar party government, pointing out that most of the Weimar political crises had arisen not from votes of no-confidence in the Reichstag, but from disintegration of the coalitions.[12]

> The great danger we have to guard against is the crippling of the government by artificial crises, and we can do that by giving the head of government fixed tenure. . . . Consider our Weimar experience. Were the crises that led to the fall of the various cabinets really genuine crises? Was Herr Luther's flag decree a proper ground, or the Young plan, or, before that, the Dawes plan? It was not the great social questions that led to the fall of governments, but any sort of situation which someone wanted to evade, or with which the parties or a goverment leader were not prepared to put up.[13]

The German people, Dehler and Becker held, must be shown that democracy could produce firm leadership.

We hope by this means to make of a people like the Germans, who are inclined to be believers in authority, stronger adherents of democracy and to cultivate in them a better impression of democracy than is afforded, on its seamy side, by the recurrent government crises of parliamentary regimes.[14]

Carlo Schmid, for the Social Democrats, rejoined:

Our colleague, Dr. Becker, has insisted that, since our people are such great believers in authority, democracy should be made as palatable for them as possible. . . . I should like to assert the contrary. We ought to do everything in our power to remove from our people this devotion to authority . . . and should refrain from creating any temptation for them to put their faith again in any kind of authority. . . . Democracy is a product of confidence in one's self, not of confidence in others.[15]

The crises of German parliamentary life were not as a rule superficial, he maintained, but were "rooted in the structure of society." As he saw it, the elasticity of the parliamentary system helped to a resolution of such crises, for the change of government which it permitted served as a "kind of safety valve to release an overcharge of pressure." On the other hand, the inflexibility of presidential government would serve only to deepen a crisis.

If the president cannot master the situation satisfactorily, he must either go—in which case we have precisely the state of affairs that you want to avoid—or he will stay on and, relying upon his power, begin a war with his parliament and try to prevail against it. . . . Such persistence could only make conditions leading to a revolutionary situation enormously more virulent, and I believe that in the times in which we are living we cannot afford to do anything to increase the likelihood of such a development.[16]

The spokesmen of both parties were wary of the limits of German tolerance for parliamentary government. But where the Free Democrats offered firm leadership as a prescription, the Social Democrats insisted that nothing less than a change in the people themselves would avail:

What we have to change is the spirit of the people and not the "rules of the game." . . . The people must try now slowly to learn to work the machinery of democracy.[17]

As the Christian Democrats were staking their hopes on a reform of the electoral system, there was never a serious prospect that the Parliamentary Council would decide for the presidential executive, and most of its attention was devoted to a study of means of strengthening a parliamentary executive.

Election of the Chancellor (Article 63 [1]) Under the Basic Law, the election of the chancellor may require three stages. The president may propose a candidate to the Bundestag, and if he obtains the votes of a majority of the members, he is elected. If not, the Bundestag may within fourteen days elect a candidate of its own by majority of the members. If within this period no election takes place, a new ballot must be held at once. If on this occasion no candidate receives the votes of a majority of the members, the president must within seven days either appoint the candidate who has received the largest number of votes, or dissolve the Bundestag.

This procedure is the outcome of efforts of the Parliamentary Council to accomplish three things: confine the president to an auxiliary role in the selection of the chancellor; exert pressure on the parties in the Bundestag to come to a speedy agreement on a chancellor; in the event of an impasse, afford a way out in addition to resorting to dissolution and new elections.

The disposition to minimize, even exclude, the president's role in the selection process was strong from the start. The Chiemsee conference proposed that he have no right of nomination, but instead a right to "object" to the Bundestag's choice of a chancellor. The Bundestag could, if it wished, over-ride this objection.[18] The Social Democrats opposed even this right of objection.[19] They and the Free Democrats argued that nomination of the chancellor by the president would be superfluous, since he could do no more than offer the name of the candidate most likely to secure majority support in the Bundestag.[20] Von Mangoldt, for the Christian Democrats, however, ultimately convinced the delegates that the participation of the president, as a neutral figure, would be indispensable in setting the process of selection in motion and facilitating negotiation between the parties.[21] In his choice for the nomination, the president is not formally bound to consider what, after consultation, he thinks may be the sense of the majority in the Bundestag. But he can gain nothing by failing to do so.[22] His position in this respect is therefore comparable with that of the British monarch and the French president.

The Council was equally concerned to prevent delay in the formation of governments. The time required to bring a coalition together had increased through the Weimar period, lengthening from an average of four days for cabinets formed up to 1923 to twenty-three days for those formed thereafter. The crisis between the first and second Luther governments in 1926 had lasted forty-six days. But the Council could not fix a limit on the time to be taken in interparty negotiations without deciding what was to be done should the prescribed time elapse without an agreement. Three solutions were considered: dissolution of the Bundestag; election of the chancellor by the Bundesrat instead of the Bundestag; election of the chancellor by less than an absolute majority of the Bundestag. There were objections to all three. To provide only for dissolution in the event of stalemate in the Bundestag might lead to repeated fruitless and demoralizing general elections. The upper house, especially with the defeat of the senate proposal, would not be a representative body. The election of a "minority" chancellor by the Bundestag might revive the Weimar practice of resorting to "caretaker" (*geschäftsführende*) governments. With the catastrophic series of elections in 1932–33 in mind, none of the parties favored relying on the first alternative alone. The federalist-minded CDU/CSU preferred a resort to the Bundesrat.[23] The Free Democrats continued to advocate an executive with fixed tenure, but in any case remained antipathetic to an executive owing its existence to the Bundesrat. The Social Democrats, after some wavering,[24] came down on the side of the Bundestag. In effect, the majority decided that if there had to be a resort to a less representative government to break an impasse, it would be more consistent with the parliamentary principle that it should owe its existence to a minority in the Bundestag rather than to the delegates of the Land governments in the Bundesrat. The president has discretion whether to admit such a minority government to office or declare a dissolution.*

The parties in the Bundestag, therefore, have as an inducement to

* The Standing Orders of the Bundestag (6/12/51) (Sec. 4, par. 5) provide that the nomination of a chancellor from the floor of the Bundestag must be supported by at least one-fourth of the members. The constitutionality of this provision is doubtful, but it is unlikely that the president would appoint a chancellor supported by fewer than a quarter of the members in preference to dissolution (see Fritz Münch, *Die Bundesregierung* [Frankfurt a.M.: Alfred Metzner Verlag, 1954], p. 141).

cut their bargaining short and come to an agreement the knowledge that, if they do not, either the candidate commanding the largest support among them will be given office anyway or they will have to face a fresh election within two to three weeks.

3. STRENGTHENED POSITION OF THE CHANCELLOR;
   WEAKENED POSITION OF THE PRESIDENT

Having contrived measures to speed the election of a chancellor, the Parliamentary Council next set about strengthening his position in office relatively to the parties in the Bundestag, the president, and his colleagues in the cabinet. To this end, it provided that the Bundestag can express lack of confidence in the chancellor only by electing a successor by the majority of its members. The Bundestag's indorsement of the members of the chancellor's cabinet is not required, nor can it bring a vote of no-confidence against them. On the other hand, the chancellor may ask the Bundestag for a vote of confidence, and if he does not get it, dissolve the Bundestag with the president's agreement, or request him to declare a legislative emergency. The president, for his part, cannot dismiss the chancellor unless the Bundestag has elected a successor, nor, once the chancellor is in office, can he dissolve the Bundestag without the chancellor's agreement. The chancellor's pre-eminence in the cabinet is assured through the formal provision that he alone is responsible for "general policy" and by the fact that he alone is elected by and directly accountable to the Bundestag, the appointment and tenure of ministers resting on his decision.[25]

Constructive Vote The so-called "constructive vote of no-confi-
of No-Confidence dence" (*das konstruktive Misstrauensvotum*) is
(Article 67) one of the few provisions of the Basic Law
which the two major parties in the Parliamentary Council united to support from the beginning.[26] In essentials, it was adopted as proposed by the Chiemsee conference: "The Bundestag can express its lack of confidence in the chancellor only by electing a successor and requesting the president to dismiss the chancellor."

There is no doubt that, given a parliamentary situation in which all or most of the parties are disposed to play the parliamentary game according to the rules, the chancellor's hand is strengthened by this provision. The German parties will often enough combine to take a negative view of this or that government policy. It is quite another matter to bring them together in the constructive agreement needed to form a government. But it would be a mistake to think that it was this consideration which roused the strong and even passionate advocacy of the provision in the Parliamentary Council. The deputies were not so much concerned about the "normal" parliamentary situation, nor, for that matter, typical Weimar conditions. The Chiemsee experts and some in the Parliamentary Council[27] held that

the experiences of the Weimar period show that to restore the functioning of the parliamentary system according to the rules of the game, provision should be made in the Basic Law that a vote of no-confidence could be brought only by a majority prepared to act constructively; in other words, the vote of no-confidence as a bare act of obstruction should be ruled out.[28]

But this had little relevance to most of Weimar parliamentary history, for of the nineteen Weimar governments only two (at most three, if the Papen government is included) fell as the result of votes of no-confidence. What in fact obsessed the delegates was the conduct of the National Socialist and Communist parties in the Reichstag and in the Prussian Landtag in 1932:

Whoever recalls the situation in the German Reichstag before 1933 knows that the extremist parties made common cause in rejecting a government—it cost them nothing to bring in a motion of no-confidence, since they had not to take the responsibility—although they themselves were quite incapable of forming a government of their own.[29]

. . . Should any spurious majority whose two wings hate each other like poison be able to block the operation of government? If the answer is yes, then we must stand by the old arrangement by which any kind of majority was sufficient to overthrow the government. If, however, we are of the opinion that a genuine opposition is not possible without the corresponding conception of responsibility . . . then we must adopt the point of view that a vote of no-confidence, with all its consequences, may be proposed only by a majority willing and able to undertake the task of government.[30]

The "constructive vote of no-confidence" can scarcely be regarded as affording insurance against obstructive conduct by an anti-parliamentary majority that can unite only for disruptive purposes. Other means are always open to determined obstructionists, if they are in the majority, to bring the parliamentary machine to a stop. But it does insure, in such a situation, that a chancellor who owes his position in the first place to the parliamentary forces loyal to parliamentary practices remains in office. To be sure, the president could make such a "minority" chancellor's position untenable by refusing him a dissolution or a declaration of legislative emergency. But without the status of a Hindenburg, and disposing of no emergency powers of his own, the president could gain nothing by such a refusal except stalemate and breakdown of the parliamentary order.

The possibility exists that in normal conditions a chancellor might lose his majority and, in the absence of one to replace him, cling to his position, although the candidate of a larger minority party might have a better claim to office.* The case of the *"klebende"* ("clinging") chancellor was not overlooked by the Parliamentary Council.[31] However, to provide the means of detaching him from office, the Council would have been obliged either to provide the president with the power in his own right to dismiss the chancellor and declare a dissolution or to give up the constructive vote of no-confidence. It was prepared to do neither. As between guarding against familiar and unfamiliar risks, it chose the former.

In practice, motions of no-confidence are not admitted to the order paper of the Bundestag except in the form of a nomination of a successor to the chancellor.[32] Motions of censure (*Missbilligungsanträge*), whether of particular actions or of general policies of the government which do not entail the government's overthrow, have been permitted. This practice has been criticized by, among others, Dr. Adenauer, as being inconsistent with the constructive vote of no-confidence.[33] But here, authority—this time in the person of the chancellor—is once again claiming more than its due. The Parliamentary Council's intention was to discourage obstructive and irresponsible party tactics in the Bundestag, not to protect governments from criticism, even the severest criticism, of their conduct and policies.[34]

---

* For example, in a Bundestag of 500 deputies composed of 130 deputies of the right, 140 of the center and 230 of the left, a coalition of the center and right, supporting a chancellor of the center, might break up, with the left unwilling to join either party to form a new government. If there is to be a "minority" government, the left has the better claim to head it, but will not have the opportunity to do so unless the chancellor resigns (see Münch, *op. cit.,* p. 180).

*Dissolution of
the Bundestag
(Article 68);
Legislation in
an Emergency
(Article 81)*
Having given the "minority" chancellor constitutional respectability, the Parliamentary Council had to afford him a means of bringing pressure to bear on a refractory majority in the Bundestag which might refuse to pass essential legislation. For this purpose, he may resort either to the threat of a dissolution or a declaration of legislative emergency.

A decision to dissolve the Bundestag, with the exception already mentioned,[35] is tied directly to this situation of parliamentary crisis and is essentially a right belonging to the chancellor. A right of the president, either on his own initiative or in response to developments in the Bundestag, to declare a dissolution was overwhelmingly rejected.[36] On the other hand, the chancellor's use of the dissolution is subject to restrictions. He must ask for and be refused a vote of confidence before he can proceed to a dissolution. The Bundestag can arrest the dissolution by electing a successor to him. The president has discretion whether to give effect to the chancellor's proposal for a dissolution. It is clear, however, that this discretion is intended to be a narrow one, directed to determining whether an election at the time is in the national interest. Should the president refuse a dissolution, he could hardly avoid acceding to a government's request for a declaration of legislative emergency. Any other course would precipitate a constitutional crisis which could be resolved only by the chancellor's resignation or his own. On the other hand, should the chancellor be defeated on a question of confidence and apply for a declaration of legislative emergency without proposing a dissolution, the president would be in a strong position to grant or withhold it as he thought best.

The declaration of a state of legislative emergency does not have the scope of Article 48 of the Weimar constitution. It applies only to the circumstances in which Article 48 was used in 1930–33. The president and Bundesrat must agree to the declaration. All legislation continues to be submitted to the Bundestag. But if the Bundestag rejects draft laws which the government has designated as "urgent," or amends them in a form unacceptable to the government, they become law if they are approved by the Bundesrat. The Basic Law, or any part of it, cannot be amended or suspended by such legislation. Only one term of legislative emergency is permitted in the life of a government. It comes to an end six months from the date of declaration, or upon the resignation or replacement of the chancellor. The tightrope-walking here is obvious. The Council attempted to prevent a breakdown of government which a would-be dictator could exploit, but without creating a dictatorship in doing so—to afford a means of tiding the parliamentary system over a crisis without leaving an opportunity for the parties in the Bundestag to evade responsibility indefinitely.

The Parliamentary Council dealt separately with the emergency which might confront a government as the result of natural catastrophe, civil disorder, military attack, and the like. The argument ran: when parliament does not function because it is in a crisis of its own making, there should be no general emergency procedure on the model of Article 48 by which responsibility for government can readily pass from parliament to other hands. If parliament is functioning, emergency measures should not be taken without its consent. Hence, emergency procedure should be confined to the situation in which parliament is prevented by *force majeure* from fulfilling its functions.[37] Accordingly, a provision was adopted by which, if the Bundestag or Bundesrat were thus incapacitated, the government, with the agreement of the presidents of the two chambers, could issue temporary decrees and temporarily suspend certain of the basic rights in an emergency.[38] The article was deleted from the Basic Law in the final reading because it was thought that so long as the occupation powers continued to reserve to themselves responsibility for the Federal Republic's defense and the maintenance of its constitutional order, the exercise of emergency powers by the federal government might lead to confusion. With the return of sovereignty to the Federal Republic, the question of powers to deal with an emergency has arisen again. At the time of writing, the Western German parliament has before it legislation on the subject.

Chancellor and Ministers   Where coalition governments are the rule, a chancellor is necessarily at a disadvantage in imposing his leadership on them. To form and keep the coalition in being, he may have to make concessions to the various parties on appointments and issues which tie his hands and tend to transform his role from that of leader of a team to chairman of a refractory committee whose members' first allegiance is directed to party interests. The chancellor may find himself spending more time at peacemaking than pacemaking. As we have seen, Weimar chancellors were frequently in this position.

With this experience in mind, the Parliamentary Council has done what can be done by constitutional means to strengthen the chancellor's hand and enable him to establish an ascendancy over his cabinet colleagues.

Only the chancellor is elected by and can be replaced by the Bundestag. Ministers are not individually responsible to the Bundestag, as they were to the Reichstag. Since the cabinet as a whole stands or falls with the chancellor, its collective responsibility is assured. In constructing his government, the chancellor is assisted by the fact that the Basic Law makes no provision about the number or kind of posts of which it is to be composed. He is therefore free, within the limits fixed by consideration for efficiency and parliamentary financial tolerance, to make as many or as few ministerial appointments as the necessities of coalition politics may require.

The ministers owe their offices and their tenure of them to the chancellor. He is entirely free both to choose his ministers and to dismiss them, without interference from parliament or the president.* The president, it is true, appoints and dismisses ministers on the proposal of the chancellor, but this is a formality. The president cannot refuse the chancellor's wishes, much less impose his own on the chancellor. Some commentators[39] dispute this point, but von Mangoldt is emphatic in upholding it.[40] Apart from the fact that von Mangoldt has the best claim to know what the Parliamentary Council intended, the argument seems conclusive that by refusing to appoint the ministers nominated, the president could effectively prevent a chancellor unacceptable to him from forming a government. This, evidently, would be inconsistent with every other provision on the formation of governments adopted by the Parliamentary Council.

The chancellor's is the dominant voice in the cabinet. His position recalls the story told of President Lincoln, who, when he put a question to the vote of his cabinet, found himself in the minority and announced the result: "Ayes, five. No's, three. The No's have it."

* Hindenburg, from January, 1928, insisted that the minister of defense should have his confidence, and on other occasions intervened in the formation of cabinets.

Article 65 admittedly does not make the chancellor's pre-eminence entirely clear:

The federal chancellor determines, and is responsible for, general policy. Within the limits of this general policy, each federal minister conducts the business of his department independently and on his own responsibility. The federal government decides on differences of opinion between the federal ministers. . . .

The ambiguity here results from an academic penchant of the Chiemsee experts for combining in one the three kinds of cabinet executive known to German constitutional experience: the chancellor (Bismarckian) type; the collegial (council of ministers) type; the independent specialist minister (*ressort*) type.[41] The provision does not mean, as it might suggest, that all decisions are to be made by majority vote in the cabinet, or that individual ministers may take an independent line for which they can be held to account apart from the government as a whole. What it means is that the chancellor may settle any question which in his judgment belongs to that realm of general policy for which he is resposible to the Bundestag. The cabinet may settle any other matter, particularly those on which differences of opinion exist between ministers. What the chancellor or the cabinet do not take upon themselves to decide, an individual minister may settle for himself.[42]

The President   The provisions for the president's election by a
(Articles 54 to 56)   national assembly, composed of members of the
Bundestag and delegates elected by the Landtage of the Länder, followed from the Parliamentary Council's decision to eliminate from the presidential office all characteristics tending to make it a focus of power and popular support competing with the Bundestag. Popular election of the president, and the popular referendum and initiative, were alike condemned as affording opportunities for the unscrupulous demagogue.[43]

The president's powers need not be recapitulated. If the analogy is not taken too far, they might be said to give him the position which Preuss believed, mistakenly, he was giving the Weimar president: a role in relation to government and parliament akin to that of the British monarchy. The formal powers of the latter are so great and the conventions which govern their use so numerous (and subtle) that the authors of written instruments of government could hardly be expected to produce an institution more than approximating it. Other disparities arise from the differences of national politics and party organization in the two countries. The British monarch is ordinarily protected from involvement in political decisions by the constitutional custom that he acts only on the advice of a responsible minister and by the fact that it is usually obvious which party leader has the best claim to take office as prime minister. The German president's actions are similarly subject to ministerial approval, but he does have a clearly defined discretion to admit a "minority" chancellor to office or declare a dissolution and to accede to a "minority" chancellor's request for emergency powers or a dissolution—a discretion which has obvious utility in conditions where it may often be difficult to form a government with a working majority and where further elections would do nothing to clarify the situation. But even in Great Britain, supposing that the political conditions which prompted these provisions in the Basic Law were also to arise in the British parliament, it seems clear that the monarch would be drawn into playing a much more active part in the formation of governments than for some time past.

Another difference is a considerable one. The formal nature of the Basic Law, particularly the federal structure which it establishes, opens the way to doubt and dispute over the constitutionality of legislation, which cannot exist in the British situation. Hence the president's signature of laws is more than a formality. He is obliged to satisfy himself that they have been enacted in accordance with the Basic Law,[44] and, if he is in doubt, he may request an opinion from the constitutional court.[45] The president thus serves as a first line of defense against an unconstitutional exercise of legislative power. The first federal president has not hesitated to take a stand on that line.

4. CONCLUSION

These arrangements have been the subject of much criticism in Germany and elsewhere. Some regret the Parliamentary Council's preoccupation with conditions that may never arise in Germany again and consider that the Council should boldly have assumed instead that the parliamentary situation in Western Germany would develop in such a way as to permit the chancellor to stand or fall on a simple question of confidence and to rely upon the weapon of dissolution to keep his majority in order. This criticism also entails that the Parliamentary Council was mistaken in thinking it unlikely that a two-party system or something near to it would develop in Western Germany. The power of dissolution, or the threat of its use, can alone do little to strengthen the hand of the government unless an appeal to the electorate is likely to result in a clear expression of opinion one way or the other on the issues before it. With many parties, such clear mandates seldom emerge, and repeated appeals to the electorate may serve only to discredit the government and play into the hands of antidemocratic forces. The reasons for thinking that the Parliamentary Council's estimate of future party developments was the more realistic one are discussed in the next chapter.

Other critics, of whom Professor Friedrich Glum[46] of Munich is a notable example, show that the provisions of the Basic Law would not, in the last analysis, prevent a recurrence of the situation that confronted Hindenburg in 1932–33 and a breakdown of constitutional government. If for an indefinite time the parliamentary parties and the electorate are so divided that a working majority for a government cannot be produced, nothing—declarations of legislative emergency, dissolutions, or anything else—can avail to save parliamentary government. Indeed, had the Basic Law been in effect prior to 1932, unless all the Reichstag parties (excepting the Communists and the Nationalists) had combined to support a chancellor, Hitler would undoubtedly have come to power as a "minority" chancellor all the sooner—with or without the Nationalists, presidential *camarilla* or no presidential *camarilla*. Equally, of course, unless all the parties from center to right had agreed upon a candidate in 1930, the president would have been obliged to accept and support a Social Democrat as "minority" chancellor.

But to regard the Basic Law in this light is to make the mistake of assuming that the Parliamentary Council was trying to do something which it did not intend or believe it possible to do: *guarantee* the operation of a parliamentary system by constitutional provisions. The Council had to make the choice between relying, in the last resort, on the parties and the people or reserving extensive powers to the president, the Bundesrat, or some other authority to govern in the event of a prolonged parliamentary crisis. Professor Glum himself has no answer to the dilemma except to suggest that the position of the president should have been strengthened. The Council, for good reason it may be thought, was wary of this solution.

Since the Council did not share the illusions of the Weimar Assembly regarding the power of formal provisions to guarantee a democratic constitutional order, it attempted merely to lay down "rules of the game" for a multiparty parliament which will encourage those who have the will to overcome the difficulties of government inherent in that situation, discourage those who do not, and tide government over short-term crises. For the rest, the fate of constitutional government is left in the hands of the parties and the people.

As Carlo Schmid writes:

We chose so to establish the relation between parliament, the government and the president in the Basic Law as to create an inducement for the settlement of political crises, to make it impossible for one federal organ to shuffle off its responsibility on another, and to prevent real crises being smoothed over and made to appear solved by fictions. Where fundamental changes in political conditions occur with which the constitution cannot cope, it is better to leave the matter to the *ultima ratio populi* than to try to regulate by institutional means what is not capable of being so regulated.[47]

CHAPTER IV

THE PARTIES AND THE ELECTORAL LAW

The two-party system is possible only in a country in which the parties are not based upon *Weltanschauung*. We have already had quite sufficient experience in these debates of the Parliamentary Council to show that none of the existing parties here in Germany is free of *Weltanschauung*.

FRAU HELENE WESSEL

1. ADOPTION OF THE ELECTORAL LAW

The Parliamentary Council devised the relationships between the federal government, parliament and the president on the assumption that there would continue to be a number of parties representing the electorate. That the assumption was a reasonable one in the light of the past and the state of the parties at the time may be granted. But the question arises: Why did the Council take what seemed to be a deliberate step to preserve a number of parties by reverting to proportional representation—everywhere identified with the multiparty system—in preference to providing for the election of deputies by simple majority on a single ballot from single-member constituencies?*

Party interest, undoubtedly, was the decisive factor. In terms of their future standing in the Bundestag—even, in some cases, of their survival as national parties—the Social Democrats, Free Democrats, Center, and Communists had as much at stake in preserving proportional representation as the Christian Democratic / Christian Social Union had in supplanting it with the majority system. However, from the point of view of the best interests of parliamentary government, the parties for proportional representation—who were

* By this method (British and American), the candidate with the largest number of votes is elected on a single ballot, whether he has won an absolute majority of the votes cast or not. In Germany, prior to 1919, a second or "runoff" ballot between the two leading candidates took place when none had an absolute majority.

138

in the majority—could not fail to acknowledge the strength of the case on the other side. They were at pains to take up their position on grounds other than party self-interest. They contended that, because the existence of a number of parties was rooted in historical and other conditions basic to German life,[1] it was doubtful that a simple-majority single-member electoral law* would produce a two-party system in Germany.[2] Should the adoption of this electoral method succeed in reducing the number of parties, it could not do so, they protested, without depriving millions of political expression.[3]

Their opponents, on the other hand, denied that the existence of a number of parties was an ineradicable condition of German political life,[4] held the electoral system mainly accountable for this state of affairs in Germany in the past,[5] and insisted that the adoption of a simple-majority law would put an end to it and bring about stable two-party government.[6] To these contentions we shall return after tracing the somewhat tortuous course of the electoral law's passage.

The electoral law owed its final form as a measure of modified proportional representation to the balance of interest of the parties represented in the Parliamentary Council and to changes imposed by the military governors. In fact, the law as it finally took effect was essentially a military government enactment, for it was promulgated by the ministers-president, over widespread party opposition, at the direct order of the military governors, relying upon their "supreme authority."

The party interests which were at stake are for the most part obvious. The *Christian Democratic / Christian Social Union*, rejecting all compromise, held out to the end for a straight simple-majority system.[7] They could expect to benefit most from such a system because they were the party which, on the showing of the Landtage and communal elections in 1946, 1947, and 1948, had the best chance of becoming the leading party in the forthcoming federal election. Moreover, their voting strength was relatively well distributed through the federal territory. They led in the two most populous Länder, North Rhine-Westphalia and Bavaria, had heavy reserves of strength in Baden, Rhineland-Palatinate, and Württemberg-Hohenzollern, and sizable polls in such opposition strongholds as Hesse, Württemberg-Baden, and Schleswig-Holstein. From the long-term

---

* Hereafter referred to as the "simple-majority" electoral system.

point of view, it was in the interest of the CDU/CSU, as the major party bidding for non-Socialist support, to establish an electoral system which would put small parties at a disadvantage and discourage splintering. The Weimar experience of proportional representation had shown that, while the left-wing voters held together behind two parties, a succession of splinter groups had set themselves up to cater for one or another shade of opinion or special interest in the center and right sector. Besides the major parties of this sector— the Center party, the Bavarian People's party, the Democratic party, the German People's party, the Nationalists, and National Socialists —there had been as many as nine other small parties.

The preference of the small parties in the Parliamentary Council for proportional representation needs little explanation. The *Free Democrats*, although possessing local concentrations of votes which might have saved them under a simple-majority system, were a national party and hence concerned to maximize their over-all representation in the Bundestag. The *Communists*, with little hope of winning outright majorities in electoral districts, were dependent on proportional representation to gain seats. The *Center party* was similarly motivated. The interests of the *German party*, on the other hand, were less definitely attached to either electoral method, and the party vacillated between them. Like the Bavarian parties, the German party had a definite, though less secure, local following in Lower Saxony upon which they could count under a simple-majority system. But they also had ambitions to extend their activities to other Länder and establish themselves on a firmer footing as a national party, at least in northern Germany. At first they supported a "second ballot" system, which could have been expected to help them in north German constituencies where the non-Socialist vote was split between them, the CDU, FDP, and the parties of the extreme right. When this system showed no chance of being adopted, they shifted to proportional representation. In the end, however, the German party joined the CDU/CSU in voting against the electoral law, because of a provision prohibiting parties from combining to put forward joint nomination lists for the allocation of seats by proportional representation. This showed that their principal interest in the electoral system lay in promoting conditions which would help them to strike favorable bargains with the other conservative parties.

The Social Democratic interest in proportional representation, at least in the conditions of 1948–49, is perhaps less clear. The German Socialists have traditionally advocated proportional representation. But opinion has been and still is divided within the party about which electoral method better serves the Social Democratic cause. On one hand, the party has little hope of putting a substantial part of its program into effect until it wins a parliamentary majority in its own right. Should the party be in sight of winning the support of a majority of the electorate, a simple-majority law might help it to gain control of the Bundestag all the sooner. On the other hand, so long as an electoral victory is not in prospect and Social Democratic voters are massed in certain areas rather than dispersed, the party stands to "waste" fewer votes and gain more parliamentary seats under proportional representation. Hence the party's view of electoral methods is equivocal and tends to be governed by estimates of the strength and distribution of its support at any particular time. While it was perhaps not as clear in 1948–49 as it later became that the Social Democrats were still very much a minority party, the continuing concentration of their voting strength in cities and industrial areas was apparent. The fact that, under a simple-majority system, they would have risked a greater wastage of votes than the Christian Democrats, while with proportional representation they could realize their popular support to the full in the Bundestag, was no doubt the decisive consideration for the Social Democrats in 1948–49.

After five months of negotiations in the electoral and main committees, the Parliamentary Council on February 24, 1949, adopted, against the votes of the CDU/CSU, an electoral law with these major provisions:

There was to be a Bundestag of 410 members, half to be elected from electoral districts by simple majority and half by proportional representation. Seats were to be allocated to the Länder ("list" seats in some cases to *groups* of Länder) relatively to the size of their populations. Each party was to put forward, in addition to its individual electoral district nominees, general Land and federal lists of nominees. A quotient was to be obtained by dividing the total valid votes in the federal territory by

410. This quotient was first to be divided into the total votes of each party in each Land, and from the mandates thus ascertained for each party were to be deducted the seats won by the parties in the electoral districts by simple majority. The seats remaining were then to be allocated to the party Land nomination lists in order of precedence.

The "remainders" of party votes at Land level were to be combined at federal level and as often as they contained the quotient, further seats were to be assigned the parties from their federal nomination lists, even if the final number of deputies in the Bundestag should exceed 410.

Precedents for this unusual combination of electoral methods had already been established in the electoral procedures of the Länder, where it had evolved partly as a concession to the belief of military government officials in the superior merit of the simple-majority system as a "democratic" electoral method. The predominance of proportional representation in this particular combination is obvious, since no party could receive many more seats than it would have been entitled to under pure proportional representation. To be sure, if the vote had been distributed in the right way, a leading party—even with something less than half the total vote—*might* have obtained all of the 205 district seats in the Bundestag. But this was offset by the provision for utilization of vote remainders at federal level and the creation of additional seats to accommodate it.

On March 2, to the consternation of the Parliamentary Council, the military governors announced that it was not competent to determine the method of electing the Bundestag and that the electoral procedure would be established by legislation in each of the Landtage, which could if they wished take the Parliamentary Council's draft law as a model. Although the ministers-president as early as July of the preceding year had pointed out to the military governors the need for a federal electoral law, the Chiemsee experts in turn had stressed it, and the Parliamentary Council had established its committee to draft a law in September, this was the first official word from the military governors on the subject.

It is difficult to account for this tardy decision. Presumably, it originated in the French and American penchant for federalist decentralization. (Justifying the step to the Germans, General Clay made much of the point that each of the American states have their own electoral laws.)* But if so, why the delay of eight months in making known to the Germans a position which, presumably,† had been agreed upon at the London conference? It seems possible—and subsequent events tend to bear this out—that it was the proportional character of the electoral law adopted by the Parliamentary Council, not taking action itself, which prompted the military governors to move at the last moment to exclude the Council's competence. To give responsibility for the electoral system to the Länder might readily have been expected to lead to a reversal of the Parliamentary Council's decision in many of the Landtage because, in four, the CDU/CSU were in a position to put through simple-majority laws and, in the Länder where the SPD and FDP were strongest, such as Hesse and Bremen, these parties would have been obliged to follow suit to prevent the CDU/CSU having the best of both worlds and benefiting from proportional representation where they were less likely to achieve majorities.

The French had held from the start that not only government, but political parties and trade unions as well, should be decentralized. Proportional representation, in the exclusive control of candidacies which it gives to central party offices, greatly enhances their power, whereas the French wanted—and said it plainly—locally controlled candidacies and decentralized party organizations. The American view may also have been influenced by this consideration. A weightier factor may well have been distaste for the advantage to be obtained by the Communists (and, possibly, also by the Social Democrats) from proportional representation.

The British military governor had insisted from the start that there must be a federal electoral law in some form and, without the need of preserving a united front with his colleagues, would prob-

---

* The analogy was not exact, as the Germans were quick to point out to the Allied liaison officers, at a meeting with the Parliamentary Council committee of seven on March 8, 1949. The United States Constitution provides that "the times, places, and manner of holding elections for Senators and Representatives shall be prescribed in each state by the legislature thereof," but adds that "the Congress may at any time by law make or alter such regulations, except as to the places of choosing Senators." By the Federal Apportionment Act of 1842, Congress required that every state populous enough to be entitled to more than one representative should be divided by the state legislatures into districts each returning one member. Since then, this procedure has become general.

† Although it was discussed, it is not clear whether a decision on the point was made at London.

ably have been disposed, as with the Basic Law, to adopt a position of neutrality between the party interests.

On the German side the reaction was prompt and unaimous. Dr. von Brentano (CDU), speaking for the Parliamentary Council as well as for his party, told the Allied liaison officers that in the German view "the federal lower house could not be chosen by differing electoral methods, for it might result in a completely false representation of the opinion of the electorate." The ministers-president, at a meeting at Königstein on March 24, resolved unanimously on the need for a uniform electoral law and requested the military governors to approve the adoption of a law by the Parliamentary Council.[8]

The announcement of the decision on the electoral law had coincided with the publication of the military governors' objections to the Basic Law. The strength of the German opposition made it clear that the military governors could not hold their ground on both issues without endangering the whole project of unifying Western Germany under its own government. On April 14 they gave way and informed the Parliamentary Council that it would have competence over the electoral system, with the reservation "that the electoral machinery will remain within the competence of each Land and that any system which provides for the utilization of remaining votes shall be limited in each Land to a list of candidates presented in that Land."[9]

On May 10 the Parliamentary Council adopted its second version of the electoral law, by 36 votes to 28, this time over the objection of both the CDU/CSU and the German party:

As before, half of the deputies were to be elected from electoral districts and half by proportional representation. In each Land all votes for each of the parties were to be totalled and their respective shares of the mandates calculated by the highest average (d'Hondt) procedure.* From these mandates were to be subtracted the seats won by each party in the electoral districts, and the remaining mandates were to be assigned to party Land lists of nominees in order of precedence. However, seats acquired in the electoral districts in excess of the number to which a party was entitled by proportional representation were to be retained. In that case, the total number of seats allocated to the Land was to be increased accord-

---

* This method insures that the party with the largest vote benefits from remainders. The "quotient" method tends to benefit small parties.

ingly and the party shares of seats from the lists recalculated under the d'Hondt procedure on the basis of the increase of seats.

Here again proportional representation predominated, but proportionality was confined to the vote in each Land. Remainders were not to be combined at federal level.

The Parliamentary Council met briefly for the last time on May 23 to promulgate the Basic Law. On May 28 the military governors addressed themselves to the ministers-president on the electoral law. Although only two weeks previously they had confirmed the Parliamentary Council's competence in the matter by approving the Basic Law,* the military governors, after mentioning minor objections of their own to the electoral law, went on to invite recommendations for changes from the ministers-president: "If a substantial majority of the ministers-president is not in favor of the law . . . , the military governors are prepared to consider such modifications of the law as may be proposed by the ministers-president in order to secure the approval by a substantial majority of the ministers-president."[10] As four of the eleven ministers-president were Christian Democrats and one from the CSU, the military governors were well aware that a "substantial majority" of them could not be in sympathy with the text as it stood. On June 1 the ministers-president replied, recommending, among other things, that the proportion of deputies to be chosen by simple majority from electoral districts and by proportional representation should be changed from fifty-fifty to sixty-forty, and that only parties obtaining at least 5 per cent of the valid vote or electing one deputy in an electoral district should qualify to have their votes taken into account in the calculation for distribution of seats to the Land nomination lists.

When news of these proposals was released, there was an outcry from the parties of the majority in the Parliamentary Council. The executives of the Social Democratic,[11] the Free Democratic,[12] and the Center parties[13] promptly denied that the ministers-president had competence to alter the electoral law and demanded that any changes should be considered by the Parliamentary Council. Dr. Schumacher met the press at Munich and denounced the Western Allies for "breaking the Bonn Constitution within a few days of approving it." They had, he said, "changed the electoral law as they

* See Art. 137(2).

thought fit, once again demonstrating their over-developed gover-ness complex."[14] He accused "CDU politicians" of working behind the scenes with the French to modify the electoral law in the direction of the simple-majority principle.[15] The Social Democratic Party, he added, would have "seriously to consider whether it can take part in the elections in these circumstances."

A storm also blew up over the status of the Parliamentary Council. Did it still exist? Or, as Dr. Adenauer contended, had it been dissolved on May 23? The Social Democrats and the Free Democrats denied that there had been any agreement to dissolve the Council and accused the Christian Democratic leader of hastening to bundle the Council off stage in the interests of his party.[16]

Meanwhile, the four Social Democrats and the one Free Democrat among the ministers-president were having their lessons read to them by their party organizations. When the minsters-president convened again on June 10 at Schlangenbad, the Social Democratic and Free Democratic ministers reopened the question of the proposed changes. A further letter to the military governors followed, in which the ministers-president questioned their constitutional right to make changes in the electoral law without the concurrence of the Parliamentary Council and submitted that "the beginning of constitutional life under the Basic Law should not be shadowed with constitutional doubts." Without prior resolution of these doubts, they concluded, they felt unable to make use of the authority which the military governors had given them.[17]

The military governors put an end to further discussion on June 13 by ordering, "in virtue of their supreme authority," the promulgation of the electoral law, amended to include the sixty-forty division of seats between the two electoral methods and the 5 per cent clause.[18] A further amendment was made, under military government authority, on August 5, eliminating the provision for recalculation of seats by the d'Hondt procedure in any case where the result in the electoral districts should necessitate the allocation of additional seats to a Land.

The opposition died away. The Social Democrats did not make good their threat to withdraw from the election. Their resentment, it became clear, had been provoked mainly by the Allied attempt to implicate one set of German authorities in undoing the work of another. Once the military governors had taken on themselves the onus of imposing the changes, the parties resisted them no further. In fact, these changes did not alter the proportional character of the law in a decisive way. One party, with the right distribution of its vote, might have won all the direct seats in each Land, but it was extremely improbable that any would do so. As it turned out, the major parties gained very few more seats than they would have won under proportional representation without the "frills." None of the smaller parties failed to win seats in the Bundestag. The Communists were not excluded, since they managed to win more than 5 per cent of the vote in several Länder. The military governors gained little by their intervention, except the fresh stirring up of party ill-feeling, which had begun to die down after the controversies over the Basic Law, and the reproach of having treated cavalierly the constitution they had just approved.

2. THE MULTIPARTY SYSTEM AND ELECTORAL
   METHODS IN GERMANY

The question whether the majority in the Parliamentary Council pursued immediate party interests in the electoral law to the detriment of the longer-term interests of stable parliamentary government cannot be answered without considering their contention that other factors than electoral methods were primarily responsible for the development of the German party system, and that, by adopting a simple-majority law, the Council would be attempting to force an unsuitable party pattern on the German electorate. The Parliamentary Council debates themselves unfortunately furnish little ground for a conclusion on these rather speculative points. There was much airing of opinion on both sides. But opinions which otherwise would be given considerable weight, particularly where held by men with long experience of political life in Germany, must be discounted because of loyalty to party and the interests at stake.

The case for holding that electoral methods produced a number of parties in Germany rests on the fact that both electoral methods used there—a majority system with second ballot until 1919 and proportional representation thereafter—are nearly everywhere associated with this condition.* Conversely, the simple-majority system with single ballot is nearly everywhere associated with countries with two-party government, or tending toward two-party government.† Impressive as this fact is, it does not, however, prove the case. The question still remains: Do countries with multiparty systems owe them to their electoral methods, or are the electoral methods incidental to the existence of a number of parties? Here there is no evidence on which to form a judgment. Instances of change from proportional representation or the second-ballot system to a simple-majority single-ballot system (or the reverse) which would throw light on the subject are extremely rare. Maurice Duverger[19] lays great stress on the effect of electoral methods on the party system. His investigations show that second ballots and proportional representation sustain multipartism, even conduce to a multiplication of parties, and operate to check any tendency to bipartism.[20] But he does not venture beyond the conclusion that the simple-majority single-ballot system favors the two-party system;[21] the simple-majority system with second ballot and proportional representation favors multipartism.[22]

What other explanation can be offered for a number of parties in Germany? Duverger, explaining this condition in his own country, says: "The multi-party system in France is a result of the non-coincidence of the main cleavages of opinion." There are certain basic issues upon which French public opinion is divided: freedom vs. planning, clericalism vs. anti-clericalism, orientation to the East vs. orientation to the West, etc. Multipartism, he says, arises because Frenchmen do not accept one of the antitheses as fundamental. Some emphasize freedom vs. planning, others clericalism vs. anti-clericalism, others East vs. West, and so on. He doubts whether a majority electoral system would produce a two-party system in France "except after a very long delay."[23]

* The majority system with second ballot was in effect in France until 1945; in Belgium until 1899; in Holland until 1917; in Switzerland, Italy, and Germany until 1919; in Norway until 1921. In every case except that of Belgium before 1894, there was a plurality of parties.

† Exceptions: Sweden before 1911; Denmark before 1920; Canada today, although the Canadian situation might be compared with that of Britain before the Labour party finally supplanted the Liberals as a major party and hence described as "tending to bi-partism."

A similar non-coincidence of main cleavages of opinion existed and still exists in Germany on three major issues: religion, the social and economic order, and nationalism vs. particularism. If one also takes into account the tendency (observable in countries with two parties) for the duality of opinion on the social and economic order to break down, pass through a phase of tripartism, and re-form on new lines as new radical parties on the left emerge, a fairly consistent, comprehensive explanation of numerous parties in Germany is afforded. Thus, in the earliest stages of the Empire, there were conservatives who were primarily nationalists, and other conservatives who were primarily Prussians, Bavarians, Hanoverians, or Schleswig-Holsteinians. There were liberals who were primarily Protestants and nationalists, and other Protestants and nationalists who were primarily liberals. There were conservatives and liberals alike, members of all classes and callings, for whom defense of the interests of the Catholic church was paramount.

Later, with the development of a Socialist and, still later, a Communist party, and with the replacement of the monarchy by a republic, there was a shift in the alignment of opinion on social, economic, and political issues reflecting these changes, but without a corresponding reduction in the number of parties. There was, instead, an increase. Here proportional representation appears to have had a decisive effect in stereotyping the old and encouraging new party divisions. Over religion and the national question (now transformed into centralism vs. federalism), cleavages continued and kept in being a specifically Catholic party as well as Bavarian, Hanoverian, and Schleswig-Holsteinian parties.

Today, for the first time in German parliamentary history,* a party, the Christian Democratic Union, has succeeded in free elections in attracting mass support cutting across all major dualisms of German opinion. Significantly, the CDU has set about doing this by substituting for one of the prime dualisms, the conflict over religion, a new dualism, of which, at one pole, the party offers itself as a rallying point for *all* religious, anticollectivist Western-oriented opinion. But the phenomenon of "non-coincidence" still persists. There remain the farmers and artisans of Bavaria—Catholic, individ-

* Excluding from consideration the National Socialists with their tactics of electoral intimidation.

ualistic, opponents of government control and interference—whose foremost desire is for an "independent viable Bavarian state" which, they feel, would best understand and know how to look after their interests: hence a *Bavarian* party, as well as a *Christian Social* party hardly daring to be less Bavarian in orientation. There remain the Catholic working people of North Rhine-Westphalia whose first concern, with all their socialist inclinations, support of a strong centralized welfare state, and dislike of CDU conservatism, is for the defense of the Church's position on school and family matters: hence a *Center* party. There remain the Protestant industrialists, business and professional men of the old liberal convictions who, as much as they may approve of Dr. Erhard's free-enterprise economy, resolutely defend the powers of the national government against concessions to Bavarian or other varieties of particularism, and dislike and resist the influence of the Church in politics: hence a *Free Democratic* party. There remain the conservative Protestant business and professional men and farmers in Lower Saxony who, with the accomplishment of their first aim in 1946, the re-creation of a Hanoverian state, have gone on to match the Bavarians in their zeal for federalist decentralization: hence a *German* party.*

It appears that, while second ballots and proportional representation maintain and encourage many parties, the root cause of them lies in historical, social, and economic factors determining the outlook of a people. While neither side in the Parliamentary Council saw, or at least admitted, the full complexity of the matter in its reading of the past, the majority had the sounder position.

The decision to retain proportional representation must also be examined in the light of contemporary conditions. Was German opinion in 1949 in a state such that a simple-majority electoral system could have brought it to a rapid crystallization in two major parties, each capable of winning a majority and governing by itself? Three points may be considered:

---

* Also represented in the second Bundestag: the special interest party of refugees and expellees, the *All-German Bloc,* which, since the time of writing, has disintegrated. Others not represented in the second Bundestag: the *Communists;* such parties of the radical right as the *German Right* and *German Conservative* parties (now combined in the *German Reich* party) and the *Socialist Reich* party (banned); the *South Schleswig Voters' Union;* ephemeral parties, such as the *Economic Reconstruction* party.

What would have been the probable effect of a simple-majority law on the smaller parties?

What is the likelihood that the CDU/CSU will be able to maintain its hold on the vote of its heterogeneous following?

What success has the Social Democratic Party had in turning itself from a sectional class party into a broad national party?

As to the first, the returns for the Bundestag elections of 1949 and 1953 indicate that had a simple-majority electoral law been adopted in 1949 neither the Free Democrats nor the German party would have lost their representation in the Bundestag.* In certain constituencies in Hesse, Baden-Württemberg, and Hamburg, the Free Democrats, and in Lower Saxony, the German party, have shown the consistent strength in every election since 1948 which suggests a firm core of voters. In fact, of the 242 seats in the Bundestag filled by election by simple majority in single-member constituencies, the Free Democrats won 12 in 1949 and 14 in 1953, and the German party 5 in 1949 and 10 in 1953. The Bavarian party also won in eleven constituencies in 1949, but lost every seat in 1953.

Under a straight simple-majority system there would have been a much stronger inducement for the non-Socialist parties to combine to put forward the candidate of the strongest party in any constituency where a split between them might have been likely to let in a minority Socialist candidate. Whether (and on what terms) the CDU/CSU would have been prepared, in general, to enter such agreements would, of course, have depended on the strength of their expectations. In 1949, close as the leading parties were on the showing of the Land elections, the CDU/CSU would certainly have had a strong incentive to do so. On the 1949 vote in the constituencies, had such agreements existed, the Free Democrats would have acquired a further 15 seats, the German party a further 13, and the Bavarian party a further 4. Even assuming the improbable, that all Communist votes had gone to the Socialist candidate, the three parties between them would have acquired an additional 23 seats. Altogether, it seems unlikely that the three minor parties between them would have returned fewer than 25 per cent of the deputies

* Admittedly, the *psychological* effect on the German voter of a change to a simple-majority law cannot be estimated. It might have lost the smaller parties all their supporters; it might just as easily have gained them supporters.

under a majority law in 1949. As it seems equally unlikely that the Social Democrats' share would have fallen below 30 per cent (their actual share of directly elected members in 1949 was 40 per cent), it can be asserted with some confidence that in 1949 the CDU/CSU, even with a simple-majority electoral law, would have been obliged to find coalition partners to form a working majority.

In 1953, on the other hand, with the enormous advantage which they would have acquired from a majority system (the CDU in fact won 130 direct seats to the Social Democrats' 45), it is just possible that the Christian Democrats might have secured a majority in the Bundestag independently of the Bavarians. The interesting thing, however, is that, although their popular vote fell sharply, the Free Democrats and the German party increased their share of constituency seats. The reason for this was that in all of the constituencies in Hamburg and in about half in Lower Saxony, the CDU, FDP, and DP had stand-down agreements. Is it likely that the Christian Democrats would be so helpful to their coalition partners on other occasions? This raises two points which have so far been neglected: the relationship between the Christian Democratic and the Christian Social Union and between the parties in the Länder.

If, under a simple-majority system, the Free Democrats and the German Party were to disappear as national parties, the Christian Democrats would be entirely dependent on Bavarian support whenever they did not possess a majority in their own right. Although the Christian Democratic and Christian Social deputies combine in one parliamentary group in the Bundestag, the relationship between the two parties has been and remains much more that of an alliance than a union. The CSU has insisted upon retaining its own identity as a separate party and has resisted efforts by the present CDU leadership to impose a tighter, more centrally controlled organization. The CSU deputies have never hesitated to take an independent line on major issues of policy,* and, indeed, where Bavarian interests are concerned, it is clear that they could not do otherwise without putting the Bavarian party back into the running as the national party representing those interests. Hence, the

---

* It will be recalled that they voted against the Basic Law and, recently, took a leading part in the Bundestag's drastic revision of the coalition government's first defense law.

Christian Democrats might feel that they would be in a tactically stronger position vis-à-vis their Bavarian colleagues, whether of one party or the other, if they encouraged the parliamentary survival of the centralist-minded Free Democrats.

Unless (improbably) all of the Länder adopted such a law, multipartism would not come to an end in the Länder with the adoption of a federal simple-majority electoral law. A party aspiring to form a government at federal level necessarily has much at stake in the party composition of Land governments, owing to the range of matters in which the Bundesrat has a decisive vote.[24] Here again, incentives might develop to induce the Christian Democrats to reach agreements in Bundestag constituencies favorable to the other non-Socialist parties.

We may conclude that it is at least doubtful that a simple-majority electoral law would have eliminated representatives of the Free Democrats and the German party from the Bundestag. It is of course certain that one or other (or possibly both) of the Bavarian parties would have survived.

The subsequent success of the CDU/CSU is itself the most impressive evidence for the contention that German public opinion was ready in 1949 to move to a two-party system. This is the first party group in German history to win a parliamentary majority of its own, and that under an electoral system predominantly one of proportional representation. It is pertinent, however, to consider the factors that made for that success and whether they are likely to endure.

In establishing itself rapidly throughout the Western Länder as a national party in 1945–46, the CDU/CSU had the advantage over other parties that it could rely upon the unofficial organizational support of the Catholic church, one of the few institutions to survive the war with an intact national organization. Since then, however, the party has made little progress in strengthening and extending the base of its party organization, which it must do if it is to sustain its appeal as a broad national party. The party organization remains small (about 300,000 members), predominantly Catholic (even in areas where there is denominational parity), and loosely knit. Protestants, relative to their numbers, are much less active than Catholics in the management of party affairs. In the Catholic constituencies, the organization is chiefly in the hands of officials loyal to the old left Zentrum tradition and least in sympathy with the CDU's present conservative orientation.

But success breeds success. The party has been able to attract the votes of an increasing number of north German Protestants, even if they have not been drawn into the party organization. Business and industrial leaders, who would perhaps originally have preferred a party more solidly committed to conservative economic policies, have been dazzled by Dr. Erhard's "miracle" and impressed and gratified by the energetic activity of his ministry on behalf of their interests—against even such Allied-sponsored policies as the iron, steel, and coal deconcentration programs and the restriction of trade between East and West. The party finances, which on the basis of paid-up membership would otherwise be rather meager, have benefited from support in this quarter.

In Dr. Adenauer, the CDU/CSU has had the supreme advantage of being led by a man with the strength of personality and political acumen adequate to impose his leadership on the diverse elements composing the party and its coalition partners and, most important, to represent Western Germany skilfully and forcefully in its relations with the Western powers in the occupation period. Perhaps Dr. Adenauer's single greatest service to his party was, while representing German interests with such effect, to win the unqualified confidence of the Western governments, particularly that of the United States, upon which support for German recovery so largely depended. His replacement will certainly raise difficulties for the party. All of the possible candidates with the stature for national leadership presently in view are identified with one or another of the particular interests or segments of opinion in the party: Herr Karl Arnold, the former minister-president of North Rhine-Westphalia and Herr Jakob Kaiser, the minister for All-German Affairs, with the left and trade unionism; Dr. Ludwig Erhard, the minister of economics, with laissez faire and the business community; Dr. Fritz Schäffer, the vice-chancellor and former minister of finance, with Bavarian particularism; Dr. Josef Wuermeling, the former minister for family affairs, with Catholic orthodoxy. The CDU/CSU's future development as an interdenominational party would perhaps better be served by the choice of a Protestant successor, but with the death of Dr. Hermann Ehlers, the able and popular president of the first Bundestag, no Protestant candidate remains. In certain circumstances, particularly if reunification should become a real prospect, it might be in the party's interest to be led by a man with sympathies more to the left than Dr. Adenauer's. But in that case some right-wing support would certainly be lost.

The CDU/CSU, as the party with the responsibility of government, has drawn a dividend from the general disposition of the German people in the postwar years to work together and stand together to restore the German economy and Germany's status among the nations. Sectional interests, particularly trade-union demands on wage rates, hours of work, and the extension of *Mitbestimmungsrecht*, have never been pressed to the point where labor-management tension might have become a serious embarrassment for a party catering both for the support of industrial management and trade unionists. But the party's very success in restoring the economy, bringing the occupation to an end, and recovering Western German sovereignty—hence relieving some of the postwar pressures which have tended to unify German opinion behind it—may lead to difficulty in the future. There are already signs that the trade unions will press more vigorously for a larger share for the German workman in the fruits of the economic "miracle" to which his industry and patience made such a contribution.* In foreign affairs, a general relaxation of tension between East and West would also remove another pressure which, so far, has produced cohesiveness in the party following. The incompatibility between certain specifically German interests—reunification, the recovery of the Eastern territories, and trade with Eastern Europe—and an exclusively Western-oriented policy would become more than a latent source of strain within the government coalition and parties.

It is a truism that coalitions tend to fly apart when the exigencies that produced them disappear. The CDU/CSU, like many other great national parties in democratic countries, is a "coalition" of diverse interests and groups. Its survival, as the exigencies of the post-

* Average hourly wage (1952–53) of the German workman, $0.38; British workman, $0.49; American workman, $1.78. Working days lost in strikes (1952–53 average) : Germany, 750,000; U.K., 2 million; U.S., 59 million.

war and (*if they do*) the cold war periods recede, may depend on whether the common denominator which it offers in the Christian ethos will, of itself, prove sufficiently attractive to hold this heterogeneous following. But for the present, it is clear that the CDU/ CSU's great and probably continuing source of strength lies in the fact that its policies and its leadership match a predominantly moderate, conservative mood in the German electorate and that it has gone a long way to establish itself as the party best suited to represent that outlook in national politics and in government.

This prevailing conservatism implies what an examination of the postwar fortunes of the Social Democratic party plainly shows: that whether or not the German electorate was ready in 1948–49 for a two-party system, it was certainly a very long way from being ready to make the Social Democrats a governing party and one of the two. The Social Democrats have made definite if somewhat halting efforts to recast the image of their party in the public mind as a broad, national, rather than a class, sectarian, party. They take their stand as firmly as ever that the basic issues before the German people are social and economic. But both doctrine and approach to the electorate since the Erfurt (1891) and Heidelberg (1925) programs have been modified to afford a basis upon which all reformist opinion can unite and to draw middle-class support.*

Their new "action program," after a perfunctory opening bow to Lassalle, Marx, Engels, and Bebel, reads very like a British Labour party manifesto: transfer to public ownership only of basic industries "ripe" for it; retention, with regulation, of the market economy; emphasis on economic planning and the rational use of resources; participation of the workers in industrial management; support of the small businessman and the farmer; basic reform of the tax structure; reorganization and extension of the social services;

---

* "The Social Democratic Party of Germany does not represent the special interests of individual groups. . . . The Social Democratic Party has grown from being the party of the working class which it originally was to be a party of the people. The industrial workers constitute the core of its members and voters. But the struggle and the endeavor of the Social Democratic Party are devoted to the interests of all who seek to further social justice, political and economic democracy, spiritual freedom and tolerance, national unity and international cooperation, undeterred by any narrow-minded concern for vested interests. . . ." (*Action Program of the Social Democratic Party*, adopted September 28, 1952, and revised July 24, 1954).

more and better housing for the low-income groups; promotion of *Gleichberechtigung* for women in the home and in trades and professions; consolidation of schools in a uniform system, extension of free schools and improvement of the conditions of teachers; judicial and penal reform. The moderate tone of Erich Ollenhauer's leadership and the rise to influence in the party of such eclectic personalities as Carlo Schmid, Georg-August Zinn, Max Brauer, Wilhelm Kaisen, Walter Menzel, and, before his death, Ernst Reuter, reflect the change. So also do the varied backgrounds of the party's parliamentary representatives, of which only about 25 per cent are trade-union officials and workmen, and the remainder civil servants (13 per cent *Beamten;* 7 per cent *Angestellte*); businessmen and farmers (14 per cent); editors and journalists, members of professions of law, medicine, engineering, and the church (10 per cent); university and school teachers (8 per cent); party officials (7 per cent); and housewives, nurses, social welfare workers, authors, and others (15 per cent).

But the party, so far, has had only moderate success in attracting a broad following in the electorate beyond its traditional trade-union and working-class support. The continued concentration of its strength in urban and industrial areas shows this. In 1949, 60 per cent, and in 1953, 82 per cent of the constituencies in which the SPD had majorities were in the thirty largest cities of Western Germany and in such lesser cities and industrial districts as Herford, Minden, Detmold, Herne-Castrop-Rauxel, Ennepe-Ruhr-Witten, Wetzlar, Hanau, Offenbach, and Darmstadt. In elections since 1947, except in 1953, the Social Democrats, although falling behind the Christian Democrats in the Land as a whole, have consistently led in the major city districts (Stadtkreise) of North Rhine-Westphalia. In 1953 the SPD share of the vote was higher in the urban areas than in the Land as a whole. Similar concentration of SPD vote in cities is observable in the election figures for Bavaria and other Länder.

But even in many of these city constituencies the Social Democrats are still a minority party. In their best year (1949), in the fifty-seven constituencies of the thirty largest cities, the Social Democrats won thirty-nine seats. But had the votes for the CDU/CSU, FDP, DP, and BP been combined against them, they would have lost twenty-one of these. Even with the Communist votes, they would have lost eight. This weakness was underscored in 1953, when the non-Socialist parties did in fact reach stand-down agreements in many of these constituencies and the Social Democrats won only twenty-one of the fifty-seven seats in the thirty largest cities. The CDU made further inroads on the Socialists' strength with the urban electorate in 1957.

This review of developments since 1949 does not show in any conclusive way that German public opinion was ready for a two-party system *at that time*. It is doubtful that a simple-majority system would have eliminated all the smaller parties. The Christian Democratic/Christian Social Union achieved spectacular successes in 1953 and 1957, but it faces serious problems in its leadership, organization, and domestic and foreign policy which must be solved if party unity and the hold upon its following in the electorate are to be maintained in the future. The Social Democrats, on the other hand, have not to date succeeded in establishing themselves as a broad national party attracting mass support across class and denominational lines.

The most certain result of adopting a simple-majority, single-member electoral system in 1949, it is clear, would not have been the elimination of multipartism but the production of overwhelming majorities for the non-Socialist parties in the 1949, 1953, and 1957 elections. In 1953, the Social Democrats might have held as few as 15 per cent of the seats in the Bundestag, although their share of the total vote was 29 per cent. Normal as such a result might be to a simple-majority system, it is questionable whether such underrepresentation in the Bundestag of the sector of the community supporting the Social Democrats would have been a healthy condition in which to resume parliamentary life in postwar Germany. On the whole, we may conclude that the decision to retain a large element of proportional representation in the electoral system was a sound one.

CHAPTER V

BASIC RIGHTS

> By laying it down that every man possesses inherent natural rights, a principle is expressed that remains open to free interpretation.
>
> It is frivolous, it is arrogant, it is—I do not know what—to suppose that in the present obscure situation one can say: thus will the economic and social order of the future take form.
>
> THEODOR HEUSS

1. DIFFERING NATIONAL TRADITIONS

It may clarify matters to state at the outset of this chapter what it seems to the writer can intelligibly be said in a general way about "basic rights."

In the course of the last two centuries, it came to be widely thought in Great Britain, France, the United States, Germany, and elsewhere (a) that in a certain sphere of action (religious belief, expression of opinion, assembly, association, etc.) the individual citizen or subject should be largely, if not altogether, free to act without interference by those exercising the authority of government; (b) that those exercising such authority should intervene in this sphere, if at all, only on the basis of law and subject to procedural and other safeguards against arbitrary exercise of authority, usually including a judicial proceeding of some kind.

Many people, where such a sphere of freedom for the individual exists, have thought that the "rights" or "freedoms" of this sphere are in some sense of special importance, and have shown this by giving them special names (*"Grundrechte,"* *"droits des citoyens,"* "civil liberties," "rights of the subject," etc.) and by devising various metaphysical and other theories to explain them (e.g., that such rights are "natural" or "God-given" rights; that they originate in a "social contract"; that they arise from the "transcendental nature of

159

man"; that they are conferred by or arise in some way from "the State," and so on).

More recently, some people have come to hold the opinion that various other "rights" are of the same or like importance, such as a right to have work and to be paid a "living wage" for it, or to have financial security in old age and against the risks of sickness, accidents, etc., or to have educational opportunities, and so on. It seems desirable to distinguish between this sphere of rights and the first sphere for one practical reason if no other. In the first, all that is needed, for the most part, for the individual citizen to be "free" is that someone in authority should *refrain* from doing something. In the second sphere it is necessary, so that the individual citizen can be "free" or have a "right" to do something, that some other body —an agency of government, an employer, a trade union, or the like— should *also* do something. In this study, the rights of the first sphere will be referred to as the "classic basic rights" and those of the second as "economic and social rights."

To recognize in this way the contingent or historical character of "basic rights" is not to disparage their importance or the importance of sound legal systems and judicial procedures. One can offer perfectly good practical arguments why people should be free to do certain things, without resorting to metaphysical ones. And it is obviously better that decisions on these important matters should be taken with care (i.e., under laws adopted in some generally accepted manner and by well-established and tested procedures with due regard paid to past experience [precedent]), than by arbitrary whim.

To discover the comparative area of freedom—the "rights" that Britons, Americans, Frenchmen, and Germans have in fact enjoyed —requires an extensive comparative study of the laws and institutions of each country and how they have worked in peace and war and in various economic and political conditions. In this chapter, little more has been done than to summarize what is already generally known and to single out developments on one or two points for special study. However, the following can be tentatively stated:

(1) Abstract statements of rights and theories tending to establish the absolute or extra-historical character of such rights appear to have had little effect on the actual sphere of freedom enjoyed anywhere. For instance, some constitutions have abstract statements

of rights to which a great deal of attention has been paid and on the basis of which a considerable body of law has been erected. Other constitutions have such statements, but little or no attention has been paid to them. Still other constitutions have no such statement at all. But this has made little practical difference to the sphere of freedom in the countries concerned. In each case where a citizen's freedom of action had to be restricted in some way, somebody had to decide under what conditions, to what extent, and for how long it was to be restricted. If the legislator did not spell out how abstract principles were to be applied in individual cases, someone else—a judge or an administrator—had to do it so that decisions in individual cases could be made. It is these particular decisions in sum that measure the sphere of freedom and tell us what "rights" are. It can be argued, of course, that the statement of certain abstract principles in a dignified and highly respected document, and the *belief* that these principles have originated in a certain way or have a peculiar status of their own, have had, in the long run, a guiding influence on the acts of legislators, judges, and administrators. A possible example of this in the exercise of police powers in different places is discussed later in this chapter. However, it appears that judges, as well as legislators and administrators, have more often been influenced by contemporary historical conditions than by belief in abstract ideas. The sphere of freedom obviously expands and contracts. In wartime and on other occasions when people are badly frightened, the sphere shrinks. Some persons and groups, notably adult women, trade unionists, and certain racial minorities, attained "rights" only after long political agitation and after great changes had taken place in the social and economic environment of the countries concerned.

(2) Making allowance for some differences in the time of developments and for the different importance attached to being free to do different things, one can say that Britons, Frenchmen, Americans, and Germans appear on the whole to have enjoyed comparable freedom during the greater part of the last century and this. Periods of war and unconstitutional or arbitrary government are obvious exceptions.

(3) The various statements of "basic rights" drawn up and incorporated in German constitutions up to World War II had comparatively little effect in determining the German's sphere of free-

dom. This was determined by ordinary legislation and other law and by courts, particularly administrative courts.

(4) There seem to be no grounds for thinking that this arrangement in Germany was any less effective in securing the citizen's freedom than arrangements elsewhere, or that, with perhaps one exception, there were extraordinary weaknesses in this arrangement that somehow prepared the way for the Nazi tyranny.

At the time of this study, it is obviously too early to say whether the Bonn "basic rights" will work any greater change in the German legal system than the Weimar or earlier statements of basic rights did. Hence, this chapter is less a study of the new constitutional law of basic rights in Germany than it is a study of the *opinions* of a group of representative Germans about these rights. This, however, is of considerable historical interest. In the long run, what the German people *think* about their rights and what they should be free to do is likely to count for more than the constitution and all the courts in the land.

The United States, Great Britain, France   Where they have attempted to answer them, the Americans, the British, the French, and the Germans have traditionally offered somewhat different answers to the theoretical questions: what is the origin and status of "basic rights"* and what relation between the citizen and the government (or the "State") do such rights imply? There are also some important differences in the way the law of basic rights is made and enforced in each country.

Although the Constitution of the United States nowhere speaks of

---

* In this chapter, no attempt has been made to distinguish between the use of the term "rights" when it refers to legal rights currently recognized by and enforced by an authority and when it refers to rights (which may or may not be enforced) for which someone claims a special status in virtue of divine sanction or their origin in a "state of nature," a "social contract," etc. It is to be hoped that it will be clear from the context which use of the term is being made. Further, since the author does not think that any precise meaning can be attached to such terms as "natural rights," the "State," the "social contract," etc., he would have preferred to set them off by quotation marks throughout the text, but has refrained from doing so to avoid over-complicating the punctuation. Finally, there are certain differences between "civil rights or liberties" (American), "rights of the subject" (British), "*droits des citoyens*" (French), and "*Grundrechte*" (German), corresponding to the respective traditions of these countries. As shifting from one term to another would be confusing, the author proposes, since this is a German study, to use "basic rights" throughout.

the "self-evident truth" of "inalienable rights" with which all men are "endowed by their Creator," as does the Declaration of Independence, a sphere of rights belonging inherently to the people is implied in the Ninth Amendment: "The enumeration in the Constitution of certain rights shall not be construed to deny or disparage others retained by the people."

The authors of the Constitution clearly thought that basic rights were natural rights, held by the citizen as against and limiting the exercise of the authority of government. That they should be recognized and respected as such was one of the terms of the compact under which the people had agreed to subordinate themselves to a common government. A resolution, sponsored by James Madison and others in the first Congress of the United States, in which the first ten, or "civil rights," amendments were adopted, expresses this view:

All power is originally vested in and consequently derives from the people. . . . Government is instituted and ought to be exercised for the benefit of the people; which consists in the enjoyment of life and liberty, with the right of acquiring and using property and generally of pursuing and obtaining happiness and safety. There are certain natural rights of which men, when they form a social compact, cannot deprive or divest their posterity, among which are the enjoyment of life and liberty.[1]

The basic rights set out in the first ten and certain other amendments to the Constitution form a part of the supreme law of the land. However, it is the federal judiciary that decides what these provisions mean and whether and how to apply them in particular circumstances. Although through the years the courts have sometimes explicitly claimed to share the view of "natural rights" held by the founders, a host of other considerations, including shifting views as to the proper role of the federal judiciary in a federal system and needs arising from economic and political developments on the American continent have evidently exercised a very great influence on the courts. For instance, until comparatively recently, the American citizen could not expect uniform protection of freedom of conscience, speech, press, or assembly throughout the Union. In the First Amendment to the Constitution, only *Congress* (the federal legislature) is forbidden to make law abridging these rights. Until 1925, the Supreme Court steadily refused to extend its protection to these rights against encroachment by the several *state* governments, although, as it has been phrased, "the enduring vitality of natural law concepts for the Court encouraged repeated appeals for judicial protection."[2]

In twenty-one cases between 1827 and 1907, the Court was required to rule upon this point, and reaffirmed Chief Justice Marshall's negative decision of 1833.[3] In 1897,[4] however, the Court extended its protection to the right of private property on the basis of the Fourteenth Amendment, which forbids a *state* to deprive a person of "life, liberty or property, without due process of law." Twenty-eight years later, the Court decided[5] that the freedoms enumerated in the First Amendment might also be regarded as "liberty" in the sense of the Fourteenth Amendment and were therefore entitled to the protection of the Constitution and the Court.[6] The interval between these two decisions can perhaps be taken as a fair measure of the extent to which the judiciary has in fact been influenced by the doctrine of natural rights.

Since it is in the domain of the states, not of the federal government, where authority bears most directly on the citizen, he has had to depend in the main for guaranty of his rights on the constitutions, legislatures, and courts of the several states. This protection, to say the least, has been far from equal. The state legislatures and local government bodies and their police forces have been the principal sources of law and ordinances and other measures infringing civil liberties. Discriminatory treatment by the states of racial minorities, labor organizations, eccentric religious sects, radical political groups, immigrants, and farmers and workmen "down and out" in economic depression are well known. The majority of American citizens, to be sure, have enjoyed a considerable degree of liberty from the beginning. But in a nation where the people are sovereign and the majority rules, it is to the condition of the minority to which one must turn to assess the state of individual liberty. The federal judiciary has intervened increasingly in the field of state legislation and law enforcement since 1925, and the protections afforded minorities have increased.

The British people behave as though their rights and freedoms have a special immunity. This special status is not conferred by "natural law" or any other abstract conception of rights, but rather by historic recognition and observance.

In the positive sense of the term, therefore, the British subject does not have basic *rights*, but he has freedom, and the limits of this freedom are set by law. What the law does not forbid, he may do. For his rights, in this sense, three features of the British constitutional system are of particular importance for the subject:

Restrictions on individual freedom, with but few exceptions, are imposed only by law, for the most part by the criminal law. It is for the courts, not the government or the police, to decide whether under the law an act is a crime.

The police act under and are bound by specific laws and if they exceed their authority they may be subject to suit. Enabling acts may confer broad powers on the police in war-time, but there is no general police power. They exercise discretion only in the sense that they have the decision whether to prosecute under the law.

Parliament by altering the law can expand or restrict the area of individual freedom at will.[7]

The security of British liberties depends, therefore, in the last resort upon the prevailing temper of Parliament and of the people. At times, notably during and after the Napoleonic wars, restrictive laws and heavy penalties reduced the area of freedom. Trade unions were for long subjected to repressive measures under statutory and common law. But on the whole, in the past century, the subject's rights have been extended and confirmed.

In France, where law is positive and systematic, basic rights, although embodied in successive "declarations" of more or less constitutional character, have never been binding as directly applicable law. They require implementation in the code of positive law. The French citizen must therefore look to the legislature and to the courts, particularly the administrative courts, for protection of his rights. In this respect, his position is more analogous to that of the German citizen before 1933 than to that of the American citizen. However, even when in the last century the more positivist "rights of citizens" had displaced the "rights of man" of 1789, one finds in the French Constitution of 1848 (where basic rights are described as "*droits des citoyens garantis par la Constitution*") that "*Elle* [*la République*] *reconnait des droits et des devoirs antérieurs et supérieurs aux lois positives.*" The French continue to regard the basic rights as norms superior to the general body of law and as having a controlling effect upon the exercise of state authority.

Germany—   The predominant German view has been that the
1848–1918   individual does not and cannot hold rights against
                     the "State," for the State itself through an act of
self-limitation is the source of these rights. The citizen's sphere of
rights and freedoms is guaranteed to him within the framework of
the State, to which he owes duties of an equally binding character.

The National Assembly, meeting in Frankfurt in May, 1848, to
consolidate the revolutionary movements of that year and unite the
German people under a national constitution, drew up the first national code of basic rights. There was no unanimity of opinion in the
Assembly about the nature of these rights. A 'natural rights" school
believed that they were *"unveräusserliche und heilige Menschenrechte,"* with an existence "independent of the State and taken with
him by each individual into the community upon the founding of
the State compact."[8] The "statists," basing themselves on the new
positivist teaching, although conceding that the basic rights were of
the "highest importance," saw their source only in the State and insisted that they could possess no status higher than *"staatliches
Recht."* This opinion was heavily in the majority, and was held by
liberals and radicals as well as conservatives, for the difference of
view did not correspond to the normal factional divisions in the
Assembly.

The issue of the Circular of the National Assembly of December
2, 1848, expressed the majority view. Comparing the Declaration of
the Rights of Man of the first French Republic with the new German Basic Rights, it said:

> The general rights of man are an abstraction from a supposed state
> of nature and are believed to belong to man prior to and outside any
> form of state association. The consequence of this is that these rights of
> man are not really properly matters for legislation by the State, but
> rather a *noli me tangere* with which legislation by the State cannot deal.
> The German basic rights are less abstract. They do not arise from a
> primitive condition existing prior to or beyond the State, and in this
> respect we are certainly more constructive than the disciples of Rousseau.
> Rights are to be those which the individual has within the State, which
> he possesses in virtue of his citizenship.[9]

Accordingly, the basic rights were characterized in the Frankfurt
constitution as *"Die Grundrechte des deutschen Volkes,"* and in

Article 130 one reads that "the following basic rights shall be guaranteed to the German people."

The intellectual presuppositions of the men of the *Paulskirche* were not those of the rationalists Locke and Jefferson, but those of the German idealists and historians. To unite the German people and bring into being the "State" of German philosophical and historical imagination was their highest hope. Indeed, a national code of basic rights was valued as a means to weld the German people into a national community as much as for itself. In such a State, the basic rights were conceived not as negatively guaranteeing the freedom of the citizen against the power of the State, but as creating the positive conditions for the participation of the citizen in the political life of the State. In the words of Rudolf Smend:

. . . dieses ganze Recht des staatsbürgerlichen Standes ist aber keine vorbehaltene private Sphäre, sondern grundrechtliche Stellung im Staat, es ist, wie Metternich es augsedrückt hat, die "Politische Existenz des Individuums,"

and again,

Über all erscheint diese Sphäre der auscheinend privaten Grundrechte nicht als trennender Vorbehalt gegenüber dem Staat, sondern als verbindende Beziehung zu ihm, als Grundlage politischer Eignung.[10]   .

Although seven of the seventeen state constitutions adopted between 1850 and 1880 included statements of basic rights, incorporating provisions from the Frankfurt and other continental constitutions,[11] these state constitutions in practice did little to advance the German citizen's rights. The basic rights were not binding upon the Landtage of the states, since no practice of judicial review existed. The constitutions themselves could be amended by simple enactment. Nor did Bismarck in 1867 and 1871 take the opportunity to bring uniformity into this field by incorporating a code of rights in the North German and Reich constitutions. He was preoccupied with the strategy of political unification and considered that basic rights could be left to the Länder.

Meanwhile, developments in other directions were under way which were to be of greater significance for German rights. In the preceding century of absolute monarchical rule, individual action and indeed nearly every aspect of life in the German states had been subordinated to royal will. Only the members of the most powerful and strongly intrenched of the "estates," some of the nobility and clergy, were able to maintain a degree of independence. Lawmaking and administrative functions were concentrated in the hands of the monarch and his servants. To meet the organizational requirements of a military state, Frederick William I and Frederick the Great in Prussia had transformed the bureaucracy into an instrument of personal government, from which they excluded any control by the courts. In the famous case of the miller Arnold, who, he considered, had been unjustly deprived of rights in a water mill, Frederick the Great in 1779 condemned and imprisoned members of the *Kammergericht* who persisted, against his will, in finding against the miller.[12]

One of Frederick's successor's first acts was to exonerate in full and indemnify the condemned judges. He thereby acknowledged the widespread resentment against royal interference with the courts. No Prussian king ever attempted it again.[13] This recovery of independence by the courts, coupled with the entry into force in 1794 of the Prussian Code of General State Law (*Allgemeines Landrecht*), constitute the beginnings of a development which, culminating eighty years later in the creation of the first administrative courts, established the rule of law—the "*Rechtsstaat*"—in Germany.

In 1848, however, government by decree and arbitrary administration were still the order of the day in many of the German states.[14] The reforms undertaken in the next half-century were specifically directed to this state of affairs, as the definitions of the *Rechtsstaat* offered by the German public law specialists of the time show:

. . . an administration of government conducted in conformity with constitutional principles under the surveillance of the judiciary.

LORENZ VON STEIN (1879)

. . . [a State] in which the powers of the administration are strictly defined by law and can be exercised only in accordance with the law.

GEORG MEYER (1878)

. . . a State which stands under the aegis of the law, the highest authority of which is not the King but the law; a community in which not only the relations between individuals but, above all, their relations to State authority are determined by the principles of law; where both the governing and the governed are ruled by law and not by the "*tel est notre plaisir*" of reigning personages.

GERHARD ANSCHÜTZ (1904)

The establishment of uniform codes of Reich law and of administrative courts to review administrative actions* for conformity to law, the rehabilitation of the judiciary, and the reform of administrative procedures by new men in the civil service with a liberal outlook combined to regularize the impact of authority on the individual. The liberties enjoyed—at any rate by the German bourgeois class—under the *Rechtsstaat* were comparable with those claimed and won elsewhere. As elsewhere, emerging working-class organizations were subjected to repressive measures, enforced at times with exceptional severity by the police.

From the standpoint of accessibility and lowness of cost, it seems probable that the safeguards for rights were more readily available in Germany than they were elsewhere, although, in making international comparisons, it has to be kept in mind that in the last quarter of the last century the pace and scale of government intervention in the economic and social sphere was greater in Germany than, for instance, in Great Britain or the United States. Administrative courts and a body of administrative law developed rapidly in Germany as a counterpart to the exercise of powers by government as yet unknown in Great Britain and the United States.

A perhaps critical difference between other states governed under the rule of law and the *Rechtsstaat* lay in the position and powers of the police. In Prussia and the other German states, through a practice surviving from the absolutist era[15] which became a fundamental principle of German administrative law, the police were either granted by law or were presumed on the basis of *Gewohnheitsrecht* to possess a general power (*Allgemeine polizeiliche Ermächtigung*) to maintain public order and security. The famous

* Such bodies were gradually established in the various German states from 1863, beginning with Baden in 1863 and Prussia in 1875. In Prussia there were "courts" at three levels, *Kreis* and *Stadt Ausschüsse, Bezirksausschüsse,* and the *Oberverwaltunsgericht.* In practice, the lower "courts" or commissions were composed entirely of civil servants active in the administration. Only the members of the higher court were professional jurists appointed for life. Parallel arrangements, different in some respects, existed in the other states. The jurisdiction of these courts also varied from state to state. In some (e.g., Württemberg), complaints brought by anyone who considered that a particular administrative action had not been taken in accordance with the law could be heard. In others (e.g., Prussia), the courts were restricted to cases arising under specified types of law, except that any complaint against the exercise of police power could be heard. In most states, however, jurisdiction was confined to enumerated fields of law.

Section 10 II 17 of the Prussian *Allgemeines Landrecht* read: "It is the function of the police to take the necessary measures for the maintenance of public peace, security, and order, and to prevent an imminent danger to these befalling the public or its individual members." This did not mean that the police were free to act as they pleased. By a development of judge-made law, analogous to English common law, the Prussian *Oberverwaltungsgericht* defined and limited the methods to be used by the police in discharging their functions.[16] Further, by legislative or constitutional enactment at Land and Reich level, a field of life or activity could be excluded entirely from the police acting on the basis of their general police power.[17] This was in fact one of the first provisions of the Reich Law on Freedom of Movement, the Reich Trades Ordinance, the Reich Press Law, and the Reich Law on Assembly.

The order of approach here clearly differed from that in Great Britain and the United States. There, the sphere of individual rights and freedom is first assumed or explicitly defined in constitutional law. This sphere of freedom can then be encroached upon by the police acting in terms only of specific laws that make specific acts illegal. In the German case, public peace, order, and security were held as the primary desiderata, and the means of securing them were given priority. The general police power once established, the sphere of individual freedom was then created by legislation and by action of the administrative courts limiting the police power. Whereas the British and American citizen can do what the law does not forbid him to do, the German citizen could do what the law permitted him to do. In the former case, the constitutional presumption favors the citizen's freedom; in the latter, it favored the exercise of authority.

With both approaches, the resulting spheres of individual freedom *could* be the same, and it seems likely that for most of the past hundred years they were. However, it is plausible to argue on the evidence of events in Germany that, in times of constitutional and political crisis when the men who are judges and administrators may be suborned, intimidated, or flouted, the existence of general police powers and a public conditioned to their use could hasten the downfall of constitutional government and the destruction of individual freedom. There is an obvious parallel between the different attitudes toward police power taken in Germany and other countries and the different theories of basic rights common to these countries. In this respect, if no other, theories about rights have perhaps had important consequences for those who held them.

Weimar   The picture of basic rights in the Weimar period is a confused one. Hugo Preuss, who prepared the first draft of the Weimar constitution, did not include a code of basic rights in this draft. He may have feared that the Weimar assembly, like its Frankfurt predecessor, would be diverted by a discussion of rights from what he regarded as more important tasks.[18] As a civil servant, trained in the traditions of the *Rechtsstaat*, he may also have felt that the protection of basic rights could be left to the existing safeguards. Friedrich Ebert and members of the committee of states, however, prevailed upon him to incorporate a list of the "classic" basic rights in his draft.

Friedrich Naumann, the *rapporteur* for basic rights in the constitutional committee, had convictions of a different kind. For him, the "abstract" rights of 1848 were an old story—"museum pieces"—without power to stir the imagination or claim the allegiance of the modern masses. He wanted a statement of rights and duties which would reflect the problems of the day and serve a new social order accommodating both socialism and capitalism. To him it was clear that, in prevailing conditions, there was as little possibility of creating a purely socialistic public law as of retaining without modification the older, individualistic rights.[19]

Whether Naumann's draft of a new set of basic rights, designed for the "popular understanding" and avoiding legal form and content, might have won the understanding and, more important, the loyalty of the German people, it met no sympathy in the constitutional committee. Such worthy but highly unjuristic thoughts as "Order and freedom are akin," or "Every kind of honest work is equally worthy of respect and is of equal dignity," or "Thrift is the prior condition of progress" failed to impress this company of lawyers. Nevertheless, many social and economic "rights" were incorporated in the constitution. The political parties, in competition to advance their own objectives, lengthened the list. The Social Democrats hoped by this means to lay the foundations for a socialist state. But although by far the largest party in the National Assembly, they lacked a majority, and could obtain agreement only to programmatic principles looking to future socialist legislation, but committing the Reichstag to nothing. On the other hand, the bourgeois parties of the center and right compensated themselves for these concessions with constitutional guaranties for the institutions of private property, inheritance, freedom of contract, marriage and the family, and so on.

For the first time, then, a code of basic rights took effect as a part of a national constitution. As to the status of these rights and duties in law, there was, however, no agreement. Were they, as supreme law, binding upon the three branches of government, above all on the legislature? If they were binding, had the courts the power of reviewing legislation for its conformity to the basic rights? Which rights were to be regarded as binding and which not, since many had obviously only a declarative or programmatic character ("It is the duty of every German to accept honorary office" [132]; "The independent middle class in agriculture, industry and commerce shall be benefited by legislation and administration" [164])? Learned professors drew up schemata ranking the basic rights—but by no means always in the same way—according to their supposed relative efficacy at law. Until the end of the Weimar period, public law experts and the courts were disputing the answers to these questions.

In practice, with the exception of property rights, the traditional procedures and safeguards of the *Rechtsstaat* continued to be of greater significance for individual rights than the formal provisions of the Weimar constitution. This may be seen in the interpretation placed on the articles of the constitution dealing with freedom of person, expression, and assembly, inviolability of dwelling, and secrecy of correspondence, where, in each case, it was provided that the right concerned might be limited on the basis of "law," or the "general laws," or the "national law." What did these terms mean in practice? Consider as an example the first, Article 114:

> The freedom of the person is inviolable. Any encroachment upon, or deprivation of, personal freedom by public authority is permissible only on the basis of law.

We find that the term "law" was interpreted to include not only existing and future Reich and Land statutory law (including *Rechts-*

verordnungen), but also the provisions of unwritten or customary law (*Gewohnheitsrecht*) in the Länder.[20] Anschütz, the leading constitutional authority of the Weimar period, says of Article 114:

"Law" in the sense of paragraph 1, sentence 2, includes also and especially those general principles on the competence and duties of the police applicable in the Länder which are based partly on statutory and partly on customary law. In particular, the relevant provision of the Prussian General Land Law (Section 10 II 17) . . . is maintained.

The whole of the pre-Weimar pattern of general police power exercised under restraints of varying degrees of effectiveness was thus retained intact. So interpreted, the constitutional articles themselves were superfluous,[21] for they offered no protections to rights beyond those already existing or which could be established by ordinary law.

Toward the constitutional provisions on property rights, however, quite a different attitude was adopted.

Property is guaranteed by the constitution. Its content and its limitations are defined by the laws. Expropriation can take place only for the general welfare, and upon statutory grounds. It is accompanied by adequate compensation, unless a national law provides otherwise [Article 153].

Basing themselves on a new construction of the word "property" in Article 153, certain public law experts and the *Reichsgericht* joined forces to extend a formidable new protection to the rights of property-owners against measures undertaken by national and local authorities "in the public interest." Hitherto, the ownership rights in property, which might be subject to expropriation in the public interest and were entitled, therefore, under the law, to be compensated, were understood in the civil law sense to be real rights in real property or movable things (*"das dingliche Recht des bürgerlichen Rechts an Grundstücken oder an beweglichen Sache"*).[22] Distinct from expropriation in this sense, there were recognized in administrative law various legal restrictions on property (*"die gesetzliche Eigentumbeschränkung"*) required for reasons of public health, safety, and convenience, e.g., building restrictions, zoning ordinances, sanitation regulations, and the like. Whether these limitations upon the use of property were to be compensated or to be borne by the owner as a social burden was solely for decision by the legislative body.

In 1924 and 1925, the *Reichsgericht*, breaking with precedent, asserted a right of judicial review of legislation. Following views already formulated by theorists in 1924, the court now adopted a definition of "property" subject to compensation under Article 153 of the constitution so broad as to include a wide range of rights restricted by law in the public interest, for which compensation had hitherto been regarded as solely within the discretion of the legislature. Thus armed, the courts proceeded to examine Reich and Land legislation and, where restrictions existed without corresponding provision for compensation, to find the legislation unconstitutional. The financial implications, particularly for the municipalities (*Gemeinden*), were serious.

Theorists devised a further doctrine which would have enormously enlarged the jurisdictional area of the courts had they chosen to make use of it. Article 109 asserted the traditional rule of law that "all Germans are equal before the law." In the past this had been taken in Germany, as elsewhere, to be a directive to the executive to administer the law without favor or discrimination because of the subject's status. Now the view was advanced that this rule was also binding upon the legislature, which, according to the formula propounded, must in its laws "treat equal states of affairs equally" (*"Er . . . gebiete dass die Rechtsordnung gleiche Tatbestände gleich behandle"*). Once the practice of judicial review had been established, a concept of such generality, susceptible to a variety of interpretations, could clearly have served as an instrument of great effectiveness to subordinate the legislature to the judiciary.[23]

The innovation of judicial review was stoutly resisted by a minority of the public law specialists, led by Gerhard Anschütz. Efforts to adjudicate in matters not within its province, in their view, could lead only to a "politicizing" of the judiciary.

The excursions of the Weimar courts into the field of judicial review do have a one-sided appearance. The readiness of the judiciary to extend constitutional protection to property rights, while leaving the citizen's liberties to traditional modes of protection, bears a certain analogy with the discriminatory use made by the Supreme Court of the United States of the "due process" clause. Willibalt Apelt says of the movement for judicial review:

In their distrust of a parliament resting upon the sovereignty of the people, all the circles who were opposed to democracy agitated for and sought means of restricting the legislative power, in order to obstruct the carrying out of far-reaching social changes.[24]

For basic rights, the developments of the Weimar era may be summed up in the phrase: "promise unfulfilled." In the constitutional provisions themselves there was a boldness of design, an opening-up of new vistas looking to the just ordering of the modern community scarcely to be found in other constitutional documents of the time. But the Weimar climate was not favorable for that steady process of development by which a constitution and the life of the people who live under it may become one—each embodying and expressing the other. All were at odds—classes, parties, legislators, jurists, professors. Nothing was settled. New conceptions ordering the life of the individual and the community could not take hold. The old, by force of inertia, continued to prevail.

2. "CLASSIC" RIGHTS UNDER THE BASIC LAW

The Bonn basic rights, although less ambitously conceived than those of Weimar, carry greater conviction as constitutional law. The unresolved issues which cast doubt on the status in law of the basic rights throughout the Weimar period are decisively settled. By bringing these rights to the forefront of the Basic Law, its authors avoid that appearance of afterthought and secondary priority created in the Weimar constitution by the relegation of basic rights to the end. The lapidary style of presentation, with a sparing use of ambiguous abstract language, always productive of difficulty and subject to exploitation in the courts, evokes confidence that this code of rights will wear well at law. Not all of the provisions meet the Parliamentary Council's test for a "basic right": Can it be directly applied as law? Declarative and programmatic provisions are not altogether excluded; but they are rare. Nor, despite the Council's declared intention to confine itself to the "classic" rights, are the so-called social and institutional rights passed over. But these again have been kept to the minimum consistent with satisfying the most clamant demands of the institutions, classes, and interest groups concerned. One might epitomize this code of basic rights as a lawyer's code—produced by lawyers as standing rules for the lawyers who would in future enact and administer the law and adjudicate under it.

Turning to the Parliamentary Council's deliberations, we shall take up first the Council's treatment of the classic individual rights and then go on to the social and institutional rights.

Theory of Rights   At first sight, the provisions of the Basic Law seem to follow the American example so closely —basic rights are described as "inviolable and inalienable"; they bind the three branches of government as law; they are protected by a constitutional court—that one is prompted to assume that a theory of natural rights must underlie them. In fact, there is nothing in the language of the Basic Law to warrant such an assumption.

Article 1 is significant, not so much for what it says but for what it does not say.

The dignity of man is inviolable; to respect and protect it is the duty of all state authority.

The German people therefore acknowledge inviolable and inalienable human rights to be the basis of every human community, of peace and of justice in the world.

In this opening declaration, there is nothing incompatible with a natural rights (whether theological or rationalist), a historical, or a statist theory. As between these rival views, it takes no position— and designedly so.

The parties influenced by Catholic doctrine, or holding a similar view of rights—the Christian Democratic / Christian Social Union, the Center, and the German party—pressed from the outset for an explicit rejection of statist pretensions and for acknowledgment of the grounding of individual rights in natural law. Dr. Süsterhenn (CDU) told the delegates at the second plenary session:

We must get back to recognizing that man does not exist for the State, but the State for man. For us, freedom and the dignity of human personality have the highest value. The State serves these ends by creating the external conditions and institutions which enable the individual to realize his physical and spiritual capacities and freely to develop his personality within the limits set by natural moral law. . . . The State ought not to be an end in itself, but must be deliberately confined to fulfilling a subsidiary function vis-à-vis the individual and the various groups within the community. . . . The State is not for us the source of all law, but is itself subject to the law. There are . . . rights prior to and superior to the State, resulting from the nature and being of man and his various associations which the State has to respect. Every power of State finds its bounds in these natural, God-given rights of the individual, the family, the local communities of town and country, and the occupational groups.[25]

First drafts of the Chiemsee conference and the basic rights committee reflected the influence of the Church parties:

The State exists for man, not man for the State.[26]

The dignity of man is founded upon eternal rights with which every man is endowed by nature.[27]

And later in the main committee:

Resolved to secure a lasting respect for and a safeguarding of human dignity, the German people acknowledge these God-given inviolable and inalienable human rights and freedoms to be the basis of freedom, justice, and peace.[28]

Except for muted support from the Free Democrats, the State as the source of rights had no friends in the Council. Dr. Heuss did permit himself one outburst against the Chiemsee formula:

"The State exists for man, not man for the State." I presume that the author who fashioned this sentence was very proud of it. . . . But, gentlemen, I ask you, what kind of a German is this? The State is—there! What on earth is it? A declaratory statement, a suable right, a legal principle, or what exactly? Forgive me if I am a little blunt. Into this article there has been slipped a furtive attack against the wrongly understood Hegel, dead now these 117 years. And just because someone feels obliged to lodge a polemic against Hegel, who is defenseless, we have one of those stale commonplaces, echoing what all the world says, that Hegel has poisoned our thinking about the State. . . . When we are establishing a basic law for the State, we ought not to begin with a disparagement of it as only a subsidiary affair of man—what then is man? Just because we have experienced . . . in the period when Hitler was calling the tune. . . how the State could be the ruin of human beings, in my opinion we don't have now to begin with so negative an approach. The State is not merely an apparatus, but it is also the bearer of an inherent worth, and as the pillar of an ordered community, it is for man, and man for it, no bare abstraction. Discard this banal philosophy of the State and turn to principles to which it is practicable to give a legally binding effect![29]

The Social Democrats, as far as they expressed a positive view of their own, took a historical line. There is a certain piquancy in the Socialist Carlo Schmid's approving references to Burke:

I recall that the amazing Burke in his reactions to the French Revolution said that, in general, men appear to have no concrete rights arising from nature, that their rights have evolved historically and are the products of decisions and institutions developed in the course of their history. . . . We must make an historical conception of natural rights (only an apparent contradiction in terms) our point of departure and say, at this stage of historical development, we Germans are not prepared to live under standards of freedom which do not include these and these and these guarantees of freedom from the State.[30]

But the Social Democrats and Free Democrats were less concerned to advance theories of their own than to resist the theory of the Church parties. An explicit reference in Article 1 to "natural law," they feared, might open opportunities for doctrinaire interpretation and for drawing implications regarding future social policy in Western Germany which they could not accept.

To erect natural law as an absolute is a dangerous business. I recommend a reading of Kant on this subject where he says that, in general, natural law tends to manifest itself to each one in a way which best suits his own desires.[31]

These misgivings of Carlo Schmid were echoed by Dr. Heuss:

For myself, I feel uneasy about beginning the basic law with a declaration of rights existing prior to the State. In laying it down that every man possesses inherent natural rights, a principle is expressed that remains open to free interpretation. . . . The formula "von Natur aus eigenen Rechten" seems to me undesirable because of the erroneous consequences which might arise from it.[32]

Schmid and Heuss therefore set themselves to devise a wording of strictly neutral character avoiding all presupposition as to the origin of basic rights. In their formulas,[33] the text ultimately adopted originates.

But although any reference to natural rights has been excluded from the Basic Law, it will be clear from the provisions next to be discussed that the conception of the relationship between individual freedom and authority underlying the Basic Law in fact differs significantly from German theory and practice in the past.

Restrictions
on Basic
Rights

Once basic rights are given the status of supreme law, the problem arises: How are the necessary safeguards against their abuse, and restrictions upon them in the public interest, to be applied without in practice undermining the rights themselves? We have seen that for the greater part of the time in Germany, the legislature could limit or extend rights at will and that the executive, particularly the police, had wide general powers, subject to restraints imposed by administrative courts and the law. The Basic Law differs in several important respects.

The parliament, wherever it is authorized to restrict a basic right by law, may do so only by a law which applies generally, not solely to an individual case, which names the basic right and the article protecting it, and which refrains from infringing upon a basic right's "essential content" (Article 19[2]). This insures against both discriminatory legislation directed at individual persons or associations and legislation of such generality as to void a basic right indefinitely.

We saw in the Weimar constitution that many of the basic rights might be limited by a "law," "laws," or the "general laws." The Parliamentary Council sought, although only with partial success, to avoid relying upon this omnibus formula and to establish criteria for legislative intervention which would serve at once as a guide for and a limit upon legislative interference with rights. Standards of varying concreteness are established for limitation upon freedom of person (Articles 2 and 104), of association (Article 9), of movement (Article 11), of the inviolability of the home (Article 13). (No limitations are to be placed on freedom of faith and conscience [Article 4].) For legislative restrictions on freedom of opinion, press, radio, and cinema (Article 5), of assembly in the open air (Article 8), of the mails and telecommunications (Article 10), of the practice of trades and professions (Article 12), no standards are fixed. The explanation for this difference of treatment lies partly in the intractability of the problem of "legislating" on complex matters within the compass of a short constitutional article and partly in the fact that special interests and conflicts of opinion in some cases assisted and in others prevented agreement on standards.

Absence of   The omission from the Basic Law of a constitu-
Grounds for   tional basis for general police power is a yet
General Police   more significant departure from tradition. The
Power   "law" in the Weimar constitution under which
individual freedom could be restricted, we saw, was interpreted to
include the general body of law, embracing the common law and
other legal bases for the exercise of a general police power in the
Länder. The Chiemsee conference adopted this position even more
explicitly in its draft:

> The basic rights, except as specifically provided in their content, are
> to be understood within the framework of the general legal order [*im
> Rahmen der Allgemeinen Rechtsordnung*].[34]

The basic rights committee initially followed the Chiemsee formula, although only in connection with one right, that of freedom
of person:

> This freedom may only be encroached upon within the compass of
> the legal order [*im Rahmen der Rechtsordnung*].

At an early stage, Carlo Schmid (SPD) attacked this provision as
leaving too wide a discretion to the administration:

> The administration must be properly authorized to act by laws. A
> law is the outcome of the *volonté générale*, not a bare expression of the
> will of the executive. The inclusion of customary law [*Gewohnheits-
> recht*] is a dangerous thing. There have been many abusive practices
> under police law. I should like it . . . to be made clear that any encroach-
> ment by the State requires authorization by democratically adopted
> legislation.[35]

Von Mangoldt (CDU) insisted that the resort to *Gewohnheitsrecht* was a practical necessity:

> The administration cannot be expected in every case to act only on
> the basis of specific legislative provisions. Not every administrative act
> depends directly on the mandate of the legislature. Rather, in many
> cases, must it be possible for the administration to take the initiative
> where no directly applicable rule has been provided. That is where the
> difficulty lies.[36]

Schmid rejoined:

> We ought not to make the exercise of authority easy. I am for making
> it difficult.

Von Mangoldt's position was indorsed by the majority of the basic rights committee. It became apparent, however, as the work of the Parliamentary Council proceeded, that to provide such latitude for discretion on the part of the administration and the police in connection with this most fundamental right was scarcely compatible with the efforts being made to give the basic rights as a whole a positive constitutional content.[37] As the result, in Article 2 ("Everyone has the right to life and to inviolability of his person. The freedom of the individual is inviolable. These rights may only be encroached upon pursuant to a law") the phrase "pursuant to a law" was substituted for "within the compass of the legal order," thus excluding *Gewohnheitsrecht* as the basis for the exercise of a general police power.[38]

A broad grant of power to the police by legislative enactment, always provided that the conditions laid down in Article 19* are met, is certainly not excluded. The presumption, however, that public order and security have overriding priority—that all else is to be subordinated to it—is missing from the Basic Law. Precedence is given neither to the need of the community for stability, order, and security, nor to the right of the individual to be free to express and develop himself and to impart the direction which he thinks proper to the social and political life of the community. Instead of attempting a forced resolution of this persisting antinomy in human affairs by suppressing one side or subordinating it to the other, the Basic Law leaves the two in tension to achieve their own adjustment empirically within a broad constitutional framework.

Judicial Review and the Constitutional Court Basic rights are afforded protection both in the courts of ordinary jurisdiction and in administrative courts. But questions regarding the conformity of legislation (federal or Land) with the basic rights are reserved solely to the federal constitutional court.[39]

We have seen that the establishment in principle of the right of judicial review by the Weimar *Reichsgericht* was an unprecedented

* "Wherever under this Basic Law a basic right may be restricted by or pursuant to a law, the law must apply generally and not solely to an individual case. Furthermore the law must name the basic right and refer to the Article which protects it. . . . In no case may a basic right be infringed upon in its essential content."

move and one which did not fail to rouse opposition from those who feared that it must lead to the subordination of the legislature to the judiciary and the "politicizing" of the courts. The unanimity of view which obtained in the Parliamentary Council on this point is, therefore, at first thought, surprising. As early as the first plenary sessions, the major parties in the Parliamentary Council committed themselves to the establishment of a constitutional court with powers of judicial review.[40]

There were many compelling considerations. The Allies themselves had stipulated

that the constitution should provide for an independent judiciary to review federal legislation, to review the exercise of federal executive power, and to adjudicate conflicts between federal and Land authorities as well as between Land authorities, and to protect the civil rights and freedom of the individual.[41]

The Council's preoccupation with re-establishing the rule of law and giving positive constitutional content to the basic rights also led inevitably to judicial review. Carlo Schmid (SPD) told the Council at its second session:

The basic rights must govern the Basic Law; they should not be merely an appendage to the Basic Law, as the catalogue of basic rights was to the Weimar constitution. These basic rights shall not be bare declamations, declarations, or directives, not just stipulations for the Land constitutions, not just a guarantee of rights in the Länder, but directly applicable federal law, on the basis of which every individual German, every individual inhabitant of our country, shall be able to bring an action in the courts.[42]

But if the basic rights were to be directly applicable law and binding upon the legislature as well as the executive and the judiciary, it followed, since the legislature could not very well be judge in its own case, that the judiciary must see to it that parliament did not overstep the constitutional bounds.

The suggestion to leave this control to the exercise of the body representing the sovereign people overlooks the fact that the legislative body would itself have to decide upon the constitutionality of its own legislation and hence be judge in its own case.[43]

The Christian Democrats were all along prepared to go the whole way to judicial supremacy. Dr. Süsterhenn (CDU) told the second plenary session:

We want a constitutional court which shall not only have the right of examining whether a law has been adopted in the prescribed form or whether it conforms to the letter of the constitution. The constitutional court for which we ask should also have the right to examine whether a law in its content corresponds to the natural and human rights basic to the constitution, as is the case with the federal court of the United States; which, above the will of the legislature, will serve as the guardian of the constitution, the protector of natural rights, and the embodied conscience of the whole nation.[44]

The Social Democrats were more reserved, but expressed no misgivings in debate over the position to be given the constitutional court. This appears the more remarkable when one considers that the influence of such a court on the life of a nation can be (as the example of the United States Supreme Court shows) a profoundly conservative one. But the Social Democrats had to weigh the advantage to them of a constitutional court as a pillar of central power[45] against its disadvantage as a conservative brake. Once it became clear that a federal structure of government could not be avoided, the Social Democrats wanted established a national court of sufficient authority to compel the Land governments to conform in their legislation and administration to national policies. Judicial review, however, could not be expected to operate in one direction only: to protect the interests of the federation but not those of the Länder. They appear to have been satisfied that provisions for the method of selection and composition of the court would safeguard them against a court hostile in principle to the Socialist program.

In these provisions, the Council frankly recognized the political character of a constitutional court: that, in many issues on which it is called to adjudicate it acts as a kind of higher third legislative chamber, whose decisions have the same effects as legislation and are usually determined, despite a play with legal concepts, by considerations of the same order as move the legislature. The Council therefore provided that the constitutional court should be composed both of federal judges and of "other members" and that half of the members should be elected by the Bundestag and the other half by the Bundesrat. (On the other hand, the federal supreme court [*Oberstes Bundesgericht*], whose constitutional function is the more limited and technical one of preserving "the uniformity of application of federal law," is to be composed solely of professional jurists.) Furthermore, neither the number of members of the court nor the proportion in which federal judges and "other members" are to be appointed to it is specified in the Basic Law. These are left for determination by ordinary federal legislation. Hence, a party possessing a majority in the Bundestag and Bundesrat could alter the composition of the court should it wish to do so.

The importance which the Social Democrats attached to these provisions for the organization and character of the constitutional court became clear when the time came to assign functions respectively to it and the federal supreme court. They firmly resisted the Christian Democratic demand that questions about the formal and substantive compatibility of federal and Land legislation with the Basic Law should be assigned to the "judicial" supreme court rather than to the "political" constitutional court.[46]

The public law experts were less readily satisfied. Within a few months of the entry into force of the Basic Law, Willibalt Apelt[47] and H. P. Ipsen[48] published attacks on the recognition in the Basic Law of the right of judicial review. Coupled with such broad provisions as those of Article 19 forbidding legislative infringement of the "essential content" of basic rights and those of Article 3 bidding equal treatment of all before the law,* judicial review, they pointed out, furnished opportunities of wide scope for bringing the legislature under the control of the courts.

The supreme representative of the *volonté générale*, of the sovereign people, is no longer the elected popular assembly but a small group of judges. Since the questions with which it will be predominantly concerned are political and ethical in character—for example, whether a

---

* Art. 3, par. 1: "All persons are equal before the law" was formerly understood in Germany, as it is in Britain, to be a directive to the executive and the courts to administer the law without favor toward or discrimination against any citizen. In the Basic Law, in analogy with the "due process" clause of the United States Constitution as interpreted by the Supreme Court, it has both a procedural and a substantive aspect. The legislature, as well as the executive, is bound by it. It governs not only the manner in which law is adopted and administered, but its content as well. In the early drafts of Article 3, it was explicitly laid down that: "*Das Gesetz muss Gleiches gleich, es kann Verschiedenes nach seiner Eigenart behandeln*" ("The law must treat equally what is equal; it may treat what is different according to its particular character"). This provision was eventually dropped by the committee of five because of fears that it might be misunderstood as countenancing discrimination on racial grounds. Nevertheless, it is taken by the experts (see Von Mangoldt's *Commentary*, p. 51) and by the constitutional court (see Mercker, *op. cit.*, *Bundesanzeiger*, No. 226, p. 3) as expressing the intent of Article 3, par. 1. The latitude which it leaves for judicial interpretation is obvious.

federal law sufficiently respects the dignity of man—the judiciary will be adjudicating in controversies which, essentially, are not justiciable. . . . This is a breach of the principle of separation of powers.[49]

It is too early to say whether these fears are justified. The constitutional court has shown restraint in refusing to review decisions of the federal legislature regarding the need for federal exercise of the concurrent legislative powers. Whether it will exercise its powers in the field of basic rights with equal circumspection remains to be seen. As the American example shows, judicial review in this field can be a double-edged sword: a powerful weapon both for the defense of individual liberties and for staying social and economic reform.

3. ECONOMIC AND SOCIAL RIGHTS

Although the Federal Republic is described in the Basic Law as a democratic and "social" federal state,[50] more attention is paid to the first of these attributes than the second. It was so intended. Indeed, had the Parliamentary Council found it possible to adhere to its first resolution, the Basic Law would have been confined to a statement of the traditional individual rights.

This position contrasts with that taken in the seven Land constitutions[51] adopted during the year preceding the Parliamentary Council meetings. In these are recognized the rights of labor to have work, to a living wage, to equal pay for the job for men and women, to decent conditions in the workplace, to be represented with management by work councils, and to be provided for when unemployed, injured, ill, and aged. The state is bidden to take any control or promotional measures that may be necessary in connection with industry, agriculture, and distribution to insure that the needs of the people are met and to prevent the formation of monopolies and cartels. Resources and the means of production are to be transferred to public ownership if "the common welfare," "the attainment of economic goals," or "prevention of monopolistic and other abuses" requires it.[52] The rights to private property (with certain conditions), to compensation for property taken by eminent domain or for public ownership and operation, and to freedom of contract are recognized. In some constitutions, the state is enjoined to protect and promote "the independent middle class" and small and medium-sized independent businesses.

What the authors of the constitutions of the Länder could do, could not the Parliamentary Council also have done? We must not lose sight of the unsettled conditions in which the Parliamentary Council met, nor forget that many of the delegates began their work with the conviction that they were producing a document of only temporary significance. Carlo Schmid (SPD) asked:

> Should we include only the rights of the individual, or provisions as well for the so-called social order, in which our new Land constitutions abound: on the economy, education, the family, etc.? It would perhaps be advisable not to attempt in a provisional constitution any final ordering of social relations, but to be content with formulating an absolutely clear and effective catalogue of individual rights, on the model of the classical "Bills of Rights" of the Anglo-Saxon states.[53]

That staunch disciple of Friedrich Naumann, Dr. Heuss, was roused to exclaim:

> The Landtage have had the courage—or the temerity—to lay down in their constitutions how the social and economic order will develop in the future. . . . It is frivolous, it is arrogant, it is—I do not know what— to suppose that in the present generally obscure situation, one can say: thus will the economic and social order of the future take form.[54]

This attitude was strengthened by the wish to avoid any ambiguity in the legal status of the basic rights which might offer opportunity, as in the Weimar constitution, to the executive, the courts, or the academic experts to call the authority of these rights into question.[55]

At this stage, the political climate in Western Germany was changing from one day to the next. In the aftermath of defeat and of collapse of the economy, in which all classes had been reduced to common misery, social tensions had relaxed. While there was still little discernible hope of restoring the private sector of the economy to its former strength, it had been comparatively easy to obtain the agreement of all parties to provisions looking toward what seemed the inevitable: the development of a full-fledged service state with a planned, centrally controlled economy. But now, following the currency reform, with signs of business recovery on every hand and with the promise of American money to help it on its way, there were in many quarters second thoughts, or at least first thoughts where there had been none before. Social welfare and the planned economy began now to be thought of in terms of higher taxes on profits and income, of controls over investment and trade, of the size of the wages bill, and of the possible expropriation of properties once again potentially valuable. As, with financial solvency, the owning and managing classes began to recover confidence, the trade unions, refugees, pensioners, veterans, and persons who suffered heavy losses in the war moved to stake their claims. Social tensions were reviving. This was the new political atmosphere—the "obscure situation"—in which the Parliamentary Council convened.

On social and economic questions, there was nearly a balance of forces between the right and left, with advantage to the right whenever it combined all the members of the Christian parties, the German party, and the Free Democrats. In these circumstances, it would have been reasonable to believe, and no doubt many delegates did believe, that there was in any case little prospect of reaching agreement on a comprehensive and self-consistent statement of social and economic rights and that it would be better to have no statement rather than a contradictory, confusing mélange of party programs.[56]

Nevertheless, the Parliamentary Council did not entirely succeed in adhering to its resolution. It could not ignore the claims of the more powerful institutions and interest groups in the country—the trade unions, property-owners, the Church—for constitutional guaranties of the rights most vital to them: of the workers to organize to safeguard and improve their working conditions; of owners to be secure in their property against arbitrary restriction or dispossession; of Catholic parents to have their children trained in schools of their faith.

Each of the provisions in the Basic Law on social and economic matters was keenly contested. For every right which a faction was bent upon securing for its own constituents there was another which it was equally bent upon excluding or restricting as far as possible. Tactical exploitation of inconsistencies in an opponent's case to advance one's own was the order of the day.

The Social Democrats demanded freedom for workers to organize and pursue their interests by collective bargaining and use of the strike, did they? Then, they must surely agree that the worker's freedom to join

an organization implied his freedom not to join it—a right equally requiring protection. The Church parties asserted the basis in natural law
of marriage, the family, and the right of parents to determine the training of their children? What had they to say of the "natural rights" of
illegitimate children? Were their rights not equal with those of other
children? Did divine law also discriminate against the illegitimate child?

—So ran the cut and thrust of debate.

On trade-union rights, the Social Democrats and the Communists,
broadly speaking, were opposed by the bourgeois parties. Yet they
had allies in the Christian Democratic and Center parties, and on the
"closed shop" issue found support even from the German party.
On property rights and the taking of property by eminent domain
or for transfer to public ownership and operation, the German
party, the Free Democrats, and a large section of the CDU/CSU
defended the interests of ownership against the Socialists, but here
again the latter had some support from the Center and the CDU.
Where the interest of the family as a center of traditional property
and other rights was concerned, as in the case of inheritance rights
and of the status of the illegitimate child, the Free Democrats ranged
themselves with the CDU/CSU, the German party, and the Center.
Where it was a question of the Church's view of parents' rights, as
in the schools question, the Free Democrats stood with the Socialists.
From these shifting alliances emerged the final pattern of compromise—as with all workable constitutional compromises, satisfactory
to none, but tolerable for all.

Thus the Social Democrats were able to obtain for the trade
unions an unconditional guaranty of the right to organize and to
fend off attempts by the right to prohibit the "closed shop," but
they had insufficient support to carry a constitutional recognition
of the right to strike. Members of the FDP, DP, and CDU/CSU
successfully resisted the Social Democrats' effort to limit constitutional guaranties of property rights to personally used property and
to exclude inheritance rights altogether, but could not evade a constitutional recognition of the principle of socialization or obtain a
guaranty of "adequate" compensation for property taken for public
purposes. The CDU/CSU, DP, and Center won recognition of the
State's duty to give special protection to marriage and the family.
They successfully resisted a Social Democratic countermove to give

the illegitimate child legal rights and status fully equal to those enjoyed by the child born within marriage. They did not succeed in their primary goal of obtaining constitutional recognition of the right of parents to have state-supported confessional schools of their choice for their children.

Trade Unions;   The first draft of this article produced by the
The Right To   basic rights committee read:
Strike
(Article 9 [3])   The right to form associations to safeguard and improve working and economic conditions is guaranteed to everyone and to all trades and professions. Agreements and measures which restrict or seek to hinder this right or compel membership are null and void; measures directed to this end are illegal. . . . The right to strike within the limitations established by law is recognized.

The right of workers to organize without interference was accepted from the start. Disagreements arose over giving constitutional recognition to the right to strike and the proposal to outlaw "agreements and measures which . . . compel membership."

The opponents of the strike provision did not attack it frontally. They weakened its effect by proposing limiting amendments. To avoid any appearance of constitutional sanction for "wildcat," spontaneous strikes, an early amendment proposed that only "the right to strike, when trade unions have declared a strike" should be recognized. To this, Dr. Heuss[57] objected, because the trade unions would thus have conferred upon them an unprecedented role in the operation of the constitution. Who, he asked, was to have the responsibility for authorizing a strike—a local or a national union? To meet these objections, and to remove any suggestion of sanction for political and general strikes, he proposed recognition of "the right (within limits established by law) by a concerted stoppage of work to bring about adjustment of wages and conditions of work." Kaufmann (CDU) and Heile (DP)[58] insisted upon language explicitly excluding political strikes and strikes by civil servants (*Beamten*) and employees in the public service (*Angestellte des öffentlichen Dienstes*). When Dr. Schmid (SPD) asked Kaufmann whether this proposal would exclude from the right to strike workers in municipal gasworks or slaughterhouses, Kaufmann replied that he did not regard these as public employees. Schmid rejoined that they *did* fall under the category of employees in the public service. Because of such difficulties of interpretation in border cases, the Social Democrats asked that detailed restrictions on the right to strike should be left to legislation. Attempts to regulate them in a phrase or two in the Basic Law would simply lead to "endless quibbling" ("*eine grosse Kasuistik*"),[59] they said.

Unable to make this view prevail, the Social Democrats and the unions dropped the strike provision at the end of the first reading debate and did not raise it again. A provision to which general conditions and exceptions were attached might prove to be more inimical to trade-union interests than none at all, they felt. They were strengthened in this decision by the knowledge that most of the Land constitutions adopted to that date contained formulations of the right to strike acceptable to the trade unions.

The "Anti-Closed-Shop" Clause　The clause invalidating any "agreement and measures which . . . compel membership" in an organization was an artful thrust by the friends of free enterprise at the Social Democrats and the trade unions. In debate, it put them into the difficulty of squaring the trade-union imperative of organizational solidarity with their championship of individual rights in other spheres.

The Trade Union Council of the Combined Zones[60] protested that the right to remain outside an association had always been regarded in the past as adequately covered by the ordinary guaranties of individual freedom. The trade unions feared that a constitutional prohibition against compulsory membership could form the ground for a legal attack on "those measures to achieve an all-embracing organization of employees, which are entirely admissible under present general legal principles."

The Social Democratic speakers amplified this point in debate. Dr. Schmid wanted to know[61] whether the condition that wage-rate agreements could apply only to workers in an enterprise who were members of the union negotiating the agreement (which he compared to the American "closed shop" agreement) would be forbidden. Herr Heile asked whether the refusal of union members to work with non-unionists would be interpreted as an act "compelling membership in a union." They were answered affirmatively by opposing speakers.

Herr Schräge, a trade unionist in the CDU, assured the main

committee[62] that the trade unions had always been devoted to the principle of voluntarism, but they did not like to see an explicit constitutional provision on the point because it would appear to encourage the opponents of unionism. Herr Schönfelder (SPD) added frankly:[63]

> On the basis of my trade-union experience, may I say the following: certain stipulations in agreements which, to a degree, have involved compulsion, have helped to bring order into many industrial fields. As, from the point of view of both employers and employees, workers outside a union can hinder such an orderly development, both have agreed that an employer will not employ a worker who does not belong to an organization. On this basis, good relations have been maintained in many different industrial fields.

From the employers' point of view, Herr Schönfelder was supported by Dr. Seebohm (DP).

When Von Mangoldt[64] found it necessary in the second reading to introduce a number of exceptions to the clause in order to permit compulsory membership in such long-established semipublic organizations as chambers of lawyers, physicians, and pharmacists, the Social Democrats seized the opportunity to propose deletion of the entire clause. As with the "strike clause," said Dr. Eberhard (SPD), here too the introduction of exceptions, qualifications, and refinements could lead to "endless quibbling." His motion was accepted. In effect, deletion of the strike clause was traded for deletion of the "anti-closed-shop" clause.

Ownership and Inheritance The Social Democrats first opposed—unsuccessfully—the constitutional guaranty for inheritance rights, arguing that there was little point in giving such a guaranty where tax legislation had already disposed of it *de facto*.[65] Dr. Heuss (FDP) argued for the retention of the guaranty, on the ground that a legal foundation was needed for testamentary dispositions upon which complicated family arrangements depended.

As regards property rights themselves, the Social Democrats succeeded in inserting in the basic rights committee's first draft of Article 14 a provision that only property "contributing to the individual's own standard of living or to his own work" would be guaranteed. This was attacked by Dr. Kroll (CDU) and Dr. Heuss (FDP) as opening to the legislature the way to all kinds of arbitrary measures against property.[66] Dr. Heuss saw in it a penalizing of the development of wealth, upon which national prosperity and culture depended. He feared that capital made available from personal savings—to which, for instance, the industrial development of Württemberg in the nineteenth century owed its existence—would be jeopardized. Neither the concept of property used in a person's work nor that contributing to his standard of living, he added, had any precise legal significance. The courts would have to start from the beginning with these concepts.

The Social Democratic proposal was defeated six to six in the basic rights committee, a Christian Democratic trade unionist joining the five Social Democrats against four Christian Democrats, one Free Democrat, and one German party member.

The Social Democrats, prompted by the Trade Union Council of the Combined Zones, next proposed a clause: "Whoever abuses the right of ownership cannot claim the protection of these provisions."[67] Introducing the proposal, Dr. Bergsträsser (SPD) gave as examples of abuses which would, in his opinion, warrant the forfeiture of property rights, the hoarding of goods in short supply or the subsidizing by industrial firms of movements inimical to the democratic order. The provision was subjected to much criticism. The editorial committee[68] objected to the lack of any definition of "abuses of ownership." Dr. Seebohm (DP)[69] demanded that it be deleted altogether because, he said, in addition to the criminal law, it would create a further and indeterminate class of conditions under which property could be declared forfeit. Nevertheless, the clause was approved in each reading of the main committee until the last, when it was deleted on the ground that the point was already covered in Article 18. This, however, was an error—although perhaps a deliberate one—for Article 18 provides for a forfeiture of basic rights only when abuses of property rights are connected with attacks on the "free democratic order." In this form, the clause has a much narrower application.

Expropriation and Compensation　　The Chiemsee draft, following the Weimar constitution[70] (Article 153, paragraph 2), had stipulated that expropriation in the public interest should take place only against "adequate" (*"angemessene"*) compensation. Dr. Schmid,[71] putting the Social Democratic case against such a provision, recalled that under the compensation law developed during the nineteenth century, persons expropriated could in all cases sue in the courts for the full value of their property. "Adequate" compensation, so interpreted, had stood in the way of carrying out basic structural changes in the economic organization of the country. Today, with such a conception of compensation, Schmid argued, a planned reconstruction of ruined cities in Germany would be impossible; they would be left to grow up in their old anarchy. It was imperative, he said, to provide constitutionally for the possibility of expropriation with limited, or even with no, compensation.

There were repeated but unsuccessful efforts by the German party and the Free Democrats, in which Dr. Seebohm (DP) took the leading part, to reintroduce the concept of "adequate" or "full" compensation in this article. In the last such effort, Dr. Seebohm explained his position as follows:[72]

Following the historical development after the so-called full compensation provision embodied in the Prussian Expropriation Law of 1874, the concept of "adequate" compensation was introduced in the Weimar constitution. This concept received juridical acceptance and, in particular, was embodied in judgments of the Reich supreme court. It was also used in all of the legislation adopted in the interval, and appears in the constitutions of Bavaria and Baden. It is of decisive importance for us that the concept of adequate compensation should be retained, for otherwise the danger exists that the place of this intelligible, judicially clarified concept will be taken by a wording which, although a reasonable interpretation would not theoretically preclude an adequate compensation, would in practice give room for any other interpretation, even to expropriation without compensation.

Socialization
Measures
Opponents of the article on socialization measures (Article 15)[73] held that there was no need for explicit constitutional recognition of such measures, for everything necessary to the execution of transfers of property to public ownership was already provided in the expropriation clause of Article 14. The Social Democrats[74] replied that the transfer of resources and the means of production to public ownership was not just an ordinary case of expropriation, but concerned a structural transformation of the economy for which no preliminary showing of the public interest had to be made, as in Article 14. Moreover, under Article 14, expropriation proceedings could be initiated by administrative action pursuant to a general enactment, whereas

each measure of socialization required specific legislative authorization.

Marriage and   The most interesting aspect of the provisions on
the Family   marriage and the family and the schools in Articles 6 and 7 is that their very presence in the Basic Law reflects the persistent and profound influence of the Catholic church in the life of Western Germany. These are not subjects dealt with in the "classic" catalogues of basic rights,[75] to which the Parliamentary Council had resolved to confine itself. Moreover, in most federal systems, educational and cultural matters are reserved to the states. The occupation authorities had specifically directed that they should be so reserved in their November 22 *aide memoire* to the Council.

The Social Democrats made the most of these objections. They stressed their embarrassment with their trade-union supporters, whose demands for a full program of social and economic rights in the Basic Law they had resisted because of the understanding that only the classic basic rights were to be included.[76] They twitted the arch-federalists in the Church parties for attempting to impose uniform principles upon the Länder in fields which were pre-eminently their concern.[77] Of these phrases in one of the basic rights committee's final drafts of Article 6—"Marriage is the legitimate form of life partnership of a man and woman; it establishes a foundation for the family"—Dr. Greve (SPD)[78] acidly observed that neither conformed to the first article of the basic rights: neither could be directly applied as law.

For those who do not acknowledge that marriage is the legitimate form of life partnership of men and women, it is of little use to assert it in a constitution. The same applies to the second sentence . . . it is declarative and could never be applied as law; no claim based upon it could succeed before any court, whether it be an ordinary court, an administrative court, or some specially created body.

But, if the Social Democrats had the best of the arguments, the alliance of the CDU/CSU, DP, and Center had the votes, for they could count upon Free Democratic support in most of these issues, except that of "parents' rights."

The Social Democrats replied with campaigns for constitutional recognition of full equality of rights for men and women and for illegitimate children.

Equality of the Sexes   The Church parties and the Free Democrats, although giving support in principle to the equality in law of the sexes, balked at stating flatly in the Basic Law that men and women have equal rights. They contended that it would create confusion in the courts by invalidating much of the existing civil code regulating family relationships[79] and might possibly even prejudice some of the special protections already afforded women in social legislation.[80] The Social Democrats,[81] while agreeing that the existing body of law would require amendment, insisted that the principle of equal rights for women should be stated unequivocally in the Basic Law, with the provision that existing law would continue to be valid for a limited period to permit time for its amendment.

At the conclusion of the first reading in the main committee, a majority rejected the Social Democratic proposal. In the following weeks, however, the Parliamentary Council was flooded with petitions and memorials from women's associations in Western Germany —from the *Frauenring Rhineland*, the *Süddeutsche Frauenarbeitskreis*, the women workers of the *Industriegewerkschaft Metall*, the *Frauenverbände Stüttgart*, the women workers of the *Freie Gewerkschaftsbund Hesse*, and the women members of the Landtage in the Länder. In the second reading, the opposition capitulated and accepted without qualification the provision for equal rights for men and women.[82] Dr. Strauss, conceding for the CDU, said that they had perhaps "regarded the problem too much from the juridical and too little from the political point of view."[83]

Rights of the Illegitimate Child   The debates on full equality of rights for the illegitimate child throw much interesting light on sociological attitudes in Western Germany today. Unfortunately, they cannot be reviewed here in detail. The opponents of the Social Democratic case were fruitful in raising practical and technical difficulties. If the illegitimate child were to bear his father's name, be entitled to support by him and to share in his estate, this would inevitably lead, it was objected, to a claim by the father of legal rights over the child, whereas legal control of and responsibility for the illegitimate child must rest with the mother.[84]

In their most arresting argument, the Social Democrats referred with candor to a perplexing European social problem. In the words of Frau Dr. Selbert:[85]

> The frequently mentioned excess of women over men amounts in Germany to seven million, in Europe to twelve million or more. We are ignoring the life of our times if we do not clearly recognize that already, outside the institution of marriage, new customs are developing which are by no means regarded as immoral and with disapproval. One cannot deny to millions of women a claim to their own personal life, to their own happiness in love, and to the happiness of children.

And, from Frau Nadig:[86]

> When we consider that this excess of women lies mainly in the age group twenty-two to forty-five, we know that an immense change in the forms of relationships between the sexes will develop. We must expect in the future to have the mother family, and we have every inducement to give an illegitimate child an equal legal position with the legitimate child.

"Parents'
Rights"

The publicly-supported compulsory elementary school system differs in the Länder of Western Germany. In Bavaria and North Rhine-Westphalia, for example, there are both denominational (Catholic and Evangelical) schools (*Bekentnisschule*) and non-denominational schools (*Gemeinschaftschule*). Parents may choose to which they will send their children, at least where a school of their choice exists. In other Länder (e.g., Baden-Württemberg, Hesse, Bremen), there are only non-denominational schools. Religious instruction taking into account the faith of the children is commonly given in these schools. The issue in the "parents' rights" controversy was whether, as the Church parties demanded, the principle of the right of parents to choose the "religious-ideological" (*"religiösweltan-schaulichen"*) character of schools should be incorporated in the federal constitution, thus compelling all the Länder to make provision for publicly-supported denominational schools where required.

The supporters of "parents' rights" were the most pertinacious minority in the Parliamentary Council. Although repeatedly defeated by eleven to ten,* they persisted with their campaign in each

---

* Eight Socialists, two Free Democrats, one Communist, against eight Christian Democrats and Christian Socialists, one Centrist, and one German party member.

successive reading to the last. Finally, they asked for a popular referendum within a year of the Basic Law's entry into force to decide upon constitutional recognition for "parents' rights." This too was rejected.

The essence of the argument for "parents' rights" is contained in the joint public declaration made by the Church parties after their defeat in the third reading debate:

> As before, we maintain our view that the parents' right of bringing up their children is a God-given, natural right, beyond the sphere of the State. This natural right of bringing up children extends, above all, to the religious-ideological education of the children, and not only within the confines of the family, but also of the schools. The school must be given a religious-ideological character which corresponds to the dictates of the parental conscience. In a State founded upon the principle of freedom of conscience, of tolerance, and of democracy, the nature of its schools should be such that, in respect to religious or ideological outlook, no one will be under a restraint of conscience. A public, compulsory, uniform school system with a definite ideological character prescribed by the State means an encroachment on the parents' freedom of conscience. We demand, therefore, that in connection with the religious-ideological character of the schools, the wishes of the parents be taken into account and that the parents be enabled, according to the dictates of conscience, to have their children educated in confessional or non-denominational or secular schools.[87]

Behind the uncompromising spirit of this demand lay the Church's reaction to the brutal revival of the *Kulturkampf*[88] by the National Socialists and the Communists, reinforcing the Church's traditional determination to assure to itself the means of maintaining influence over the young. In particular, the Church wanted to keep in its hands the education of children of refugee families from Catholic areas in the East now moving in large numbers into predominantly Protestant areas of Western Germany.

The implications which they saw in the demand for "parents' rights" were more, however, than the Protestant and secular elements could accept. Some saw a threat to the long-established tradition of *Gemeinschaftschule* and the atmosphere of tolerance which they had promoted in such localities as Baden and Hamburg.[89] Others resented an attempt to interfere with local autonomy in this question and saw no reason why parents in Länder such as Bavaria should wish to impose their school pattern on parents of other Länder who were quite content that the Bavarians should have their own.[90] For others, it was a financial and administrative impossibility to provide denominational and non-denominational schools in every community.

Something should be said of the history of "parents' rights" as natural rights. . . . One might observe with some irony that "parents' rights" were never demanded in Church circles at the time when confessional elementary schools were obligatory. . . . If we took the principle seriously . . . then every father and mother individually could determine that their children should be trained in a certain way. That is impossible, because we cannot very well create special schools to cover every individual notion and whim.[91]

Finally, still others, of whom Dr. Heuss was one, saw the spread of confessional schools as tending to isolate national minorities. The Catholic expellee families who settled, as a great majority of them did, in Evangelical areas, would claim their own denominational schools. In these separate schools, children from the Sudetenland, Silesia, and Hungary would be segregated, whereas the most pressing national need was to secure their integration with their own generation in the homeland.[92]

CHAPTER VI

THE POLITICAL MATURITY OF THE WESTERN GERMAN PEOPLE: AN APPRAISAL

The course of German history in the past one hundred years has been such as to make it virtually impossible for historians to write about it with detachment. Outside Germany, the optimistic overconfidence that characterized writing about Germany in the first half of the century gave way in the second half to disillusionment and caustic historical indictments of the entire German people. In the heat of the second world war, these indictments could not but carry conviction for minds reeling at the horror of unprecedented and unspeakable crimes committed by Germans in the name of the German people.

Yet, can these wholesale indictments of the German people stand the test of reflection in cooler moments? For those who consider that there is both a unity underlying Western civilization,* and a presumptive collective moral and political responsibility among peoples who share in this heritage, the doubt may arise whether, if there is to be a general imputation of guilt to the Germans, we are not all in some way and to some degree implicated in this guilt. Others who reject such a presumption must ask themselves whether *they* are ready to accept responsibility for all the acts of the national states of which they are citizens—whether, for example, as Americans, Britons, or Frenchmen, they feel individually culpable for the many acts of omission and commission that stain the record of these peoples in their dealings with other peoples.

* Some may say, of Christendom.

While appalled at the wrongs that had been done by Germans to their own people and to their neighbors, the writer became increasingly dissatisfied in the postwar years with the view of recent German history that explained all in terms of a kind of recurring national conspiracy, into which, it was claimed, *all* Germans had more or less consciously entered to aggrandize the German nation at the expense of other peoples. Were future developments in Germany to lie under the suspicion of being but further episodes in the history of such a national conspiracy? Was there not evidence in German laws and institutions to show that men in Germany had labored before and might labor again for justice and peace between men and between nations? Granting that these Germans had been ineffective, confused, even that they had suffered a deplorable failure of nerve, was it just to disparage their motives and deny them the tragedy of their defeat? Could these Germans rise from their defeat and, at last, assert an enduring influence on the course of German history?

Prompted by the belief that periods of constitution-making and significant constitutional change provide an exceptional opportunity to gain insight into the moral and political condition of a people, the author undertook this study of the new institutions of Western Germany and the circumstances in which they developed to see whether it might shed light on these questions. In the author's opinion, it has done so.

From this point of view, the abstract merits of the Basic Law as a constitutional document are largely irrelevant. The Weimar constitution was and still is regarded by many experts as a model of constitution-making; yet it was subverted. What is relevant (and this the study impressively shows) is that the Basic Law is the product of a deliberate effort on the part of its framers to face the realities of German constitutional and political history and to devise provisions for a federal order, for parliamentary government, and for the rights of citizens in a free society, taking into account the needs and the strengths and weaknesses of the German people. Although it is too early to be entirely sure that the Parliamentary Council succeeded in this effort, for the time being it counts for much that the effort was made. The men of Bonn kept well clear both of the visionary idealism of Frankfurt and the pedantry of Weimar.

The drawing up of the Basic Law was a genuine act of representative democracy. All the interests and points of view of present-day Western Germany had their due representation in the Parliamentary Council. If the accounts of the Council's deliberations in the foregoing pages show nothing else, they show that every major provision in the Basic Law was the outcome of interplay between these varying views and interests in debate and negotiation. Unlike its Bismarckian and Weimar predecessors, the Bonn constitution is the product of many minds and wills, not of one or a few. Awkwardly elaborate though some may be, the compromises in which the Basic Law abounds constitute a hopeful sign for the future. They suggest that this constitution will endure, as others have endured elsewhere, because its provisions, although wholly satisfactory to none, are tolerable for all.

The Basic Law was written in a time of crises arising from the continuing inability of the Western German economy to provide for the basic needs of the people and from the deepening antagonism between Soviet Russia and the Western powers. It is greatly to the credit of the German representatives in Bonn that they kept their heads in these circumstances. Russian threats did not frighten them from taking measures in Western Germany to restore self-government and the orderly administrative processes necessary for reconstruction and recovery. Neither were they "stampeded" by the Western Allies into accepting laws and institutional arrangements that might have crippled the recovery efforts of the Western Germans and intensified political differences between them. In recent years, the Western German parties have managed to rise above the ugly mood of bitterness stirred up between them in the last days of the negotiations of the Basic Law and the first year of renewed parliamentary life. No doubt the successful operation of the constitutional provisions they themselves devised has helped in this.

All Western Europe and the rest of the free world have marveled at the pace and scale of the economic recovery of Western Germany since 1949. When due allowance is made for incidental circumstances that enabled Western Germany to make the best use of foreign economic assistance—absence of overseas commitments, a modest contribution to "occupation" or defense costs, the destruction of obsolescent capital equipment in the war—a large share of credit must go to the resourcefulness of German management and the industry of the German people.

The political "miracle" in Western Germany has received much less attention. The Bonn Republic is now half as old as the Weimar Republic. In its first seven years, not a single parliamentary crisis of the kind that plagued the Weimar Republic has occurred. Extremist parties of the right and left, intent upon exploiting minority discontents, have had short shrift. At the same time, far-reaching measures of reconstruction and reform have been undertaken. The Western German people have received and accommodated in their economic and social life millions of dispossessed persons and political refugees from outside their borders. Vital decisions on national defense and the relations of Western Germany to the European community— decisions concerning which there are deep divisions of German opinion—have been taken in an orderly manner. An intensive study of the operation of the constitution in the first two terms of the federal parliament has yet to be made, but it is already clear that the Basic Law has proved to be an effective working instrument of government.

The Germans are by no means yet "out of the woods." The reunification of their country and the ultimate settlement of their political and economic relations with the wider European and world communities in which they must live still lie before them. But there is good reason to expect that in the decisive part they are bound sooner or later to play in the solution of these problems, the Western Germans will act with a due sense of responsibility to their neighbors and of the need to keep the peace.

NOTES TO THE TEXT

ABBREVIATIONS USED IN CITATIONS

German Documents

References to stenographic reports of meetings of the Parliamentary Council and its committees are shown as follows:

Plen. 3s. 9/9/48, p. 32   *Plenum*, third sitting, September 9, 1949, p. 32 of stenographic report

GsA.   *Grundsatzausschuss* (Committee on Basic Rights)

Zus.A.   *Zuständigkeitsausschuss* (Committee on Division of Powers)

Org.A.   *Organisationsausschuss* (Committee on Organization)

FA   *Finanzausschuss* (Committee on Finance)

RA   *Rechtspflegeausschuss* (Committee on the Judiciary)

Wr.A.   *Wahlrechtsausschuss* (Committee on the Electoral Law)

HA 2R, p. 61   *Hauptausschuss* (Main Committee), second reading debate, p. 61 of stenographic report

Drs.   Parliamentary Council document

Allied Documents

CFM/47/M/48   Paper No. 48 of the Council of Foreign Ministers, Moscow meeting, 1947

203

CONL/M(45)7   Minutes of the seventh meeting of the Allied
                     Control Council, 1945

CORC/M(46)23   Minutes of the twenty-third meeting of the
                     Allied Control Council Co-ordinating Com-
                     mittee, 1946

ASEC(47)154   Paper No. 154 of the Allied Control Council
                     Secretariat, 1947

BIB/P(47)81/1   Paper No. 81 (first revision) of the Bipartite
                     Board, 1947

MGMP/M(48)3   Minutes of the third meeting of the Military
                     Governors and Ministers-President, 1948

Abbreviations of German public law journals (*"AOR," "NJW,"* etc.)
are explained in the Bibliography, p. 280.

CHAPTER I

1. Potsdam Agreement of August 2, 1945, Sec. III, par. 14. [11] (Note:
Numbers in brackets following footnote references refer to the numbered
entries in the "Documents" section of the Bibliography.)

2. *Ibid.*, Sec. III, par. 15 (c).

3. *Ibid.*, par. 9 (iv).

4. *Ibid.*, Sec. IV.

5. *Ibid.*, Sec. III, par. 19.

6. Lucius D. Clay, *Decision in Germany* (New York: Doubleday &
Co., 1950),.p. 120.

7. Statement by the Soviet Member of the Allied Control Council Co-
ordinating Committee (CORC/M[46]23, Minute 243, p. 2); Report of the
Allied Control Authority to the Council of Foreign Ministers of February
25, 1947 (ASEC[47]154, Sec. IV, Part 8). [13]

8. Statement of the French Member of the Allied Control Council of
October 1, 1945 (Annex B to CONL/M[45]7); of January 21, 1946 (Appendix A to CONL/M[46]2); of August 10, 1946 (Appendixes A and B
to CONL/M[46]21). [13]

9. Statement by the French Member of the Council of Foreign Ministers
of March 22, 1947 (CFM/47/M/48). [13]

10. Statement by the Soviet Member of the Council of Foreign Ministers
of March 17, 1947 (CFM/47/M/23). [13]

11. Statement by the U.S. Member of the Allied Control Council of July
20, 1946 (Appendix A to CONL/M[46]19). [13]

12. Statement of the French Member of the Allied Control Council of
August 10, 1946 (Appendix B to CONL/M[46]21). [13]

13. Statements by the Soviet Member of the Allied Control Council of

February 25, 1947 (Appendix A to CONL/M[47]5) and of August 30, 1947 (Appendix B to CONL/M[47]19). [13]

14. Report from the Deputies to the Council of Foreign Ministers of April 23, 1947 (CFM/47/M/148). [13]

15. Report of the U.S. Secretary of State on the Fourth Session of the Council of Foreign Ministers of April 28, 1947. [13]

16. Proposal of the U.K. Member to the Council of Foreign Ministers of March 31, 1947 (CFM/47/M/89). [13]

17. Proposal of the French Member of the Council of Foreign Ministers of March 21, 1947 (CFM/47/M/40 and 41). [13]

18. CFM/47/L/7, November 27, 1947. [13]

19. *Ibid.*

20. *Ibid.*

21. Clay, *op. cit.*, p. 397.

22. *Ibid.*, p. 399.

23. *Ibid.*, p. 398.

24. CFM/45/17 (London), September 13, 1945. [13]

25. Clay, *op. cit.*, pp. 413–14. (See also the text of his telegram to the United States Department of the Army, paraphrased on p. 414.)

26. *New York Times*, June 5, 1948.

27. *Manchester Guardian*, July 8, 1948.

28. *Die Welt*, July 1, 1948; *Flensburger Tageblatt*, July 5, 1948; *Der Tagesspiegel*, July 8, 1948; *Die Welt*, July 8, 1948.

29. Accompanying Memorandum and Comments on Documents I, II, and III by the Ministers-President, July 10, 1948. [2]

30. *New York Herald-Tribune*, July 10, 1948.

31. *New York Times*, July 10, 1948.

32. *Ibid.*, July 12, 1948.

33. Clay, *op. cit.*, p. 410.

34. Extract from minutes of the Meeting of the Military Governors and Ministers-President of July 26, 1948 (MGMP/M [48] 3). [14]

35. *Ibid.*

36. *Bericht über den Verfassungskonvent auf Herrenchiemsee von 10. bis 23. August 1948* (Munich: Richard Pflaum Verlag). (Hereinafter cited as "*Bericht.*")

37. *Bericht*, p. 18.

38. The record of the protracted negotiations between the Western governments is available only in part.

39. Accompanying Memorandum and Comments on Documents I, II, and III by the Ministers-President of July 10, 1948. [2]

CHAPTER II

1. K. C. Wheare, *Federal Government* (Oxford: Oxford University Press, 1953). For his views on the Weimar constitution, see p. 26.

2. Arnold Brecht, *Federalism and Regionalism in Germany: The Division of Prussia* (Oxford: Oxford University Press, 1945), p. 47. Those who are familiar with this admirable study will recognize how much of this chapter is derived from it.

3. Edmond Vermeil observed of the Weimar constitution: "Without according to this questionable term 'federal state' more significance than it possesses, it can be said on the whole that the Reich of 1919 is a federal state like the Bismarckian Reich . . . with the same form and the same purposes. However, within the structure there is a very clear displacement of the center of gravity from the States to the Reich" (*La Constitution de Weimar et le Principe de la Démocratie Allemande* [Strasbourg: l'Imprimerie Alsacienne, 1923], p. 280).

4. Darmstädter, *Bismarck and the Creation of the Second Reich*, p. 199.

5. Brecht, *op. cit.*, pp. 73 ff.

6. Heinrich Brüning, "Ein Brief," *Deutsche Rundschau*, LXX, No. 7 (July, 1947), 9.

7. Plen. 3s. 9/9/49, p. 41. (NOTE: Where dates of official German documents and enactments are given in summary form, the day of the month precedes the month and year, following official German usage.)

8. Schmid (SPD) Plen. 9s. 6/6/49, p. 171, cited and endorsed by von Mangoldt (Hermann von Mangoldt, *Das Bonner Grundgesetz* [*Kommentar*] [Berlin and Frankfurt a.M.: Verlag Franz Vahlen G.m.b.H., 1953], p. 32).

9. Chiemsee draft, pp. 18, 19, 61; GsA. 19s. 9/11/48, p. 25; and Drs. 215.

10. Proposed by Dr. Seebohm (DP) Plen. 9s. 6/5/49, p. 180.

11. Cf. Georg August Zinn, "Der Bund und die Länder," *AOR*, LXXV (1949), 295–96.

12. Plen. 2s. 8/9/48, p. 16.

13. Menzel (SPD), Plen. 3s. 9/9/48, pp. 29, 32, 34.

14. Schmid (SPD), Plen. 2s. 8/9/48, p. 16; Menzel, Plen. 3s. 9/9/48, p. 33.

15. Plen. 3s. 9/9/48, pp. 41–42.

16. Brockmann (Z), Plen. 3s. 9/9/48, pp. 55, 56; Plen. 7s. 21/10/48, p. 97; Frau Wessel (Z), HA 1R, p. 136.

17. Schwalber (CSU), Plen. 3s. 9/9/48, p. 36.

18. Seebohm (DP), Plen. 3s. 9/9/48, p. 49.

19. Schwalber, *loc. cit.*

20. *Ibid.*

21. Süsterhenn (CDU), Plen. 2s. 8/9/48, p. 21.

22. This summary is based on the Chiemsee report, pp. 37 ff.; the stenographic reports of the second, third, and seventh plenary sessions of the Parliamentary Council, and of the first to tenth sittings of the organization committee.

23. Katz (SPD), Org.A. 4s. 22/9/48, p. 8.

24. Org.A. 10s. 6/10/48, p. 46.

25. Letter from Dr. Walter Menzel to the author, 2/7/54.

26. Cf. von Mangoldt, *op. cit.*, p. 265.

27. E.g., Dr. Katz (SPD): "On the proposal made here today to establish a mixed Bundesrat and Senate, I can offer only my personal opinion: that this hybrid arrangement is a step backward, not forward. . . . In my view, a . . . confusion of functions would develop and, as so often with hybrids, the worst characteristics of each parent type would come out" (Plen. 7s. 21/10/48, p. 91).

28. Drs. 298.

29. Letter from Dr. Menzel to the author, 2/7/54.

30. Süsterhenn (CDU), HA 1R, p. 124.

31. Dehler (FDP), Plen. 7s. 21/10/48, p. 89; Becker (FDP), HA 1R, pp. 138, 140.

32. HA 1R, p. 129.

33. HA 1R, p. 141.

34. Plen. 10s. 8/5/49, p. 207.

35. For this and the following statements of party positions, see HA 1R, pp. 123 ff.

36. HA 2R, pp. 507–8.

37. HA 2R, p. 508.

38. A right of which it never made use.

39. HA 1R, p. 146.

40. In Art. 79(3).

41. HA 1R, p. 141.

42. Art. 105, *Bericht*, p. 77.

43. Arts. 70–75.

44. Resolution of the Weinheimer Tagung (*Bundesrecht und Bundesgesetzgebung: Bericht über die Weinheimer Tagung des Instituts zur Förderung öffentlicher Angelegenheiten in Frankfurt a.M. am 22. und 23. Oktober 1949* [Frankfurt a.M.: Wolfgang Metzner Verlag, 1950], p. 192). (Hereinafter cited as *"Bundesrecht und Bundesgesetzgebung."*)

45. Reinhold Mercker, "Zwei Jahre Rechtsprechung des Bundesverfassungsgerichts," *Bundesanzeiger*, No. 226 (November 24, 1953), p. 5.

46. HA 1R, p. 136.

46a. Chiemsee draft, Art. 34.

47. Third reading draft, Art. 36, par. 2.

48. Military Governors' Memorandum to the Parliamentary Council on the Basic Law, March 2, 1949. [14]

49. The Military Governors' Letter of Approval of the Basic Law of May 12, 1949, records in paragraph 7 a restrictive interpretation of this clause by which, the Germans are warned, the future Allied high commissioners would be guided. In fact, no German legislation was rejected by the high commissioners for transgressing the federal division of powers.

50. Cf. Professor Wilhelm Grewe's remarks at the Weinheimer Tagung, *Bundesrecht und Bundesgesetzgebung*, p. 31.

51. *Bundesrecht und Bundesgesetzgebung*, pp. 119, 176.

52. Art. 125.

53. *Bundesrecht und Bundesgesetzgebung*, pp. 97, 99.

54. Mercker, *op. cit.*, p. 5, and BVerfGE 2, 224.

55. Cf. Ringelmann in *Bundesrecht und Bundesgesetzgebung*, pp. 24–29.

56. E.g., Gerhard Anschütz, *Die Verfassung des Deutschen Reiches* (12th ed.; Berlin: Verlag von Georg Stilke, 1930), Commentary on Art. 107, n. 5C, p. 441.

57. Cf. Grewe, *Bundesrecht und Bundesgesetzgebung*, pp. 48–51; Mercker, *op. cit.*, p. 5; and BVerfGE 2, 221 ff.

58. HA 1R, pp. 79, 80.

59. HA 2R, pp. 361 ff.

60. Brecht, *op. cit.*, pp. 66, 67.

61. Plen. 3s. 9/9/48, p. 38.

62. Von Mangoldt, *op. cit.*, p. 464.

63. Hoch (SPD), HA 1R, p. 195; HA 2R, p. 447.

64. HA 1R, p. 196.

65. *Ibid.*, p. 196.

66. HA 4R, p. 756.

67. HA 2R, p. 447.

68. Von Mangoldt, *op. cit.*, p. 461.

69. *Ibid.*, p. 221.

70. *Ibid.*, p. 222; Friedrich Giese, *Grundgesetz für die Bundesrepublik Deutschland* (*Kommentar*) (Frankfurt a.M.: Verlag Kommentator G.m.b.H., 1953), p. 70.

71. Cf. Laforet (CDU) HA 2R, pp. 433 ff.

72. Menzel and Schmid (SPD) HA 2R, p. 433.

73. HA 2R, p. 434.

74. Giese, *op. cit.*, p. 138.

75. *Ibid.*, p. 138; Herrfahrdt's commentary on Art. 84 in Bodo Dennewitz *et al.*, *Kommentar zum Bonner Grundgesetz* (Hamburg: Hansischer Gildenverlag, Joachim Heitmann u. Co., 1950).

76. Menzel and Zinn (SPD) HA 2R, p. 438.

77. Laforet, HA 2R, pp. 436, 437.

78. For a documented account of the anomalies, inconsistencies, and discriminations of the American state tax structures, the effects of state fiscal practices on national economic and financial policy, and the wide differences between the states in expenditure on education, health services, social security, and other public services, see Alvin H. Hansen and Harvey S. Perloff, *State and Local Finance in the National Economy* (New York: W. W. Norton & Co., 1944), and Rolf A. Weil, "Federal Aid and Countercyclical Fiscal Policy" (unpublished Ph.D. dissertation, University of Chicago, 1950).

79. Plen. 7s. 21/10/48, p. 100.
80. Arts. 4 and 11.
81. Arts. 14 and 83.
82. Herman Höpker-Aschoff, "Das Finanz- und Steuersystem des Bonner Grundgesetzes," *AOR*, LXXV, No. 3, 313.
83. *Bericht*, pp. 34 and 66.
84. Höpker-Aschoff (FDP), Plen. 7s. 21/10/48, p. 98.
85. Höpker-Aschoff, in *Schriftlicher Bericht zum Entwurf des Grundgesetzes für die Bundesrepublik Deutschland erstattet von den Berichterstattern des Hauptausschusses für das Plenum* (Bonn: Bonner Universitäts-Buchdruckerei Gebr. Scheur G.m.b.H.), p. 54. (Hereinafter cited as *"Schriftlicher Bericht."*)
86. *Ibid.*, p. 54.
87. *Ibid.*, p. 55.
88. Par. 5, Memorandum of the Military Governors of March 2, 1949. [14]
88a. See part 6, p. 61, above.
89. FA 5s. 22/9/48, p. 26; 8s. 29/9/48, pp. 13, 34, 75.
90. Plen. 7s. 21/10/48, pp. 99 ff.
91. Ministerialdirektor Ringelmann (Bavaria) HA 2R, p. 525.
92. Höpker-Aschoff (FDP) and Greve (SPD) Plen. 7s. 21/10/48, pp. 99 ff.
93. Binder (CDU) Plen. 7s. 21/10/48, p. 103.
94. Ministerialdirektor Ringelmann (Bavaria) HA 1R, p. 160.
95. Binder, Plen. 7s. 21/10/48, p. 104.
96. Ringelmann, HA 1R, p. 161.
97. Military Governors' Aide Memoire of November 22, 1948. [14]
98. Military Governors' Memorandum of March 2, 1949. [14]
99. Höpker-Aschoff in *Schriftlicher Bericht*, p. 58.
100. *Ibid.*, p. 58.
101. Cf. speech by Dr. Gülich (SPD), former finance minister of Schleswig-Holstein, in debate on the constitutional amendment in the Bundestag, May 6, 1953; also leading article by Hans Herbert Goetz in *Frankfurter Allgemeine Zeitung*, "Leider keine echte Finanz-Reform," March 21, 1954.
102. Schlör (CSU) and Binder (CDU), HA 2R, pp. 511–18.
103. *Ibid.*
104. HA 2R, pp. 514, 515.
105. *Ibid.*, p. 515.
106. *Ibid.*, p. 518.
107. See pp. 85–86 above.   108. Art. 106(3).
109. Speech of the federal minister of finance to the Bundestag of January 28, 1953, on the federal budget for the fiscal year 1953; from Curt S. Goldsmith, *Report of the 247th and 248th Meetings of the Bundestag to the U.S. High Commissioner for Germany*, p. 6. [18]

109a. *Schriftlicher Bericht,* pp. 57, 58.

110. FA 2S, 16/9/48, remarks of the chairman, pp. 1–6, 17–24.

111. Curt S. Goldsmith, *Report of the 252nd and 253rd Meetings of the Bundestag to the United States High Commissioner for Germany,* p. 10. [18]

112. Communication of April 22, 1949, to the Parliamentary Council from the Military Governors, par. d., text quoted on p. 104.

113. See p. 85 above.

114. Clay, *op. cit.,* p. 419.

115. For text, see Appendix B.

116. See, for example, the *Christian Science Monitor,* March 7, 1949; *Manchester Guardian,* April 8, 1949.

117. Clay, *op. cit.,* pp. 408, 413–19.

118. Maier and Schmid (SPD), HA 28s. 18/12/48, p. 337.

119. HA 28s. 18/12/48, pp. 331 ff.

120. HA 29s. 5/1/49, pp. 342, 345.

121. See Clay, *op. cit.,* p. 226.

122. On the record, so far as it is available.

123. See the *Times* and the *Manchester Guardian,* issues of April 12, 1949.

124. See parts 6 and 8 of this chapter.

125. DENA report of March 15, 1949.

126. *Manchester Guardian,* March 12, 1949.

127. *Der Tagesspiegel,* March 6, 1949.

128. *New York Times,* March 31, 1949.

129. Clay, *op. cit.,* p. 425.

130. Resolution of the CDU/CSU faction of March 30, 1949. [14]

131. Resolution of the SPD faction of March 30, 1949. [14]

132. Clay, *op. cit.,* p. 432.

133. HA 4R, p. 735.

134. Menzel, *ibid.,* pp. 731, 736.

135. *Der Kurier,* April 8, 1949.

136. Interview, reported in *Der Telegraf,* April 6, 1949.

137. *Manchester Guardian,* April 13, 1949.

138. *Die Allgemeine Zeitung,* April 21, 1949.

139. Clay, *op. cit.,* p. 432.

140. *Ibid.,* p. 434.

141. *Ibid.,* pp. 431, 432.

142. Hans Schneider, "Fünf Jahre Grundgesetz," *NJW,* VII, No. 25 (June 24, 1954), 937–41.

143. Werner Weber, *Spannungen und Kräfte im Westdeutschen Verfassungssystem* (Stuttgart: Vorwerk, 1951); Schneider, *op. cit.*

CHAPTER III

1. Plen. 3s. 9/9/48, p. 40; see also Fritz Münch, *Die Bundesregierung* (Frankfurt a.M.: Alfred Metzner Verlag, 1954), pp. 82–90.

2. Gustav Stresemann, *Diaries, Letters and Papers*, ed. and trans. Eric Sutton (London: Macmillan & Co., 1940), III, 458 ff.

3. For a review of the use of special powers in the Weimar period, see Hans Schneider, *Das Ermächtigungsgesetz vom 24. März 1933: Bericht über das Zustandekommen und die Anwendung des Gesetzes* (Bonn: Bundeszentrale für Heimatdienst, 1955).

4. Agnes Headlam-Morley, *The New Democratic Constitutions of Europe* (Oxford: Oxford University Press, 1928), pp. 197, 211.

5. R. Redslob, *Die parlamentarische Regierung in ihrer wahren und in ihrer unechten Form* (Tübingen, 1918), pp. 5, 94.

6. Headlam-Morley, *op. cit.*, p. 214.

7. See Edward Dreher, "Das parlamentarische System des Bonner Grundgesetzes im Vergleich zur Weimarer Verfassung," *NJW* (1950), pp. 130–33.

8. Menzel (SPD) Plen. 3s. 9/9/48, p. 30; see also Süsterhenn (CDU) Plen. 2s. 8/9/48, p. 22; Dehler (FDP), HA 2R, p. 399; Carlo Schmid, "Regierung und Parlament," *RSW*, Vol. III (1951), p. 95.

9. Von Mangoldt, "Das Verhältnis von Staatschef und Regierung," in *Deutsche Landesreferate zum III. Internationalen Kongress für Rechtsvergleichung in London 1950* (Sonderveröffentlichung der *Zeitschrift für ausländisches und internationales Privatrecht*), p. 835.

10. Von Brentano (CDU), HA 3R, p. 639.

11. Becker (FDP), HA 2R, p. 396.

12. Dehler (FDP), Org.A. 5s. 23/9/48.

13. Dehler (FDP), HA 2R, p. 399.

14. Becker (FDP) HA 2R, p. 396.

15. Schmid (SPD) HA 2R, pp. 397, 400.

16. *Ibid.*, p. 397.

17. Katz (SPD), HA 3R, p. 638.

18. *Bericht*, p. 43, and p. 73, Art. 87.

19. Org.A. 7s. 29/9/48, pp. 25 ff.

20. HA 1R, pp. 42–43.

21. HA 1R, p. 42; HA 3R, p. 644.

22. Von Mangoldt, *Commentary*, p. 340.

23. Walter (CDU), HA 1R, pp. 41, 42.

24. See Org.A. 7th and 8th sittings.

25. This point is disputed in the public law literature. But see p. 133 above.

26. Süsterhenn (CDU), Plen. 2s 8/9/48, p. 26; Menzel (SPD), Plen. 3s. 9/9/48, p. 28.

27. Süsterhenn (CDU), Plen. 2s. 8/9/48, p. 22.
28. *Bericht*, p. 44.
29. Menzel (SPD), Plen. 3s. 9/9/48, p. 28.
30. Schmid (SPD), HA 1R, p. 45.
31. Dehler (FDP), von Brentano (CDU), HA 1R, pp. 44, 45.
32. *Geschäftsordnung des Deutschen Bundestages*, 6/12/51, Sec. 98, par. 2.
33. See Münch, *op. cit.*, p. 179.
34. See Von Mangoldt, *Commentary*, p. 359.
35. See p. 126.
36. HA 1R, p. 45; HA 2R, p. 415.
37. Menzel (SPD), Org.A. 14s. 14/10/48, pp. 43–45.
38. Art. 111 of the third reading draft.
39. E.g., Giese, *op. cit.*, p. 107; Hans Nawiasky, *Die Grundgedanken des Grundgesetzes* (Stuttgart and Cologne: W. Kohlhammer Verlag, 1950), pp. 90, 96 ff.
40. Von Mangoldt, *Commentary*, p. 345.
41. *Bericht*, p. 43.
42. See HA 2R, Laforet and others, pp. 410–12; Von Mangoldt, *Commentary*, p. 350.
43. Süsterhenn (CDU), Plen. 2s. 8/9/48, p. 25; Heuss (FDP), Plen. 3s. 9/9/48, p. 43.
44. See Art. 82.
45. *Gesetz über des Bundesverfassungsgericht*, 12/5/51, Sec. 97, par. 2.
46. Friedrich Glum, *Das parlamentarische Regierungssystem in Deutschland, Grossbritanien und Frankreich* (Munich and Berlin: C. H. Beck'sche Verlags Buchhandlung, 1950), pp. 334–38.
47. Schmid, *op. cit.*, pp. 95 ff.

CHAPTER IV

1. Frau Wessel (Z), HA 52s. 22/2/49, p. 692; Diederichs (SPD), Wr.A. 3s. 23/9/48, p. 31.
2. Diederichs (SPD), Plen. 7s. 21/10/48, pp. 104–12; Becker (FDP), Plen. 8s. 24/2/49, pp. 127, 128.
3. Heuss (FDP), Plen. 8s. 24/2/49, pp. 132 ff.
4. Kroll (CDU), Plen. 7s. 21/10/48, pp. 112–14.
5. Reichskanzler a.D. Luther, Wr.A. 7s. 5/8/48, p. 41.
6. Kroll (CDU), Wr.A. 3s. 23/9/48. p. 41.
7. At one stage they did propose a Bundestag of 350 members, 300 to be elected from single-member constituencies and 50 by proportional representation (Plen. 8s. 24/2/49, p. 153).
8. List of Resolutions adopted by the Conference of Ministers-President at Königstein on March 24, 1949. [14]

9. Communication of the military governors to representatives of the Parliamentary Council of April 14, 1949. [14]

10. Letter from military governors to the ministers-president of May 28, 1949. [14]

11. *Der Telegraf*, June 4, 1949.

12. Letter from Dr. Dehler (FDP) to Dr. Adenauer, reported by DPD on June 14, 1949.

13. *Der Morgen*, June 4, 1949.

14. *Manchester Guardian*, June 4, 1949.

15. *Der Tag*, June 4, 1949.

16. *Der Kurier*, June 4, 1949.

17. Letter of the ministers-president to the military governors of June 10, 1949. [14]

18. Letter of the military governors to the ministers-president of June 13, 1949. [14]

19. Maurice Duverger, *Political Parties: Their Organization and Activity in the Modern State* (London: Methuen, 1954), p. 241.

20. *Ibid.*, pp. 239–55.

21. *Ibid.*, p. 217.

22. *Ibid.*, p. 239.

23. *Ibid.*, p. 228.

24. See chap. ii, part 5.

CHAPTER V

1. R. MacIver, *Great Expressions of Human Rights* (New York: Harper & Bros., 1950), p. 137.

2. *The Constitution of the United States of America: Analysis and Interpretation*, Introduction by E. S. Corwin (Legislative Reference Service, Library of Congress [Washington, D.C., 1953]), p. 751.

3. *Barron v. Baltimore*, 7 Pet. 243 (1833).

4. *Chicago, B. and Q.R. Co. v. Chicago*, 166 U.S. 226 (1897).

5. *Gitlow v. New York*, 268 U.S. 652 (1925).

6. See also R. Carr, *Federal Protection of Civil Liberties* (Ithaca, N.Y.: Cornell University Press, 1947), pp. 5–14.

7. W. Ivor Jennings, *The Law and the Constitution* (London: University of London Press, 1948), p. 242.

8. Ernst Eckhardt, *Die Grundrechte vom Wiener Kongress bis zur Gegenwart* (Breslau: Verlag Mund H. Marcus, 1913), p. 85.

9. *Flugblätter aus der deutschen Nationalversammlung* (Herausg. v. Bernhardi).

10. Address, "Bürger und Bourgeois in Deutschen Staatsrecht," at Reichsgründungsfeier, January 19, 1933, in Smend, *Staatsrechtliche Abhandlungen und andere Aufsätze* (Berlin, 1955), pp. 309, 328.

11. Eckhardt, *op. cit.*, pp. 165–95.

12. Ernst Forsthoff, *Lehrbuch des Verwaltungsrechts* (Munich and Berlin: C. H. Beck'sche Verlags Buchhandlung, 1951), pp. 23 ff.

13. Walter Jellinek, *Verwaltungsrecht* (Berlin: Verlag von Julius Springer, 1928), pp. 80 ff.

14. Forsthoff, *op. cit.*, p. 30.

15. Jellinek, *op. cit.*, p. 412.

16. *Ibid.*, pp. 413 ff.

17. Richard Thoma, "Grundrechte und Polizeigewalt," in *Verwaltungsrechtliche Abhandlungen: Festgabe zur Feier des fünfzigjährigen Bestehens des Preussischen Oberverwaltungsgerichts 1875–1925* (Berlin: Carl Heymanns Verlag, 1925), p. 202.

18. Willibalt Apelt, *Geschichte der Weimarer Verfassung* (Munich: Biederstein Verlag, 1946), p. 107.

19. *Ibid.*, p. 108.

20. Anschütz, *Die Verfassung des Deutschen Reiches* (12th ed.; Berlin: Verlag von Georg Stilke, 1930), p. 480; Friedrich Giese, *Die Verfassung des Deutschen Reiches* (8th ed.; Berlin: Carl Heymanns Verlag, 1927), pp. 254, 255; Jellinek, *op. cit.*, p. 429; Apelt, *op. cit.*, pp. 312, 313.

21. Thoma, *op. cit.*, p. 202.

22. Apelt, *op. cit.*, pp. 339–44.

23. *Ibid.*, pp. 305, 306.

24. *Ibid.*, p. 343.

25. Plen. 2s. 8/9/48, p. 20.

26. Art. 1, Chiemsee draft.

27. GsA. 4s. 23/9/48.

28. CDU-DP-Z proposal, HA 2R, 18/1/49, pp. 545, 546.

29. Plen. 3s. 9/9/48, p. 44.

30. GsA. 4s. 23/9/48, pp. 5, 8.

31. GsA. 4s. 23/9/48, p. 5.

32. *Ibid.*, pp. 9, 17.

33. Schmid: "Die Würde, menschlichen Lebens wird vom Staate geschützt. Sie ist begründet in Rechten, die dem Menschen jedermann gegenüber Schutz gewähren"; Heuss: "Die Würde des menschlichen Wesens steht im Schutz der staatlichen Ordnung."

34. Art. 21, Chiemsee draft.

35. GsA. 4s. 23/9/48, p. 24.

36. *Ibid.*, p. 26.

37. See editorial committee's comment, Drs. 370.

38. See HA 4R, 5/5/49, p. 744.

39. The matters over which the constitutional court has jurisdiction are listed in Article 93.

40. See Süsterhenn (CDU), Plen. 2s. 8/9/48, p. 25; Menzel (SPD), Plen. 3s. 9/9/48, p. 32; HA 1R, pp. 271–72. The Communist delegation

opposed this arrangement, proposing instead the creation of a parliamentary committee to consider and decide upon issues involving the compatibility of legislation with the Basic Law.

41. Par. (e), Aide Memoire of the US/UK/French military governors of November 22, 1948.

42. Plen. 2s. 8/9/48, p. 4.

43. Menzel (SPD), Plen. 3s. 9/9/48, p. 32.

44. Plen. 2s. 8/9/48, p. 25.

45. It will be recalled that the United States Supreme Court, by overruling state particularism in the first decades of the last century, opened the way to the exercise of central power in the interest of national economic development.

46. RA 7s. 6/12/48, p. 45; HA 23s. 8/12/48, pp. 274, 275.

47. Willibalt Apelt, "Betrachtungen zum Bonner Grundgesetz," *NJW* (1949), pp. 481–85.

48. Hans Peter Ipsen, "Die Nachprüfung der Verfassungsmässigkeit von Gesetzen," in *Deutsche Landesreferate zum III: Internationalen Kongress für Rechtsvergleichung, in London, 1950* (Sonderveröffentlichung der *Zeitschrift für ausländisches und internationales Privatrecht*) (Berlin and Tübingen, 1950), pp. 791–818.

49. Willibalt Apelt, "Betrachtungen zum Bonner Grundgesetz," *NJW*, No. 13 (July 1, 1949), p. 482.

50. Art. 20.

51. Württemberg-Baden, Bavaria, Hesse, Bremen, Rhineland-Palatinate, Württemberg-Hohenzollern, and Baden.

52. The Hessian and Bremen constitutions schedule certain enterprises for transfer to public ownership.

53. Plen. 2s. 8/9/48, p. 4.

54. Plen. 3s. 9/9/48, p. 44.

55. Wolfgang Abendroth, "Zum Begriff des demokratischen und sozialen Rechtsstaates im Grundgesetz der Bundesrepublik Deutschland," in *Aus Geschichte und Politik: Festschrift zum 70. Geburtstag von Ludwig Bergsträsser* (Düsseldorf, 1954), pp. 291 ff.

56. See Zinn's remarks, GsA. 3s. 21/9/48, pp. 16, 17. Other German authorities have found the absence in the Basic Law of a code of social and economic rights its single most serious defect (see H. P. Ipsen, *Über das Grundgesetz* [Hamburg, 1950], pp. 14–17; also, Abendroth, *op. cit.*, pp. 291, 295).

57. GsA. 25s. 24/11/48, p. 80.

58. HA 1R, pp. 211 ff.

59. HA 1R, p. 215 (Eberhard).

60. GsA. 25s. 24/11/48, pp. 63 ff.

61. HA 1R, pp. 210–15.

62. HA 1R, p. 211.

63. HA 2R, p. 570.
64. HA 2R, p. 569.
65. Zinn, GsA. 6s. 5/10/48, pp. 61, 63.
66. GsA. 8s. 7/10/48, pp. 63–101.
67. GsA. 26s. 30/11/48, pp. 30 ff.
68. Drs. 370.
69. HA 2R, pp. 578–80.
70. Although, under the Weimar constitution, exceptions could be made by law.
71. GsA. 8s. 7/10/48, pp. 64 ff.
72. Plen. 9s. 6/5/49, p. 178.
73. Strauss (CDU), HA 1s. p. 216; Seebohm, Plen. 9s. 6/5/49, p. 179.
74. Schmid and Greve, HA 1s. p. 216.
75. They are, however, dealt with in the United Nations Declaration on Human Rights, Articles 16 and 26.
76. Menzel and Bergsträsser, GsA. 29s. 14/12/48, pp. 39–60.
77. Bergsträsser, HA 1R, p. 250.
78. HA 2R, p. 554.
79. Dehler, GsA. 26s. 30/11/48, p. 58.
80. Kaufmann, HA 1R, p. 208.
81. Frau Dr. Selbert, HA 1R, p. 206.
82. Subject to the transitional provision in Art. 117.
83. HA 2R, p. 538.
84. Frau Wessel, HA 2R, p. 549.
85. HA 2R, p. 552.
86. HA 1R, p. 241.
87. HA 3R, p. 615; Drs. 612.
88. Frau Dr. Weber (CDU), HA 2R, p. 556.
89. Bergsträsser (SPD), HA 1R, p. 248; Zimmerman (SPD), HA 1R, p. 252; Schönfelder (SPD), HA 2R, p. 555.
90. Ehlers (SPD), HA 2R, p. 556.
91. Schmid (SPD), HA 2R, p. 566.
92. Heuss (FDP), HA 1R, p. 295; Plen. 3s. 9/9/48, p. 45.

BASIC LAW FOR THE FEDERAL REPUBLIC OF GERMANY*

The Parliamentary Council, meeting in public session at Bonn am Rhein on 23 May 1949, noted that the Basic Law for the Federal Republic of Germany, which was adopted by the Parliamentary Council on 8 May 1949, was ratified in the week of 16–22 May 1949 by the legislatures of more than two-thirds of the participating German Länder.

By virtue of this fact the Parliamentary Council, represented by its Presidents, has engrossed and promulgated the Basic Law.

The Basic Law is hereby published in the Federal Gazette pursuant to Article 145, Section 3:

PREAMBLE

Conscious of its responsibility before God and Men, animated by the resolve to preserve its national and political unity and to serve the peace of the World as an equal partner in a united Europe, the German people,

in the Länder Baden, Bavaria, Bremen, Hamburg, Hesse, Lower Saxony, North Rhine-Westphalia, Rhineland-Palatinate, Schleswig-Holstein, Württemberg-Baden and Württemberg-Hohenzollern,

has enacted, by virtue of its constituent power, this Basic Law of the Federal Republic of Germany

to give a new order to political life for a transitional period.

It has also acted on behalf of those Germans to whom participation was denied.

* The German text is the official text of the Basic Law. This English text is the translation approved by the Allied high commission in Germany. Its inconsistencies of style and spelling have not been corrected.

The entire German people is called on to achieve by free self-determination the unity and freedom of Germany.

I. BASIC RIGHTS

Article 1

(1) The dignity of man is inviolable. To respect and protect it is the duty of all state authority.

(2) The German people therefore acknowledge inviolable and inalienable human rights to be the basis of every community, of peace and of justice in the world.

(3) The following basic rights bind the legislature, the executive and the judiciary as immediately enforceable law.

Article 2

(1) Everyone has the right to the free development of his personality insofar as he does not violate the rights of others or offend against the constitutional order or the moral code.

(2) Everyone has the right to life and to inviolability of his person. The freedom of the individual is inviolable. These rights may only be encroached upon pursuant to a law.

Article 3

(1) All persons are equal before the law.

(2) Men and women have equal rights.

(3) No one may be prejudiced or favored because of his sex, his parentage, his race, his language, his homeland and origin, his faith or his religious and political opinions.

Article 4

(1) Freedom of faith and of conscience, and freedom of creed, religious and secular (weltanschaulich), are inviolable.

(2) The undisturbed practice of religion is guaranteed.

(3) No one may be compelled against his conscience to render military service as an armed combatant. Details will be regulated by a federal law.

Article 5

(1) Everyone has the right freely to express and to publish his opinion by speech, writing and pictures and freely to inform himself from generally accessible sources. Freedom of the press and freedom of reporting by radio and motion pictures are guaranteed. There shall be no censorship.

(2) These rights are limited by the provisions of the general laws, the provisions of law for the protection of youth and by the right to inviolability of personal honor.

(3) Art and science, research and teaching are free. Freedom to teach does not absolve from loyalty to the constitution.

Article 6

(1) Marriage and family enjoy the special protection of the state.

(2) Care and upbringing of children are the natural right of the parents and a duty primarily incumbent on them. The state watches over performance of this duty.

(3) Separation of children from the family against the will of the persons entitled to bring them up may take place only pursuant to a law, if those so entitled fail in their duty or if the children are otherwise threatened with neglect.

(4) Every mother is entitled to the protection and care of the community.

(5) Illegitimate children are to be provided by legislation with the same opportunities for their physical and spiritual development and their position in society as are enjoyed by legitimate children.

Article 7

(1) The entire system of schools is under the supervision of the state.

(2) The persons entitled to bring up a child have the right to decide whether it shall receive religious instruction.

(3) Religious instruction forms part of the ordinary curriculum in state and municipal schools, except in non-denominational schools. Without prejudice to the state's right of supervision, religious instruction is given in accordance with the tenets of the religious communities. No teacher may be obliged to give religious instruction against his will.

(4) The right to establish private schools is guaranteed. Private schools, as a substitute for state or municipal schools, require the approval of the state and are subject to the laws of the Länder. This approval is to be given if the private schools are not inferior to the state or municipal schools in their educational aims, their facilities and the professional training of their teaching staff, and if a segregation of the pupils according to the means of the parents is not promoted. This approval is to be withheld if the economic and legal position of the teaching staff is not sufficiently assured.

(5) A private elementary school is to be admitted only if the educational authority finds that it serves a special pedagogic interest, or if, on application of the persons entitled to bring up the children, it is to be established as an inter-denominational school or as a denominational or ideological (weltanschaulich) school and a state or municipal elementary school of this type does not exist in the Gemeinde.

(6) Preparatory schools (Vorschulen) remain abolished.

Article 8

(1) All Germans have the right to assemble peacefully and unarmed without prior notification or permission.

(2) With regard to open-air meetings this right may be restricted by or pursuant to a law.

Article 9

(1) All Germans have the right to form associations and societies.

(2) Associations, the objects or activities of which conflict with the criminal laws or which are directed against the constitutional order or the concept of international understanding, are prohibited.

(3) The right to form associations to safeguard and improve working and economic conditions is guaranteed to everyone and to all trades and professions. Agreements which restrict or seek to hinder this right are null and void; measures directed to this end are illegal.

Article 10

Secrecy of the mail and secrecy of postal services and of telecommunications are inviolable. Restrictions may be ordered only pursuant to a law.

Article 11

(1) All Germans enjoy freedom of movement throughout the federal territory.

(2) This right may be restricted only by a law and only in cases in which an adequate basis of existence is lacking and special burdens would arise to the community as a result thereof or in which the restriction is necessary for the protection of youth against neglect, for combatting the danger of epidemics or for the prevention of crime.

Article 12

(1) All Germans have the right to choose their trade or profession, their place of work and their place of training. The practice of trades and professions may be regulated by law.

(2) No one may be compelled to perform a particular work except within the framework of a customary public duty to render services which applies generally and equally to all.

(3) Forced labor may be imposed only in the event that a person is deprived of his freedom by the sentence of a court.

Article 13

(1) The home is inviolable.

(2) Searches may be ordered only by a judge or, in the event of danger in delay, by other authorities as provided by law and may be carried out only in the form prescribed by law.

(3) Otherwise, this inviolability may be encroached upon or restricted only to avert a common danger or a mortal danger to individuals, and, pursuant to a law, to prevent imminent danger to public security and order, especially to alleviate the housing shortage, to combat the danger of epidemics or to protect endangered juveniles.

Article 14

(1) The rights of ownership and of inheritance are guaranteed. Their content and limits are determined by the laws.

(2) Property imposes duties. Its use should also serve the common weal.

(3) Expropriation is permitted only in the public interest. It may take place only by or pursuant to a law which provides for kind and extent of the compensation. The compensation is to be determined upon just consideration of the public interest and of the interests of the persons affected. In case of dispute regarding the amount of compensation, recourse may be had to the ordinary courts.

Article 15

Land, natural resources and means of production may for the purpose of socialisation be transferred into public ownership or other forms of publicly controlled economy by a law which provides for kind and extent of the compensation. In respect of such compensation Article 14, paragraph (3), sentences 3 and 4, apply correspondingly.

Article 16

(1) No one may be deprived of his German nationality. Loss of nationality may arise only pursuant to a law, and, against the will of the person affected, it may arise only if such person does not thereby become stateless.

(2) No German may be extradited to a foreign country. Persons persecuted for political reasons enjoy the right of asylum.

Article 17

Everyone has the right individually or jointly with others to address written requests or complaints to the competent authorities and to the representative assemblies.

Article 18

Whoever abuses freedom of expression of opinion, in particular freedom of the press (Article 5, paragraph (1)), freedom of teaching (Article 5, paragraph (3)), freedom of assembly (Article 8), freedom of association (Article 9), the secrecy of mail, the postal services and telecommunications (Article 10), the rights of ownership (Article 14), or the right of asylum (Article 16, paragraph (2)) in order to attack the free democratic basic order, forfeits these basic rights. The forfeiture and its extent are pronounced by the Federal Constitutional Court.

Article 19

(1) Whenever under this Basic Law a basic right may be restricted by or pursuant to a law, the law must apply generally and not solely to an individual case. Furthermore, the law must name the basic right and refer to the Article which protects it.

(2) In no case may a basic right be infringed upon in its essential content.

(3) The basic rights apply also to domestic juristic persons to the extent that their nature permits.

(4) Should any person's right be violated by public authority, recourse to the court shall be open to him. If no other court has jurisdiction, recourse shall be to the ordinary courts.

II. THE FEDERATION AND THE LÄNDER

Article 20

(1) The Federal Republic of Germany is a democratic and social federal state.

(2) All state authority emanates from the people. It is exercised by the people by means of elections and plebiscites and by separate legislative, executive and judicial agencies.

(3) Legislation is subject to the constitutional order; the executive and the judiciary are bound by the law.

Article 21

(1) The political parties participate in the forming of the political will of the people. They can be freely formed. Their internal organisation must conform to democratic principles. They must publicly account for the sources of their funds.

(2) Parties which, by reason of their aims or the behaviour of their members, seek to impair or destroy the free democratic basic order or to endanger the existence of the Federal Republic of Germany are unconstitutional. The Federal Constitutional Court decides on the question of unconstitutionality.

(3) Details will be regulated by federal legislation.

Article 22

The federal flag is black-red-gold.

Article 23

For the time being, this Basic Law applies in the territory of the Länder Baden, Bavaria, Bremen, Greater Berlin, Hamburg, Hesse,

Lower-Saxony, North Rhine-Westphalia, Rhineland-Palatinate, Schleswig-Holstein, Württemberg-Baden and Württemberg-Hohenzollern. In other parts of Germany it is to be put into force on their accession.

Article 24

(1) The Federation may, by legislation, transfer sovereign powers to international institutions.

(2) For the maintenance of peace, the Federation may join a system of mutual collective security; in doing so it will consent to limitations upon its sovereign powers apt to bring about and secure a peaceful and lasting order in Europe and among the nations of the world.

(3) For the settlement of disputes between nations, the Federation will accede to conventions concerning a general, comprehensive and obligatory system of international arbitration.

Article 25

The general rules of public international law form part of the federal law. They take precedence over the laws and directly create rights and duties for the inhabitants of the federal territory.

Article 26

(1) Activities tending and undertaken with the intent to disturb the peaceful relations between nations, especially the preparation of aggressive war, are unconstitutional. They are to be made a criminal offence.

(2) Weapons designed for warfare may be manufactured, transported or marketed only with permission of the Federal Government. Details will be regulated by a federal law.

Article 27

All German merchant vessels form one merchant fleet.

Article 28

(1) The constitutional order in the Länder must conform to the principles of republican, democratic and social government based on the rule of law which underlies this Basic Law. In the Länder, Kreise and Gemeinden the people must be represented by a body chosen in universal, direct, free, equal and secret elections. In the Gemeinden the Assembly of the Gemeinde may take the place of an elected body.

(2) The Gemeinden must be guaranteed the right to regulate on their own responsibility all the affairs of the local community within the limits set by law. The Gemeindeverbände also have the right of self-government in accordance with the law within the limits of the functions given them by law.

(3) The Federation guarantees that the constitutional order of the

Länder conforms to the basic rights and to the provisions of paragraphs (1) and (2).

Article 29

(1) The division of the federal territory into Länder is to be revised by a federal law with due regard to regional ties, historical and cultural connections, economic expediency and social structure. Such reorganisation should create Länder which by their size and capacity are able effectively to fulfil the functions incumbent upon them.

(2) In areas which upon the reorganisation of the Länder after 8 May, 1945, became, without plebiscite, part of another Land, a specific change in the decision then taken regarding the Land boundaries can be demanded by popular initiative within a year from the coming into force of the Basic Law. The popular initiative requires the assent of one-tenth of the population entitled to vote in Landtag elections. If the popular initiative receives such assent the Federal Government must include in the draft of the reorganisation law a provision determining to which Land the area concerned shall belong.

(3) After the law has been adopted, such part of the law as provides for the transfer of an area from one Land to another must be submitted to a referendum in that area. If a popular initiative received the assent required under paragraph (2), a referendum must in any event be held in the area concerned.

(4) Insofar as the law is rejected in at least one area, it must be re-introduced into the Bundestag. After it has been passed again, it requires to that extent acceptance by a referendum in the entire federal territory.

(5) In a referendum the majority of the votes cast decides.

(6) The procedure is established by a federal law. The reorganisation should be concluded before the expiration of three years after promulgation of the Basic Law and, should it become necessary as a result of the accession of another part of Germany, within two years after such accession.

(7) The procedure regarding any other change in the territory of the Länder is established by a federal law which requires the approval of the Bundesrat and of the majority of the members of the Bundestag.

Article 30

The exercise of the governmental powers and the discharge of the governmental functions is the concern of the Länder insofar as this Basic Law does not otherwise prescribe or permit.

Article 31

Federal law overrides Land law.

Article 32

(1) The conduct of relations with foreign states is the concern of the Federation.

(2) Before the conclusion of a treaty affecting the special interests of a Land, this Land must be consulted in sufficient time.

(3) Insofar as the Länder have power to legislate, they can, with the consent of the Federal Government, conclude treaties with foreign states.

Article 33

(1) Every German has in every Land the same civic (staatsbürgerlich) rights and duties.

(2) Every German has equal access to every public office according to his aptitude, qualifications and professional achievements.

(3) Enjoyment of civil and civic rights, admission to public offices and rights acquired in the public service are independent of religious denomination. No one may suffer disadvantage by reason of his adherence or non-adherence to a denomination, religious or secular.

(4) The exercise of state authority as a permanent function is as a rule to be entrusted to members of the public service whose service and loyalty are governed by public law.

(5) Rules of law concerning the public service shall be established with due regard to the traditional principles of the permanent civil service (Berufsbeamtentum).

Article 34

If any person, in the exercise of a public office entrusted to him, violates his official obligations to a third party, liability rests in principle on the state or the public authority which employs him. In the case of wilful intent or gross carelessness the right of recourse is reserved. In respect of the claim for compensation or the right of recourse, the jurisdiction of the ordinary courts may not be excluded.

Article 35

All federal and Land authorities render each other mutual legal and administrative assistance.

Article 36

Civil servants employed in the highest Federal authorities are to be drawn from all Länder in appropriate proportion. Persons employed in other Federal authorities should, as a rule, be drawn from the Land in which they serve.

Article 37

(1) If a Land fails to comply with its obligations of a federal character imposed by the Basic Law or another federal law, the Federal

Government may, with the consent of the Bundesrat, take the necessary measures to enforce such compliance by the Land by way of federal compulsion.

(2) To carry out such federal compulsion the Federal Government or any agent commissioned by it has the right to give instructions to all Länder and their authorities.

III. THE BUNDESTAG

Article 38

(1) The deputies to the German Bundestag are elected in universal, direct, free, equal and secret elections. They are representatives of the whole people, are not bound by orders and instructions and are subject only to their conscience.

(2) Anyone who has attained the age of twenty-one is entitled to vote; anyone who has attained the age of twenty-five is eligible for election.

(3) Details will be regulated by a federal law.

Article 39

(1) The Bundestag is elected for a four-year term. Its legislative term ends four years after its first meeting or in its dissolution. The new election takes place during the last three months of the term or within sixty days after dissolution.

(2) The Bundestag assembles within thirty days after the election, but not before the end of the term of the previous Bundestag.

(3) The Bundestag determines the termination and resumption of its meetings. The President of the Bundestag may convene it at an earlier date. He must do so if a third of the members, the Federal President or the Federal Chancellor so demand.

Article 40

(1) The Bundestag elects its President, his deputies and the secretaries. It draws up its Rules of Procedure.

(2) The President exercises the proprietary and police powers in the Bundestag building. No search or seizure may take place in the premises of the Bundestag without his permission.

Article 41

(1) The scrutiny of elections is the responsibility of the Bundestag. It also decides whether a representative has lost his seat in the Bundestag.

(2) Against the decision of the Bundestag an appeal lies to the Federal Constitutional Court.

(3) Details will be regulated by a federal law.

Article 42

(1) The meetings of the Bundestag are public. Upon a motion of one-tenth of its members, or upon a motion of the Federal Government, the public may, by a two-thirds majority, be excluded. The decision on the motion is taken at a meeting not open to the public.

(2) Decisions of the Bundestag require a majority of votes cast unless this Basic Law provides otherwise. For the elections to be made by the Bundestag the Rules of Procedure may provide exceptions.

(3) True and accurate reports of the public meetings of the Bundestag and of its committees shall not give rise to any liability.

Article 43

(1) The Bundestag and its committees may demand the presence of any member of the Federal Government.

(2) The members of the Bundesrat and of the Federal Government as well as persons commissioned by them have access to all meetings of the Bundestag and its committees. They must be heard at any time.

Article 44

(1) The Bundestag has the right, and upon the motion of one-fourth of its members the duty, to set up a committee of investigation to take the requisite evidence at a public hearing. The public may be excluded.

(2) The rules of criminal procedure shall apply mutatis mutandis to the taking of evidence. Secrecy of the mail, postal services and telecommunications remains unaffected.

(3) Courts and administrative authorities are bound to render legal and administrative assistance.

(4) The decisions of the committees of investigation are withdrawn from judicial consideration. The courts are free to evaluate and determine the facts which are the subject of the investigation.

Article 45

(1) The Bundestag appoints a Standing Committee, which has to safeguard the rights of the Bundestag as against the Federal Government in the interval between two legislative terms. The Standing Committee has also the powers of a committee of investigation.

(2) Wider powers, such as the right to legislate, to elect the Federal Chancellor, and to impeach the Federal President, are not within the province of the Standing Committee.

Article 46

(1) A deputy may not at any time be proceeded against in the courts or subjected to disciplinary action or otherwise called to account outside the Bundestag on account of a vote cast or an utterance made by him in the

Bundestag or one of its committees. This does not apply to defamatory insults.

(2) A deputy may be called to account or arrested for a punishable offence only by permission of the Bundestag, unless he is apprehended in the commission of the offence or during the course of the following day.

(3) The permission of the Bundestag is also necessary for any other restriction of the personal freedom of a deputy or for the initiation of proceedings against a deputy under Article 18.

(4) Any criminal proceedings and any proceedings under Article 18 against a deputy, every detention and every other restriction of his personal freedom shall be suspended upon request by the Bundestag.

Article 47

Deputies may refuse to give evidence concerning persons who have confided facts to them in their capacity as deputies or to whom they have confided facts in such capacity, as well as concerning these facts themselves. Insofar as this right to refuse to give evidence exists, no seizure of documents may take place.

Article 48

(1) Any person standing for election to the Bundestag is entitled to the leave necessary for his election campaign.

(2) No one may be prevented from accepting and exercising the office of deputy. He may not be dismissed from employment, with or without notice, on this ground.

(3) Deputies are entitled to compensation adequate to ensure their independence. They are entitled to the free use of all state-owned transport. Details will be regulated by a federal law.

Article 49

In respect of the members of the Presidium and of the Standing Committee as well as their principal deputies, Articles 46, 47 and paragraphs (2) and (3) of Article 48 apply also in the interval between two legislative terms.

IV. THE BUNDESRAT

Article 50

The Länder participate through the Bundesrat in the legislation and administration of the Federation.

Article 51

(1) The Bundesrat consists of members of the Länder Governments, which appoint and recall them. Other members of such Governments may act as substitutes.

(2) Each Land has at least three votes; Länder with more than two

million inhabitants have four, Länder with more than six million inhabitants five votes.

(3) Each Land may delegate as many members as it has votes. The votes of each Land may be cast only as a block vote and only by members present or their substitutes.

Article 52

(1) The Bundesrat elects its President for one year.

(2) The President convenes the Bundesrat. He must convene it if the members for at least two Länder or the Federal Government so demand.

(3) The Bundesrat takes its decisions by at least a majority of votes. It draws up its Rules of Procedure. Its meetings are public. The public may be excluded.

(4) Other members of, or persons commissioned by, Länder Governments may serve on the committees of the Bundesrat.

Article 53

The members of the Federal Government have the right, and on demand the duty, to take part in the meetings of the Bundesrat and of its committees. They must be heard at any time. The Bundesrat must be currently kept informed by the Federal Government of the conduct of affairs.

V. THE FEDERAL PRESIDENT

Article 54

(1) The Federal President is elected, without debate, by the Federal Convention (Bundesversammlung). Every German is eligible who is entitled to vote for the Bundestag and who has attained the age of forty.

(2) The term of office of the Federal President is five years. Re-election for a consecutive term is permitted only once.

(3) The Federal Convention consists of the members of the Bundestag and an equal number of members elected by the representative assemblies of the Länder according to the rules of proportional representation.

(4) The Federal Convention meets not later than thirty days before the expiration of the term of office of the Federal President or, in the case of premature termination, not later than thirty days after this date. It is convened by the President of the Bundestag.

(5) After expiration of the legislative term, the period specified in paragraph (4), first sentence, begins with the first meeting of the Bundestag.

(6) The person receiving the votes of the majority of the members of the Federal Convention is elected. If such majority is not obtained by any candidate in two ballots, the candidate who receives the largest number of votes in a further ballot is elected.

(7) Details will be regulated by a federal law.

Article 55

(1) The Federal President may not be a member of the Government or of the legislative body of the Federation or of a Land.

(2) The Federal President may not hold any other salaried office, nor engage in a trade, nor practise a profession, nor belong to the management or the board of directors of an enterprise carried on for profit.

Article 56

On assuming his office the Federal President takes the following oath before the assembled members of the Bundestag and the Bundesrat:

"I swear that I will dedicate my efforts to the well-being of the German people, enhance its benefits, ward harm from it, uphold and defend the Basic Law and the laws of the Federation, fulfil my duties conscientiously, and do justice to all. So help me God."

The oath may also be taken without religious affirmation.

Article 57

If the Federal President is prevented from exercising his powers, or if his office falls prematurely vacant, his powers will be exercised by the President of the Bundesrat.

Article 58

Orders and decrees of the Federal President require for their validity the countersignature of the Federal Chancellor or the functional Federal Minister. This does not apply to the appointment and dismissal of the Federal Chancellor, the dissolution of the Bundestag under Article 63 and the request under Article 69, paragraph (3).

Article 59

(1) The Federal President represents the Federation in its international relations. He concludes treaties with foreign states on behalf of the Federation. He accredits and receives envoys.

(2) Treaties which concern the political relations of the Federation or relate to matters of federal legislation require the approval or participation of the appropriate bodies competent for federal legislation in the form of a federal law. For administrative agreements the provisions concerning the federal administration apply mutatis mutandis.

Article 60

(1) The Federal President appoints and dismisses the federal judges and the federal civil servants, unless otherwise provided for by law.

(2) He exercises the power of pardon on behalf of the Federation in individual cases.

(3) He may delegate these powers to other authorities.

(4) Article 46, paragraphs (2) to (4), apply mutatis mutandis to the Federal President.

Article 61

(1) The Bundestag or the Bundesrat may impeach the Federal President before the Federal Constitutional Court for wilful violation of the Basic Law or any other federal law. The motion for impeachment must be supported by at least one-fourth of the members of the Bundestag or one-fourth of the votes of the Bundesrat. The decision to impeach requires a majority of two-thirds of the members of the Bundestag or of two-thirds of the votes of the Bundesrat. The prosecution is conducted by a person commissioned by the impeaching body.

(2) If the Federal Constitutional Court finds the Federal President guilty of a wilful violation of the Basic Law or of another federal law, it may declare him to have forfeited his office. After impeachment, it may issue an interim order preventing the Federal President from exercising the authority of his office.

VI. THE FEDERAL GOVERNMENT

Article 62

The Federal Government consists of the Federal Chancellor and the Federal Ministers.

Article 63

(1) The Federal Chancellor is elected, without debate, by the Bundestag on the proposal of the Federal President.

(2) The person obtaining the votes of the majority of the members of the Bundestag is elected. The person elected is to be appointed by the Federal President.

(3) If a person proposed is not elected, the Bundestag may elect within fourteen days of the ballot a Federal Chancellor by more than one half of its members.

(4) If there is no election within this period, a new ballot shall take place without delay, in which the person obtaining the largest number of votes is elected. If the person elected obtained the votes of the majority of the members of the Bundestag, the Federal President must appoint him within seven days of the election. If the person elected did not receive this majority, the Federal President must within seven days either appoint him or dissolve the Bundestag.

Article 64

(1) The Federal Ministers are appointed and dismissed by the Federal President upon the proposal of the Federal Chancellor.

(2) The Federal Chancellor and the Federal Ministers, on assuming office, take before the Bundestag the oath provided in Article 56.

Article 65

The Federal Chancellor determines, and is responsible for, general policy. Within the limits of this general policy, each Federal Minister conducts the business of his department independently and on his own responsibility. The Federal Government decides on differences of opinion between the Federal Ministers. The Federal Chancellor conducts the business of the Federal Government in accordance with Rules of Procedure adopted by it and approved by the Federal President.

Article 66

The Federal Chancellor and the Federal Ministers may not hold any other salaried office, nor engage in a trade, nor practise a profession, nor belong to the management or, without approval of the Bundestag, to the board of directors of an enterprise carried on for profit.

Article 67

(1) The Bundestag can express its lack of confidence in the Federal Chancellor only by electing a successor by the majority of its members and by requesting the Federal President to dismiss the Federal Chancellor. The Federal President must comply with the request and appoint the person elected.

(2) Forty-eight hours must elapse between the motion and the election.

Article 68

(1) If a motion of the Federal Chancellor for a vote of confidence is not assented to by the majority of the members of the Bundestag, the Federal President may, upon the proposal of the Federal Chancellor, dissolve the Bundestag within twenty-one days. The right to dissolve lapses as soon as the Bundestag by the majority of its members elects another Federal Chancellor.

(2) Forty-eight hours must elapse between the motion and the vote thereon.

Article 69

(1) The Federal Chancellor appoints a Federal Minister as his deputy.

(2) The tenure of office of the Federal Chancellor or a Federal Minister ends in any event on the meeting of a new Bundestag; the tenure of office of a Federal Minister ends also on any other termination of the tenure of office of the Federal Chancellor.

(3) At the request of the Federal President the Federal Chancellor, or at the request of the Federal Chancellor or of the Federal President

a Federal Minister, is bound to continue to transact the business of his office until the appointment of a successor.

VII. LEGISLATIVE POWERS OF THE FEDERATION

Article 70

(1) The Länder have the power to legislate insofar as this Basic Law does not confer legislative powers on the Federation.

(2) The division of competence between the Federation and the Länder is determined by the provisions of this Basic Law concerning exclusive and concurrent legislative powers.

Article 71

On matters within the exclusive legislative powers of the Federation the Länder have authority to legislate only if, and to the extent that, a federal law so authorises them.

Article 72

(1) On matters within the concurrent legislative powers the Länder have authority to legislate as long as, and to the extent that, the Federation does not use its legislative power.

(2) The Federation has the right to legislate on these matters to the extent that a need for a federal rule exists because

1. a matter cannot be effectively dealt with by the legislation of individual Länder, or
2. dealing with a matter by a Land law might prejudice the interests of other Länder or of the entire community, or
3. the maintenance of legal or economic unity, especially the maintenance of uniformity of living conditions beyond the territory of a Land, necessitates it.

Article 73

The Federation has the exclusive power to legislate on:—

1. foreign affairs;
2. citizenship in the Federation;
3. freedom of movement, passports, immigration and emigration, and extradition;
4. currency, money and coinage, weights and measures, as well as computation and time;
5. the unity of the territory as regards customs and commerce, commercial and navigation agreements, the freedom of traffic in goods, and the exchanges of goods and payments with foreign countries, including customs and frontier control;
6. federal railroads and air traffic;

7. postal and telecommunication services;
8. the legal status of persons employed by the Federation and by the corporate bodies of federal public law;
9. industrial property rights, coyprights and publication rights;
10. cooperation of the Federation and the Länder in matters of criminal police and of protection of the constitution, establishment of a federal office of the criminal police, as well as international prevention of crime;
11. statistics for federal purposes.

Article 74

Concurrent legislative powers extend to the following matters:—

1. civil law, criminal law and execution of sentences, the constitution of the courts, the procedure of the courts, the legal profession, notaries and legal advice (Rechtsberatung);
2. registration of births, deaths, and marriages;
3. the law of association and assembly;
4. the law relating to the transient and permanent admission of aliens;
5. the protection of German cultural treasures against removal abroad;
6. the affairs of refugees and expellees;
7. public relief;
8. citizenship in the Länder;
9. war damage and reparation;
10. benefits to war disabled persons and to dependents of those killed in the war, assistance of former prisoners of war, and care of war graves;
11. the law relating to economic matters (mining, industry, supply of power, crafts, trades, commerce, banking and stock exchanges, private insurance);
12. labor law, including labor relations, protection of workers, employment exchanges and agencies, as well as social insurance, including unemployment insurance;
13. the promotion of scientific research;
14. the law regarding expropriation, to the extent that matters enumerated in Articles 73 and 74 are concerned;
15. transfer of land, natural resources and means of production into public ownership or other forms of publicly controlled economy;
16. prevention of the abuse of economic power;
17. promotion of agricultural and forest production, safeguarding of the supply of food, the import and export of agricultural and forest products, deep sea and coastal fishing, and preservation of the coasts;
18. dealings in real estate, land law and matters concerning agricultural leases, housing, settlements and homesteads;
19. measures against epidemic and infectious diseases of humans and

animals, admission to medical and other professions and practices in the field of healing, traffic in drugs, medicines, narcotics and poisons;

20. protection with regard to traffic in food and stimulants as well as in necessities of life, in fodder, in agricultural and forest seeds and seedlings, and protection of trees and plants against diseases and pests;

21. ocean and coastal shipping as well as aids to navigation, inland shipping, meteorological services, sea waterways and inland waterways used for general traffic;

22. road traffic, motor transport, and construction and maintenance of long distance highways;

23. railroads other than federal railroads, except mountain railroads.

Article 75

Subject to the conditions of Article 72 the Federation has the right to enact general rules concerning:

1. the legal status of persons in the public service of the Länder, Gemeinden and other corporate bodies of public law;

2. the general rules of law concerning the status of the press and motion pictures;

3. hunting, protection of nature and care of the countryside;

4. land distribution, regional planning and water conservation;

5. matters relating to registration (Meldewesen) and identity cards.

Article 76

(1) Bills are introduced in the Bundestag by the Federal Government, by members of the Bundestag or by the Bundesrat.

(2) Bills of the Federal Government are to be submitted first to the Bundesrat. The Bundesrat is entitled to state its position on these bills within three weeks.

(3) Bills of the Bundesrat are to be submitted to the Bundestag by the Federal Government. In doing so the Federal Government must state its own views.

Article 77

(1) Federal laws are adopted by the Bundestag. Upon their adoption, they shall, without delay, be transmitted to the Bundesrat by the President of the Bundestag.

(2) The Bundesrat may, within two weeks of the receipt of the adopted bill, demand that a committee for joint consideration of bills, composed of members of the Bundestag and the Bundesrat, be convened. The composition and the procedure of this committee are regulated by Rules of Procedure agreed upon by the Bundestag and requiring the approval of the Bundesrat. The members of the Bundesrat on this com-

mittee are not bound by instructions. If the approval of the Bundesrat is required for a law, the demand for convening of this committee can also be made by the Bundestag or the Federal Government. Should the committee propose any amendment to the adopted bill, the Bundestag must again vote on the bill.

(3) Insofar as the approval of the Bundesrat is not required for a law, the Bundesrat may, if the proceedings under paragraph (2) are completed, enter a protest within one week against a law passed by the Bundestag. This period begins, in the case of paragraph (2), last sentence, on the receipt of the bill as readopted by the Bundestag, in all other cases, on the conclusion of the proceedings of the committee provided for in paragraph (2).

(4) If the protest is supported by a majority of the votes of the Bundesrat, it can be rejected by decision of the majority of the members of the Bundestag. If the Bundesrat adopted the protest by a majority of at least two-thirds of its votes, the rejection by the Bundestag requires a majority of two-thirds, including at least the majority of the members of the Bundestag.

Article 78

A law adopted by the Bundestag is deemed to have been passed if the Bundesrat approves it, does not make a demand pursuant to Article 77, paragraph (2), does not enter a protest within the time limited by Article 77, paragraph (3), or withdraws such protest, or if the protest is overridden by the Bundestag.

Article 79

(1) The Basic Law can be amended only by a law which expressly amends or supplements the text thereof.

(2) Such a law requires the affirmative vote of two-thirds of the members of the Bundestag and two-thirds of the votes of the Bundesrat.

(3) An amendment of this Basic Law affecting the division of the Federation into Länder, the participation in principle of the Länder in legislation or the basic principles laid down in Articles 1 and 20 is inadmissible.

Article 80

(1) The Federal Government, a Federal Minister or the Land Governments may be authorized by a law to issue ordinances having the force of law (Rechtsverordnungen). The content, purpose and scope of the powers conferred must be set forth in the law. The source of authority must be stated in the ordinance. If a law provides that a power may be further delegated, an ordinance having the force of law is necessary in order to delegate the power.

(2) The approval of the Bundesrat is required, unless otherwise provided by federal legislation, for ordinances having the force of law issued by the Federal Government or a Federal Minister concerning basic

rules for the use of facilities of the federal railroads and of postal and telecommunication services, or charges therefor, or concerning the construction and operation of railroads, as well as for ordinances having the force of law issued on the basis of such federal laws as require the approval of the Bundesrat or as executed by the Länder as agents of the Federation or as their own matters.

Article 81

(1) Should in the circumstances of Article 68 the Bundestag not be dissolved, the Federal President may, at the request of the Federal Government and with the consent of the Bundesrat, declare a state of legislative emergency with respect to a bill, if the Bundestag rejects the bill although the Federal Government has declared it to be urgent. The same applies if a bill has been rejected although the Federal Chancellor had combined with it the motion under Article 68.

(2) If, after a state of legislative emergency has been declared, the Bundestag again rejects the bill or adopts it in a version declared to be unacceptable to the Federal Government, the bill is deemed to have been passed insofar as the Bundesrat approves it. The same applies if the bill is not adopted by the Bundestag within four weeks of its reintroduction.

(3) During the term of office of a Federal Chancellor, any other bill rejected by the Bundestag can be passed in accordance with paragraphs (1) and (2) within a period of six months after the first declaration of a state of legislative emergency. After expiration of this period, a further declaration of a state of legislative emergency is inadmissible during the term of office of the same Federal Chancellor.

(4) The Basic Law may not be amended nor be repealed nor be suspended in whole or in part by a law enacted pursuant to paragraph (2).

Article 82

(1) Laws passed in accordance with the provisions of this Basic Law will, after countersignature, be signed by the Federal President and promulgated in the Federal Gazette. Ordinances having the force of law will be signed by the agency which issues them, and, unless otherwise provided by law, will be promulgated in the Federal Gazette.

(2) Every law and every ordinance having the force of law should specify its effective date. In the absence of such a provision, it becomes effective on the fourteenth day after the end of the day on which the Federal Gazette was published.

VIII. THE EXECUTION OF FEDERAL LAWS AND THE
FEDERAL ADMINISTRATION

Article 83

The Länder execute the Federal laws as matters of their own concern insofar as this Basic Law does not otherwise provide or permit.

Article 84

(1) If the Länder execute the Federal laws as matters of their own concern, they provide for the establishment of administrative procedures insofar as Federal laws approved by the Bundesrat do not otherwise provide.

(2) The Federal Government may, with the consent of the Bundesrat, issue general administrative rules.

(3) The Federal Government exercises supervision to ensure that the Länder execute the federal laws in accordance with applicable law. For this purpose the Federal Government may send commissioners to the highest Land authorities and, with their consent or, if this consent is refused, with the consent of the Bundesrat, also to subordinate authorities.

(4) Should any shortcomings which the Federal Government has found to exist in the execution of federal laws in the Länder not be corrected, the Bundesrat decides, on the application of the Federal Government or the Land, whether the Land has infringed the law. The decision of the Bundesrat may be challenged in the Federal Constitutional Court.

(5) For the execution of federal laws, the Federal Government may, by federal law requiring the approval of the Bundesrat, be authorised to issue individual instructions for particular cases. They are to be addressed to the highest Land authorities unless the Federal Government considers the matter urgent.

Article 85

(1) Where the Länder execute federal laws as agents of the Federation, the establishment of the administrative agencies remains the concern of the Länder insofar as federal laws approved by the Bundesrat do not otherwise provide.

(2) The Federal Government may, with the consent of the Bundesrat, issue general administrative rules. It may regulate the uniform training of civil servants and government employees. The heads of administrative agencies at intermediate level shall be appointed with its agreement.

(3) The Land authorities are subject to the instructions of the appropriate highest federal authorities. The instructions are to be addressed to the highest Land authorities unless the Federal Government considers the matter urgent. Execution of the instructions is to be ensured by the highest Land authorities.

(4) Federal supervision extends to the conformity with law and appropriateness of the execution. The Federal Government may, for this purpose, require the submission of reports and documents and send commissioners to all authorities.

Article 86

Where the Federation executes laws by federal agencies or by corporate or other bodies of federal public law, the Federal Government issues, insofar as the law contains no special provision, the general administrative rules. It provides for the establishment of administrative agencies insofar as the law does not otherwise provide.

Article 87

(1) The foreign service, the federal finance administration, the federal railroads, the federal postal service and, in accordance with the provisions of Article 89, the administration of the federal waterways and of shipping are conducted as matters of federal administration with their own subordinate administrative structure. Federal frontier control authorities and central offices for police information and communications, for the compilation of data for the purpose of protecting the Constitution and for the criminal police may be established by federal legislation.

(2) Social insurance institutions whose sphere of competence extends beyond the territory of one Land are conducted as corporate bodies of federal public law.

(3) In addition, independent federal superior administrative agencies and corporate and other bodies of federal public law can be established by federal law for matters on which the Federation has the power to legislate. If new functions arise for the Federation in matters on which it has the power to legislate, federal administrative agencies at intermediate and lower level can be established, in case of urgent need, with the consent of the Bundesrat and of the majority of the members of the Bundestag.

Article 88

The Federation establishes a note-issuing and currency bank as the federal bank.

Article 89

(1) The Federation is the owner of the former Reich waterways.

(2) The Federation administers the federal waterways through its own agencies. It exercises the public functions relating to inland shipping which extend beyond the territory of one Land, and those relating to maritime shipping which are conferred on it by law. Upon request, the Federation may transfer the administration of federal waterways, insofar as they lie within the territory of one Land, to this Land as its agent. If a waterway touches the territories of several Länder, the Federation may give the mandate to the Land designated by the Länder concerned.

(3) In the administration, development and new construction of

waterways, the needs of soil cultivation and of regulating water supply are to be safeguarded in agreement with the Länder.

Article 90

(1) The Federation is the owner of the former Reichsautobahnen (motor highways) and Reich highways.

(2) The Länder, or such self-governing corporate bodies as are competent under Land law, administer as agents of the Federation the federal Autobahnen and other federal highways used for long-distance traffic.

(3) At the request of a Land, the Federation may take under direct federal administration federal Autobahnen and other federal highways used for long-distance traffic, insofar as they lie within the territory of that Land.

Article 91

(1) In order to avert any imminent danger to the existence of the free democratic basic order of the Federation or of a Land, a Land may request the services of the police forces of other Länder.

(2) If the Land in which the danger is imminent is not itself willing or able to fight the danger, the Federal Government may place the police in that Land and the police forces of other Länder under its own instructions. The order for this is to be rescinded after the danger is past, or else at any time on the demand of the Bundesrat.

IX. THE ADMINISTRATION OF JUSTICE

Article 92

The judicial authority is vested in the judges; it is exercised by the Federal Constitutional Court, by the Supreme Federal Court, by the federal courts provided for in this Basic Law and by the courts of the Länder.

Article 93

(1) The Federal Constitutional Court decides: —

1. on the interpretation of this Basic Law in the event of disputes concerning the extent of the rights and duties of a supreme federal authority or of other parties concerned who have been endowed with independent rights by this Basic Law or by Rules of Procedure of a supreme federal authority;

2. in case of differences of opinion or doubts on the formal and material compatibility of federal law or Land law with this Basic Law, or on the compatibility of Land law with other federal law, at the request of the Federal Government, of a Land Government or of one-third of the Bundestag members;

3. in case of differences of opinion on the rights and duties of the Fed-

eration and the Länder, particularly in the execution of federal law by the Länder and in the exercise of federal supervision;

4. on other disputes of public law between the Federation and the Länder, between different Länder or within a Land, unless recourse to another court exists;

5. in the other cases provided for in this Basic Law.

(2) The Federal Constitutional Court shall also act in such cases as are otherwise assigned to it by federal law.

Article 94

(1) The Federal Constitutional Court consists of federal judges and other members. Half of the members of the Federal Constitutional Court are elected by the Bundestag and half by the Bundesrat. They may not belong to the Bundestag, the Bundesrat, the Federal Government or the corresponding bodies of a Land.

(2) Its constitution and procedure will be regulated by a federal law, which will specify in what cases its decisions shall have the force of law.

Article 95

(1) To preserve the uniformity of application of federal law a Supreme Federal Court will be established.

(2) The Supreme Federal Court decides cases in which the decision is of fundamental importance for the uniformity of the administration of justice by the higher federal courts.

(3) The judges of the Supreme Federal Court are selected jointly by the Federal Minister of Justice and a committee for the selection of judges consisting of the Land Ministers of Justice and an equal number of members elected by the Bundestag.

(4) In other respects, the constitution of the Supreme Federal Court and its procedure will be regulated by federal legislation.

Article 96

(1) Higher federal courts are to be established for the fields of ordinary, administrative, finance, labor and social jurisdiction.

(2) Article 95, paragraph (3), applies to the judges of the higher federal courts, provided that the Ministers competent for the particular matter take the place of the Federal Minister of Justice and the Land Ministers of Justice. The terms of service of these judges are to be regulated by a special federal law.

(3) The Federation may establish federal disciplinary courts for disciplinary proceedings against federal civil servants and federal judges.

Article 97

(1) The judges are independent and subject only to the law.

(2) Judges appointed permanently on a full time basis to an estab-

lished post can, against their will, be dismissed, or permanently or temporarily suspended from office, or transferred to other employment, or retired before expiration of their term of office only under authority of a judicial decision and only on grounds and in the form provided for by law. Legislation may set age limits for the retirement of judges appointed for life. In the event of changes in the structure of the courts or their areas of jurisdiction, judges may be transferred to another court or removed from their office, provided they retain their full salary.

Article 98

(1) The legal status of the federal judges is to be regulated by a special federal law.

(2) If a federal judge, in his official capacity or unofficially, infringes upon the principles of the Basic Law or the constitutional order of a Land, the Federal Constitutional Court may decide by a two-thirds majority, upon the request of the Bundestag, that the judge be transferred to another office or placed on the retired list. In a case of an intentional infringement, his dismissal may be ordered.

(3) The legal status of the judges in the Länder is to be regulated by special Land laws. The Federation may enact general rules.

(4) The Länder may provide that the Land Minister of Justice together with a committee for the selection of judges shall decide on the appointment of judges in the Länder.

(5) The Länder may, in respect to Land judges, enact provisions corresponding with paragraph (2). Existing Land constitutional law remains unaffected. The decision in a case of impeachment of a judge rests with the Federal Constitutional Court.

Article 99

The decision on constitutional disputes within a Land may be assigned by a Land law to the Federal Constitutional Court, and the decision of last instance in matters involving the application of Land law, to the higher federal courts.

Article 100

(1) If a court considers unconstitutional a law, the validity of which is relevant to its decision, the proceedings are to be stayed, and a decision is to be obtained from the Land court competent for constitutional disputes if the matter concerns the violation of the Constitution of a Land, or from the Federal Constitutional Court if the matter concerns a violation of the Basic Law. This also applies if the matter concerns the violation of this Basic Law by Land law or the incompatibility of a Land law with a Federal law.

(2) If, in the course of litigation, doubt exists whether a rule of public international law forms part of the federal law and whether it directly

creates rights and duties for the individual (Article 25), the court has to obtain the decision of the Federal Constitutional Court.

(3) If the constitutional court of a Land, in interpreting the Basic Law, intends to deviate from a decision of the Federal Constitutional Court or of the constitutional court of another Land, it must obtain the decision of the Federal Constitutional Court. If, in interpreting other federal law, it intends to deviate from the decision of the Supreme Federal Court or a higher federal court, it must obtain the decision of the Supreme Federal Court.

Article 101

(1) Extraordinary courts are inadmissible. No one may be removed from the jurisdiction of his lawful judge.

(2) Courts for special fields may be established only by a law.

Article 102

Capital punishment is abolished.

Article 103

(1) In the courts everyone is entitled to a hearing in accordance with the law.

(2) An act can be punished only if it was a criminal offence by law before the act was committed.

(3) No one may be punished for the same act more than once in pursuance of the general criminal laws.

Article 104

(1) The freedom of the individual may be restricted only on the basis of a formal law and only with due regard to the forms prescribed therein. Detained persons may be subjected neither to mental nor to physical ill-treatment.

(2) Only judges may decide on the admissibility or extension of a deprivation of liberty. Where such deprivation is not based on the order of a judge, a judicial decision must be obtained without delay. The police may hold no one on their own authority in their own custody longer than the end of the day after the arrest. Details shall be regulated by legislation.

(3) Any person provisionally detained on suspicion of having committed a punishable offence must be brought before a judge at the latest on the day following the arrest. The judge shall inform him of the reasons for the detention, examine him and give him an opportunity to raise objections. The judge must, without delay, either issue a warrant of arrest setting forth the reasons therefor or order the release from detention.

(4) A relative of the person detained or a person enjoying his con-

fidence must be notified without delay of any judicial decision ordering or extending a deprivation of liberty.

X. FINANCE

Article 105

(1) The Federation has the exclusive power to legislate on customs and fiscal monopolies.

(2) The Federation has concurrent power to legislate on:

1. excise taxes and taxes on transactions, with the exception of taxes with localised application, in particular of the taxes on the acquisition of real estate, on increments in value, and for fire protection;

2. taxes on income, on property, on inheritances and on donations;

3. taxes on real estate and businesses (Realsteuern), with exception of the fixing of the tax rates,

if it claims the taxes in whole or in part to cover federal expenditure or if the conditions laid down in Article 72, paragraph (2), exist.

(3) Federal laws relating to taxes the yield of which accrues in whole or in part to the Länder or the Gemeinden (Gemeindeverbände) require the approval of the Bundesrat.

Article 106

(1) Customs duties, the yield of monopolies, the excise taxes with the exception of the beer tax, the transportation tax, the turnover tax and capital levies for non-recurrent purposes accrue to the Federation.

(2) The beer tax, the taxes on transactions with the exception of the transportation tax and turnover tax, the income and corporation taxes, the property tax, the inheritance tax, the taxes on real estate and on businesses (Realsteuern), and the taxes with localized application accrue to the Länder and, as provided by Land legislation, to the Gemeinden (Gemeindeverbände).

(3) The Federation may, by a federal law which requires the approval of the Bundesrat, claim a part of the income and corporation taxes to cover its expenditures not covered by other revenues in particular to cover grants which are to be made to Länder to meet expenditures in the fields of education, public health and welfare.

(4) In order to secure the financial capacity also of the Länder with low tax revenues and to equalise among the Länder a differing burden of expenditure, the Federation may grant subsidies and take the funds for these from specified taxes accruing to the Länder. A federal law which requires the approval of the Bundesrat determines which taxes will be utilised for this purpose, and in what amounts and on what basis the subsidies will be distributed among the Länder entitled to equalization; the subsidies are to be remitted direct to the Länder.

Article 107

The final distribution, as between the Federation and the Länder, of the taxes subject to concurrent legislative powers is to be effected not later than 31 December 1952, by means of a federal law which requires the approval of the Bundesrat. This does not apply to the taxes on real estate and on businesses (Realsteuern) and the taxes with localized application. Each party is to be allowed a legal claim to specified taxes or portions of taxes according to its tasks.

Article 108

(1) Customs, fiscal monopolies, the excise taxes subject to concurrent legislative powers, the transportation tax, the turnover tax and the non-recurrent capital levies are administered by federal finance authorities. The organization of these authorities and the procedure to be applied by them will be regulated by federal law. The heads of the administrative agencies at intermediate level are to be appointed after consultation of the Land Governments. The Federation may transfer the administration of the non-recurrent capital levies to the Land finance authorities as its agents.

(2) If the Federation claims part of the income and corporation taxes for itself, it is entitled to administer them to that extent; it may, however, transfer the administration to the Land finance authorities as its agents.

(3) The remaining taxes are administered by Land finance authorities. The Federation may, by federal laws which require the approval of the Bundesrat, regulate the organization of these authorities, the procedure to be applied by them and the uniform training of the officials. The heads of the administrative agencies at intermediate level are to be appointed in agreement with the Federal Government. The administration of the taxes accruing to the Gemeinden (Gemeindeverbände) may be transferred by the Länder in whole or in part to the Gemeinden (Gemeindeverbände).

(4) Insofar as taxes accrue to the Federation, the Land finance authorities act as agents of the Federation. The Länder are liable to the extent of their revenues for an orderly administration of the taxes; the Federal Minister of Finance may supervise the orderly administration, acting through authorised federal agents, who have a right to give instructions to the administrative agencies at intermediate and lower levels.

(5) The jurisdiction of finance courts will be uniformly regulated by federal law.

(6) The general administrative rules will be issued by the Federal Government and, insofar as the administration is incumbent upon the Land finance authorities, will require the consent of the Bundesrat.

Article 109

The Federation and the Länder are autonomous and independent of each other as regards their budgets.

Article 110

(1) All revenues and expenditure of the Federation must be estimated for each fiscal year and included in the budget.

(2) The budget will be established by a law before the beginning of the fiscal year. It is to be balanced as regards revenue and expenditure. Expenditures will as a rule be approved for one year; in special cases, they may be approved for a longer period. Otherwise no provisions may be inserted in the federal budget law which extend beyond the fiscal year or which do not relate to the revenues and expenditures of the Federation or its administration.

(3) The assets and liabilities are to be set forth in an appendix to the budget.

(4) In the cases of commercially operated enterprises of the Federation the individual receipts and expenditures need not be included in the budget, but only the final balance.

Article 111

(1) If, by the end of a fiscal year, the budget for the following year has not been established by a law, the Federal Government may, until such law comes into force, make all payments which are necessary:—

(a) to maintain institutions existing by law and to carry out measures authorised by law;

(b) to meet legal obligations of the Federation;

(c) to continue building projects, procurements and other services or to continue the grant of subsidies for these purposes, provided amounts have already been authorized in the budget of a previous year.

(2) Insofar as revenues provided by special legislation and derived from taxes, levies or other sources, or the working capital reserves, do not cover the expenditures set forth in paragraph (1), the Federal Government may borrow the funds necessary for the conduct of current operations to a maximum of one quarter of the total amount of the previous budget.

Article 112

Expenditures in excess of budget items and extraordinary expenditures require the consent of the Federal Minister of Finance. The consent may only be given if there exists an unforeseen and compelling necessity.

Article 113

Decisions of the Bundestag and of the Bundesrat which increase the budget expenditure proposed by the Federal Government or include new expenditure or will cause new expenditure in the future, require the consent of the Federal Government.

Article 114

(1) The Federal Minister of Finance must submit annually to the Bundestag and to the Bundesrat an account of all revenues and expenditures as well as of the assets and liabilities.

(2) This account shall be audited by an Audit Office (Rechnungshof), the members of which shall enjoy judicial independence. The general account and a summary of the assets and liabilities are to be submitted to the Bundestag and the Bundesrat in the course of the following fiscal year together with the comments of the Audit Office in order to secure a discharge for the Federal Government. The audit of accounts will be regulated by a federal law.

Article 115

Funds may be obtained by borrowing only in case of extraordinary need and as a rule only for expenditure for productive purposes and only on the basis of a federal law. The granting of credits and the provision of security by the Federation the effect of which extends beyond the fiscal year may take place only on the basis of a federal law. The amount of the credit, or the extent of the obligation for which the Federation assumes liability, must be fixed in the law.

XI. TRANSITIONAL AND CONCLUDING PROVISIONS

Article 116

(1) Unless otherwise provided by law, a German within the meaning of this Basic Law is a person who possesses German nationality or who has been received in the territory of the German Reich, as it existed on 31 December 1937, as a refugee or expellee of German stock (Volkszugehörigkeit) or as the spouse or descendant of such person.

(2) Former German nationals who, between 30 January 1933 and 8 May 1945, were deprived of their nationality for political, racial or religious reasons, and their descendants, shall be regranted German nationality on application. They are considered as not having been deprived of their German nationality if they have established their domicile (Wohnsitz) in Germany after 8 May 1945 and have not expressed a contrary intention.

Article 117

(1) Law which conflicts with Article 3, paragraph (2), remains in force until adapted to this provision of the Basic Law, but not beyond 31 March 1953.

(2) Laws which restrict the right of freedom of movement because of the present housing shortage remain in force until repealed by federal legislation.

Article 118

The reorganization of the territory comprising the Länder Baden, Württemberg-Baden and Württemberg-Hohenzollern can be effected, notwithstanding the provisions of Article 29, by agreement between the Länder concerned. If no agreement is reached, the reorganization will be regulated by a federal law, which must provide for a referendum.

Article 119

In matters relating to refugees and expellees, in particular as regards their distribution among the Länder, the Federal Government may, with the consent of the Bundesrat, issue ordinances having the force of law (Verordnungen mit Gesetzeskraft), pending settlement of the matter by federal legislation. The Federal Government may thereby be authorised to issue individual instructions for particular cases. Except where there is danger in delay, the instructions are to be addressed to the highest Land authorities.

Article 120

(1) The Federation bears the expenditure for occupation costs and the other internal and external burdens caused by war, as provided for in detail by a federal law, and the subsidies towards the burdens of social insurance, including unemployment insurance and public assistance for the unemployed.

(2) The revenues are transferred to the Federation at the same time as the Federation assumes responsibility for the expenditures.

Article 121

Within the meaning of this Basic Law, a majority of the members of the Bundestag and of Federal Convention (Bundesversammlung) is the majority of the number of their members established by law.

Article 122

(1) From the time of the first meeting of the Bundestag, laws shall be passed exclusively by the legislative authorities recognized in this Basic Law.

(2) Legislative bodies and bodies participating in legislation in an

advisory capacity whose competence ends by virtue of paragraph (1) are dissolved from that date.

Article 123

(1) Law in force before the first meeting of the Bundestag remains in force, insofar as it does not conflict with the Basic Law.

(2) Subject to all rights and objections of the interested parties, the state treaties concluded by the German Reich concerning matters for which, under this Basic Law, Land Legislation is competent, remain in force, if they are and continue to be valid in accordance with general principles of law, until new state treaties are concluded by the authorities competent under this Basic Law, or until they are in any other way terminated pursuant to their provisions.

Article 124

Law affecting matters within the exclusive power to legislate of the Federation becomes federal law wherever it is in force.

Article 125

Law affecting matters within the concurrent power to legislate of the Federation becomes federal law wherever it is in force:—

1. insofar as it applies uniformly within one or more zones of occupation;
2. insofar as it is law by which former Reich Law has been amended after 8 May 1945.

Article 126

The Federal Constitutional Court decides disputes regarding the continuance of law as federal law.

Article 127

Within one year of the promulgation of this Basic Law the Federal Government may, with the consent of the governments of the Länder concerned, extend to the Länder Baden, Greater Berlin, Rhineland-Palatinate and Württemberg-Hohenzollern the legislation of the Bizonal Economic Administration, insofar as it continues to be in force as federal law under Articles 124 or 125.

Article 128

Insofar as law continuing in force provides for powers to give instructions within the meaning of Article 84, paragraph (5), these powers remain in existence until otherwise provided by law.

Article 129

(1) Insofar as legal provisions which continue in force as federal law contain an authorisation to issue ordinances having the force of law

(Rechtsverordnungen) or general administrative rules or to perform administrative acts, the authorisation passes to the agencies henceforth competent in the matter. In cases of doubt, the Federal Government will decide in agreement with the Bundesrat; the decision is to be published.

(2) Insofar as legal provisions which continue in force as Land law contain such an authorisation, it will be exercised by the agencies competent under Land law.

(3) Insofar as legal provisions within the scope of paragraphs (1) and (2) authorise their amendment or amplification or the issue of legal provisions in place of laws, these authorisations have expired.

(4) The provisions of paragraphs (1) and (2) apply correspondingly whenever legal provisions refer to regulations no longer valid or to institutions no longer in existence.

Article 130

(1) Administrative agencies and other institutions which serve the public administration or the administration of justice and are not based on Land law or state treaties between Länder, as well as the Association of Management of South West German Railroads and the Administrative Council for the Postal Services and Telecommunications of the French Zone of Occupation are placed under the Federal Government. The Federal Government provides with the consent of the Bundesrat for their transfer, dissolution or liquidation.

(2) The highest disciplinary superior of the personnel of these administrations and institutions is the functional Federal Minister.

(3) Public law corporations and institutions not directly under a Land, and not based on state treaties between Länder, are under the supervision of the functional highest federal authority.

Article 131

Federal legislation is to regulate the legal status of persons, including refugees and expellees, who, on 8 May 1945, were employed in the public service, have left the service for reasons other than those arising from the civil service regulations or agreed employment rules, and have not until now been employed or are employed in a position not corresponding to their former one. The same applies to persons, including refugees and expellees, who, on 8 May 1945, were entitled to a pension or other assistance and who no longer receive any assistance or any commensurate assistance for reasons other than those arising from the civil service regulations or agreed employment rules. Until the federal law comes into force, no legal claims can be made, unless otherwise provided by Land legislation.

Article 132

(1) Civil servants (Beamte) and judges who, when the Basic Law comes into force, are appointed for life, may, within six months after

the first meeting of the Bundestag, be placed on the retired list or waiting list or be transferred to another office with lower remuneration, if they lack the personal or professional aptitude for their office. This provision applies correspondingly also to employees (Angestellte) whose service cannot be terminated by notice. In the case of employees (Angestellte) whose service can be terminated by notice, periods of notice in excess of the periods fixed by the agreed employment rules may be cancelled within the same period.

(2) This provision does not apply to members of the public service who are not affected by the provisions regarding the "Liberation from National Socialism and Militarism" or who are recognised victims of National Socialism, unless there exists an important reason in respect of their personality.

(3) Those affected may have recourse to the courts in accordance with Article 19, paragraph (4).

(4) Details are determined by an ordinance of the Federal Government which requires the approval of the Bundesrat.

Article 133

The Federation succeeds to the rights and obligations of the Bizonal Economic Administration.

Article 134

(1) Reich property becomes in principle federal property.

(2) Insofar as the property was originally intended predominantly for use for administrative purposes which, under this Basic Law, are not within the administrative functions of the Federation, it is to be transferred without payment to the authorities hereafter charged with such functions, and to the Länder insofar as it is being used at present, and not merely temporarily, for administrative purposes which under the Basic Law are hereafter within the administrative functions of the Länder. The Federation may also transfer other property to the Länder.

(3) Property which was placed at the disposal of the Reich by the Länder and Gemeinden (Gemeindeverbände) without compensation shall again become the property of the Länder and Gemeinden (Gemeindeverbände), insofar as it is not required by the Federation for its own administrative purposes.

(4) Details will be regulated by a federal law which requires the approval of the Bundesrat.

Article 135

(1) If after 8 May 1945 and before the coming into force of this Basic Law an area has passed from one Land to another, the Land to which the area now belongs is entitled to the property located therein of the Land to which it belonged.

(2) Property of Länder and other public law corporations and insti-

tutions which no longer exist passes, insofar as it was originally intended to be used predominantly for administrative tasks or is being used at present, and not merely temporarily, predominantly for administrative tasks, to the Land or the public law corporation or institution which now fulfils these tasks.

(3) Real estate of Länder which no longer exists, including appurtenances, passes to the Land within which it is located insofar as it is not included among property within the purview of paragraph (1).

(4) If an overriding interest of the Federation or the particular interest of the area so requires, a settlement deviating from paragraphs (1) to (3) may be effected by federal law.

(5) Otherwise, the succession in law and the settlement of the property, insofar as it has not been effected before 1 January 1952 by agreement between the Länder or public law corporations or institutions concerned, will be regulated by a federal law which requires the approval of the Bundesrat.

(6) Interests of the former Land Prussia in enterprises organised under private law pass to the Federation. A federal law will regulate details and may make contrary provisions.

(7) Insofar as, at the coming into force of the Basic Law, property to which a Land or a public law corporation or institution would be entitled under paragraphs (1) to (3) had been disposed of through or under authority of a Land Law or in any other manner by the party thus entitled, the passing of the property is deemed to have taken place before such disposition.

Article 136

(1) The Bundesrat assembles for the first time on the day of the first meeting of the Bundestag.

(2) Until the election of the first Federal President his powers will be exercised by the President of the Bundesrat. He has not the right to dissolve the Bundestag.

Article 137

(1) The right of civil servants (Beamte), of employees (Angestellte) of the public services and of judges to stand for election in the Federation, in the Länder and in the Gemeinden may be restricted by legislation.

(2) The Electoral Law to be adopted by the Parliamentary Council applies to the election of the first Bundestag, of the first Federal Convention and of the first Federal President of the Federal Republic.

(3) The function of the Federal Constitutional Court pursuant to Article 41, paragraph (2), shall, pending its establishment, be exercised by the German High Court for the Combined Economic Area, which shall decide in accordance with its Rules of Procedure.

Article 138

Changes in the rules relating to notaries as they now exist in the Länder Baden, Württemberg-Baden and Württemberg-Hohenzollern, require the consent of the governments of these Länder.

Article 139

The provisions of law enacted for the "Liberation of the German People from National Socialism and Militarism" are not affected by the provisions of this Basic Law.

Article 140

The provisions of Articles 136, 137, 138, 139 and 141 of the German Constitution of 11 August 1919 are an integral part of this Basic Law.*

Article 141

Article 7, paragraph (3), first sentence, has no application in a Land in which different provisions of Land law were in force on 1 January 1949.

Article 142

Notwithstanding the provision of Article 31, also such provisions of Land-Constitutions remain in force as guarantee basic rights in conformity with Articles 1 to 18 of this Basic Law.

Article 143

(1) Whoever by force or threat thereof changes the constitutional order of the Federation or of a Land, by force or dangerous threats deprives the Federal President of the powers conferred on him by this Basic Law, or compels him to exercise or prevents him from exercising his powers at all or in a certain manner, or severs an area belonging to the Federation or a Land, shall be punished by penal servitude for life or for not less than ten years.

(2) Whoever publicly incites to the commission of an act within the scope of paragraph (1) or plots with another or in any other way prepares such an act, shall be punished by penal servitude up to ten years.

(3) In less serious cases, a sentence of not less than two years penal servitude in the cases specified in paragraph (1), and of not less than one year's imprisonment in the cases specified in paragraph (2), may be imposed.

(4) Whoever of his own free will abandons his action, or, if more than one person participate, prevents the commission of the act agreed, cannot be punished under the provisions of paragraphs (1) to (3).

(5) Where such an act is directed exclusively against the constitutional order of a Land, the highest Land court having jurisdiction in criminal

* See Appendix, p. 254.

cases shall, in the absence of any other provision in Land law, have jurisdiction to try the offender. In other cases the Oberlandesgericht in whose district the first Federal Government has its seat has jurisdiction.

(6) The aforementioned provisions apply until other provisions are enacted by Federal legislation.

Article 144

(1) This Basic Law requires adoption by the representative assemblies in two-thirds of the German Länder in which it is for the time being to apply.

(2) Insofar as the application of this Basic Law is subject to restrictions in any Land listed in Article 23 or in any part of such Land, the Land or the part thereof has the right to send representatives to the Bundestag in accordance with Article 38 and to the Bundesrat in accordance with Article 50.

Article 145

(1) The Parliamentary Council determines in public session, with participation of the representatives of Greater Berlin, the adoption of this Basic Law and signs and promulgates it.

(2) This Basic Law comes into force at the end of the day of promulgation.

(3) It is to be published in the Federal Gazette.

Article 146

This Basic Law ceases to be in force on the day on which a Constitution adopted by a free decision of the German people comes into force.

Bonn am Rhein,
on 23 May 1949

DR. ADENAUER
President of the Parliamentary Council
SCHÖNFELDER
First Vice-President
DR. SCHÄFER
Second Vice-President

APPENDIX

Articles 136, 137, 138, 139 and 141 of the Section "Religion and Religious Associations" of the Weimar Constitution, which have been incorporated in the Basic Law for the Federal Republic of Germany by Article 140 thereof.

Article 136

Civil and civic rights and duties are neither conditioned nor limited by the practice of a religious belief.

The enjoyment of civil and civic rights and the eligibility to public offices are independent of religious belief.

No one is obliged to reveal his religious convictions. The authorities have the right to inquire into membership in a religious association only so far as rights and duties depend thereon, or as statistical action ordered by law makes it necessary.

No one may be compelled to perform any religious act or ceremony, to participate in religious exercises or to use a religious form of oath.

Article 137

There is no state church.

Freedom of association in religious societies is guaranteed. The association of religious societies within the territory of the Reich is not subject to any limitations.

Every religious society regulates and administers its affairs independently within the limits of the law applicable for all. It chooses its officers without the intervention of the state or the civil commune.

Religious societies acquire juristic personality according to the general provisions of the civil law.

Religious societies remain public law corporations insofar as they were such heretofore. Other religious societies are to be granted like rights upon their application, if their constitution and the number of their members assures their permanence. If several such public law religious societies join together in an association, this association is also a public law corporation.

The religious societies which are corporations of public law are entitled to levy taxes on the basis of the civil taxation lists in accordance with Land law.

The same status as religious societies is guaranteed to societies whose purpose is the cultivation in common of a philosophy of life (Weltanschauung).

Insofar as the implementation of these provisions necessitates further regulation, this shall be done by Land legislation.

Article 138

State subsidies to religious societies which rest on law, contract or other special legal title will be redeemed by Land legislation. The Reich establishes the principles for this.

The rights of ownership and other rights of the religious societies and religious associations to their institutions, foundations and other property devoted to purposes of worship, education or charity are guaranteed.

Article 139

Sunday and the recognised public holidays remain protected by law as days of freedom from labor and of spiritual elevation.

Article 141

Insofar as there exists a need for public worship and spiritual care in the army, in hospitals, prisons and other public institutions, the religious societies are to be admitted for the performance of such religious acts, in connection with which compulsion is to be avoided.

AMENDMENTS* TO THE BASIC LAW FOR THE FEDERAL REPUBLIC OF GERMANY

A. Amendments effected by the Law to Amend and Supplement the Finance Clauses of the Basic Law, of 23 December 1955 (*Federal Law Gazette*, I, 817)

Articles 106 and 107 shall read as follows:

Article 106

(1) The yield of fiscal monopolies and receipts from the following taxes shall accrue to the Federation:

1. customs duties,
2. such excise taxes as do not accrue to the Länder in accordance with paragraph (2),
3. turnover tax,
4. transportation tax,
5. non-recurrent capital levies, and equalization taxes imposed for the purpose of implementing the equalization of burdens legislation,
6. Berlin emergency aid tax,
7. supplementary levies on income and corporation taxes.

(2) Receipts from the following taxes shall accrue to the Länder:

1. property tax,
2. inheritance tax,
3. motor-vehicle tax,
4. such taxes on transactions as do not accrue to the Federation in accordance with paragraph (1),
5. beer tax,
6. levies on gambling establishments,
7. taxes on real estate and businesses,
8. taxes with localized application.

(3) Receipts from income tax and corporation tax shall accrue:

until 31 March 1958, to the Federation and the Länder in a ratio of $33\frac{1}{3}$ per cent to $66\frac{2}{3}$ per cent, and

* Translation supplied from official German sources. Printed verbatim and without style or spelling corrections.

from 1 April 1958, to the Federation and the Länder in a ratio of 35 per cent to 65 per cent.

(4) The ratio of apportionment of the income and corporation taxes (paragraph [3]) should be modified by a Federal law requiring the consent of the Bundesrat whenever the development of the relation of revenues to expenditures in the Federation differs from that in the Länder and whenever the budgetary needs of the Federation or those of the Länder exceed the estimated revenues by a margin substantial enough to call for a corresponding adjustment of the ratio of apportionment in favour of either the Federation or the Länder. Any such adjustment shall be based on the following principles:

1. The Federation and the Länder shall each bear the expenditures resulting from the administration of their respective tasks; Article 120 paragraph (1) shall not be affected;
2. there shall be equality of rank between the claim of the Federation and the claim of the Länder to have their respective necessary expenditures covered from ordinary revenues;
3. the requirements of the Federation and of the Länder in respect of budget coverage shall be coordinated in such a way that a fair equalization is achieved, any overburdening of taxpayers precluded, and uniformity of living standards in the Federal territory ensured.

The ratio of apportionment may be modified for the first time with effect from 1 April 1958, and subsequently at intervals of not less than two years after the entry into force of any law determining such ratio; provided that this stipulation shall not affect any modification of such ratio effected in accordance with paragraph (5).

(5) If a Federal law imposes additional expenditures on, or withdraws revenues from, the Länder, the ratio of apportionment of the income and corporation taxes shall be modified in favour of the Länder, provided that conditions as envisaged in paragraph (4) have developed. If the additional burden placed upon the Länder is limited to a period of short duration, such burden may be compensated by grants from the Federation under a Federal law requiring the consent of the Bundesrat and which shall lay down the principles for assessing the amounts of such grants and for distributing them among the Länder.

(6) For the purposes of the present Article, revenues and expenditures of communes (associations of communes) shall be deemed to be Land revenues and expenditures. Whether and to what extent receipts from Land taxes are to accrue to communes (associations of communes), shall be determined by Land legislation.

Article 107

(1) Receipts from Land taxes shall accrue to the individual Länder to the extent that such taxes are collected by revenue authorities within

their respective territories (local receipts). Federal legislation requiring the consent of the Bundesrat may provide in detail for the determination and allotment of local receipts from specific taxes (tax shares).

(2) A Federal law requiring the consent of the Bundesrat shall ensure a reasonable financial equalization between financially strong Länder and financially weak Länder, due account being taken of the financial capacity and requirements of communes (associations of communes). Such law shall provide for equalization grants to be paid to financially weak Länder from equalization contributions made by financially strong Länder; it shall furthermore specify the conditions governing equalization claims and equalization liabilities as well as the criteria for determining the amounts of equalization payments. Such law may also provide for grants to be made by the Federation from Federal funds to financially weak Länder in order to complement the coverage of their general financial requirements (complemental grants).

B. Amendments effected by the Law to Supplement the Basic Law, of 19 March 1956 (*Federal Law Gazette*, I, 111)

1. *Article 1 paragraph (3) shall read as follows:*

(3) The following basic rights bind the legislature, the executive and the judiciary as directly enforceable law.*

2. *Article 12 shall read as follows:*

Article 12

(1) All Germans have the right freely to choose their trade or profession, their place of work and their place of training. The practice of trades and professions may be regulated by law.

(2) No one may be compelled to perform a particular work except within the framework of a traditional compulsory public service which applies generally and equally to all. Anyone who refuses on conscientious grounds to render war service involving the use of arms may be required to render an alternative service. The duration of this alternative service shall not exceed the duration of military service. Details shall be regulated by a law which shall not prejudice freedom of conscience and shall provide also for the possibility of an alternative service having no connection with any unit of the Armed Forces.

(3) Women shall not be required by law to render service in any unit of the Armed Forces. On no account shall they be employed in any service involving the use of arms.

(4) Forced labour may be imposed only in the event that a person is deprived of his freedom by the sentence of a court.

3. *The following Article 17a shall be inserted after Article 17:*

* No change in English text.

Article 17a

(1) Laws concerning military service and alternative service may by provisions applying to members of the Armed Forces and of alternative Services during their period of military or alternative service, restrict the basic right freely to express and to disseminate opinions by speech, writing and pictures (Article 5 paragraph [1] first half-sentence), the basic right of assembly (Article 8), and the right of petition (Article 17) insofar as it permits to address requests or complaints jointly with others.

(2) Laws for defence purposes, including the protection of the civilian population, may provide for the restriction of the basic rights of freedom of movement (Article 11) and inviolability of the home (Article 13).

4. *Article 36 shall read as follows:*

Article 36

(1) Civil servants employed in the highest Federal authorities shall be drawn from all Länder in appropriate proportion. Persons employed in other Federal authorities should, as a rule, be drawn from the Land in which they serve.

(2) Military laws shall take into account the division of the Federation into Länder and the latter's particular ethnic conditions.

5. *The following provisions shall be inserted after Article 45 as Article 45a and Article 45b:*

Article 45a

(1) The Bundestag shall appoint a Committee on Foreign Affairs and a Committee on Defence. Both committees shall function also in the intervals between any two legislative terms.

(2) The Committee on Defence shall also have the rights of a committee of investigation. Upon the motion of one-fourth of its members it shall have the duty to make a specific matter the subject of investigation.

(3) Article 44 paragraph (1) shall not be applied in matters of defence.

Article 45b

A Defence Commissioner of the Bundestag shall be appointed to safeguard the basic rights and to assist the Bundestag in exercising parliamentary control. Details shall be regulated by a Federal law.

6. *Article 49 shall read as follows:*

Article 49

In respect of the members of the Presidency, the Standing Committee, the Committee on Foreign Affairs and the Committee on Defence, as well as their principal substitutes, Articles 46, 47 and paragraphs (2) and (3) of Article 48 shall apply also in the intervals between any two legislative terms.

7. *The following Article 59a shall be inserted after Article 59:*

Article 59a

(1) The Bundestag shall determine when a case of defence has occurred. Its decision shall be promulgated by the Federal President.

(2) If insurmountable difficulties prevent the Bundestag from assembling, the Federal President may, when there is danger in delay, make and promulgate this determination, subject to counter-signature by the Federal Chancellor. The Federal President should previously consult the Presidents of the Bundestag and the Bundesrat.

(3) Statements concerning the existence of a case of defence which involve international relations shall not be issued by the Federal President until after such promulgation.

(4) Any decision on the conclusion of peace shall be taken by means of a Federal law.

8. *Article 60 paragraph (1) shall read as follows:*

(1) The Federal President appoints and dismisses the Federal judges, the Federal civil servants, the officers and non-commissioned officers, unless otherwise provided for by law.

9. *The following Article 65a shall be inserted after Article 65:*

Article 65a

(1) Power of command in respect of the Armed Forces shall be vested in the Federal Minister of Defence.

(2) Upon promulgation of the determination concerning the case of defence, the power of command shall devolve on the Federal Chancellor.

10. *The following provisions shall be inserted after Article 87 as Article 87a and Article 87b:*

Article 87a

The numerical strength and general organizational structure of the Armed Forces raised for defence by the Federation shall be shown in the budget.

Article 87b

(1) The administration of the Federal Defence Forces shall be conducted as a Federal administration with its own administrative substructure. Its function shall be to administer matters pertaining to personnel and to the immediate supply of the material requirements of the

Armed Forces. Tasks connected with benefits to invalids or construction work shall not be assigned to the administration of the Federal Defence Forces except by Federal legislation which shall require the consent of the Bundesrat. Such consent shall also be required for any legislative provisions empowering the administration of the Federal Defence Forces to interfere with rights of third parties; this shall, however, not apply in the case of laws concerning personnel.

(2) Moreover, Federal laws concerning defence including recruitment for military service and protection of the civilian population may, with the consent of the Bundesrat, stipulate that they shall be carried out, wholly or in part, either under Federal administration with its own administrative sub-structure or by the Länder acting as agents of the Federation. If such laws are executed by the Länder acting as agents of the Federation, they may, with the consent of the Bundesrat, stipulate that the powers vested by virtue of Article 85 in the Federal Government and appropriate highest Federal authorities shall be transferred wholly or partly to higher Federal authorities; in such an event it may be enacted that these authorities shall not require the consent of the Bundesrat in issuing general administrative rules as referred to in Article 85 paragraph (2) first sentence.

11. *Article 96 paragraph (3) shall read as follows:*

(3) The Federation may establish Federal disciplinary courts for disciplinary proceedings against Federal civil servants and Federal judges, as well as Federal service courts for disciplinary proceedings against soldiers and for proceedings concerning complaints of soldiers.

12. *The following Article 96a shall be inserted after Article 96:*

Article 96a

(1) The Federation may establish military criminal courts for the Armed Forces as Federal courts. They shall not exercise criminal jurisdiction except in the case of defence or over members of the Armed Forces serving abroad or on board warships. Details shall be regulated by a Federal law.

(2) The military criminal courts shall be within the sphere of business of the Federal Minister of Justice. Their full-time judges must be professional judges.

(3) The Federal Supreme Court shall be the superior Federal court for the military criminal courts.

13. *Article 137 paragraph (1) shall read as follows:*

(1) The right of civil servants, of salaried employees of the public services, of professional soldiers, of temporary volunteer soldiers and of

judges to stand for election in the Federation, in the Länder or in the communes may be restricted by legislation.

14. *The following provision shall be inserted as Article 143:*

Article 143

The conditions under which it will be admissible to have recourse to the Armed Forces in case of a state of internal emergency may be regulated only by a law which fulfils the requirements of Article 79.

MILITARY GOVERNORS' AIDE MEMOIRE FOR THE PARLIAMENTARY COUNCIL

1. As you are well aware, the Parliamentary Council was convened in order to draft a democratic constitution which will establish for the participating states a governmental structure of federal type, will protect the rights of the participating states, provide adequate central authority and contain guarantees of individual rights and freedoms. During the last eleven weeks the Parliamentary Council in plenary session as well as in its several committees has freely discussed those principles and drafted a basic law (provisional constitution) which is now before the main committee.

2. In view of the advanced stage now reached in the work of the Parliamentary Council, the Military Governors consider it advisable at this time to give the Council some indication of the interpretation which they will apply to the general principles set out in Document No. I. Since there are several ways in which democratic federal government can be obtained, they intend to consider the provisions of the basic law in their whole context. Nevertheless, they believe that the basic law should, to the maximum extent possible, provide:

(a) for a bicameral legislative system in which one of the houses must represent the individual states and must have sufficient power to safeguard the interests of the states;

(b) that the executive must only have those powers which are definitely prescribed by the constitution, and that emergency powers, if any, of the executive must be so limited as to require prompt legislative or judicial review;

(c) that the powers of the federal government shall be limited to those expressly enumerated in the constitution and, in any case, shall not include education, cultural and religious affairs, local government

263

and public health (except in this last case, to safeguard the health of the people in the several states), that its powers in the field of public welfare be limited to those necessary for the co-ordination of social security measures, that its powers in the police field be limited to those especially approved by the Military Governors, during the occupation period;

(d) that the powers of the federal government in the field of public finance shall be limited to the disposal of monies, including the raising of revenue for purposes for which it is responsible, that the federal government may set rates and legislate on the general principles of assessment with regard to other taxes for which the uniformity is essential, the collection and utilization of such taxes being left to the individual states, and that it may appropriate funds only for the purpose for which it is responsible under the constitution;

(e) that the constitution should provide for an independent judiciary to review federal legislation, to review the exercise of federal executive power, and to adjudicate conflicts between federal and land authorities as well as between land authorities, and to protect the civil rights and freedom of the individual;

(f) that the powers of the federal government to establish federal agencies for the execution and administration of its responsibilities should be clearly defined and should be limited to those fields in which it is clear that state implementation is impracticable;

(g) that each citizen has access to public office, with appointment and promotion being based solely on his fitness to discharge the responsibilities of the position, and that the civil service should be non-political in character;

(h) that a public servant, if elected to the federal legislature, shall resign his office with the agency where he is employed before he accepts election.

The Military Governors will be guided by these principles in their final examination of the basic law (provisional constitution) and any subsequent amendments thereto, and they will consider the basic law (provisional constitution) as a whole in order to determine whether or not the broad requirements of Document I have been met.

Frankfurt, 22 November 1948

LEADING PERSONALITIES OF THE PARLIAMENTARY COUNCIL*

CDU/CSU

The Christian Democratic delegation in the Parliamentary Council was led by *Dr. Konrad Adenauer* (CDU—North Rhine-Westphalia) who had been one of the party founders and, at that time, was chairman of the CDU in the British zone and the leader of his party in the legislature of North Rhine-Westphalia. Adenauer began his professional career with the practice of law in Cologne in 1902. He took an active part in the local government of Cologne, in which he held various positions, until he became lord mayor of Cologne, a position which he held from 1917 to 1933. He had been a member of the Prussian upper house before World War I, and in the Weimar era became president of the Prussian Staatsrat. On two occasions during this period he was called upon as a member of the Center party to form a government as Reich chancellor, but did not succeed. He was excluded from holding public office by the Nazis, by whom he was imprisoned for a time in 1934 and 1944. Reinstated by the American army of occupation as lord mayor of Cologne, he was later removed by the British commander in North Rhine-Westphalia for "obstructionism and non-co-operation." He was elected by the first Bundestag chancellor of the first government of the Federal Republic and was re-elected chancellor in 1957. He was born in Cologne in 1876, the son of a clerk of the law courts. He was educated at the Universities of Munich, Freiburg, and Bonn, where he studied law and economics. He holds the degree of doctor of law.

Dr. Heinrich von Brentano (CDU—Hesse) was deputy chairman of the main committee and of the Occupation Statute committee and also took part in the committee on distribution of powers. He was the CDU's

* Listed alphabetically by parties.

265

representative on the three-man editorial committee. His political activities began in 1945 when he helped to found the CDU in Hesse. He was a member of the constitutional assembly in Hesse and later became the floor leader of his party in the Hessian Landtag. After the establishment of the Federal Republic he was unanimously chosen leader of the CDU/CSU parliamentary group after Dr. Adenauer had resigned upon his election as federal chancellor. Von Brentano has taken a particular interest in European affairs. He was elected a vice-president of the consultative assembly of the Council of Europe in 1950. In 1955, he succeeded Dr. Adenauer as foreign minister. He was born in 1904 at Offenbach of a family which has long been identified with German intellectual and political life. He took his doctorate in law in 1926 and, after service with the judicial administration, settled in Darmstadt as a lawyer.

The late *Dr. Paul de Chapeaurouge* (CDU–Hamburg) was senator for police in the Hamburg Bürgerschaft from 1925 to 1933. During the whole of the Weimar period he was also chairman of the German People's party (DVP) in Hamburg. After the war, he became chairman of the CDU faction in the Hamburg Bürgerschaft, as well as a member of the executive of the party in Hamburg. He was a member of the committees on the constitutional court and judiciary and the Occupation Statute. De Chapeaurouge was born in 1876 in Hamburg and died in 1952. After studying law in Freiburg, Munich, and Bremen, he settled in Hamburg in 1903 as a notary.

Herr Jakob Kaiser (CDU–Berlin) was a bookbinder until 1912, and thereafter, until 1933, a leading official of the Christian trade unions. He was a member of the Center party until 1933 and a member of the Reichstag from 1932 to 1933. He was active in the resistance movement after 1933. He was arrested in 1938 and charged with high treason, but was released after seven months for lack of evidence. He participated in the preparations for the July 20, 1944, plot against Hitler and, when it failed, went into hiding and successfully eluded the Gestapo. In 1945, he was one of the founders of the CDU in the Eastern zone and became chairman in December of that year. For some time, Kaiser advocated what he called "the bridge policy" between Eastern and Western Germany and tried to provide a liaison between the political leaders of both zones through a body which he called "the national representation." But this movement failed, and Kaiser came to lean more and more toward the Western point of view. In the summer of 1947, he publicly defended the Marshall Plan. Despite this, Kaiser was re-elected chairman of the CDU in the Eastern zone at the annual convention of the party held in Berlin in September, 1947. When, however, he ventured to oppose the calling of the Soviet-sponsored East-Zone German people's congress at the time of the meeting of the Council of Foreign Ministers in London in November, 1947, he was deposed as chairman of the CDU by the

Soviet military administration. He later became a member of the CDU in Western Germany and deputy chairman of the party, and was one of the Berlin "observers" at the Parliamentary Council. He was elected to the first Bundestag and subsequently became federal minister for all-German affairs. He was born in 1888 at Hammelburg, Lower Franconia.

Professor Dr. Wilhelm Laforet (CSU–Bavaria), a leading advocate of federalist principles in the Parliamentary Council, served both on the committee on distribution of powers and the main committee. After World War I he rose in the civil service of Bavaria to become Ministerialrat in the Bavarian ministry of the interior. From the time of its founding he was an active member of the Bavarian People's party. He later became professor of constitutional and administrative law at Würzburg University. After World War II he became a member of the CSU and served in the Bavarian constituent assembly. Later he was elected to the Bavarian Landtag. He was elected to the first Bundestag, in which he was chairman of the committee on legal affairs and constitutional law. He was born in 1877 at Edenkoben, Rhineland-Palatinate. He was educated at the Universities of Munich and Berlin.

The late *Dr. Robert Lehr* (CDU–North Rhine-Westphalia), the chairman of the committee on governmental organization and a member of the main committee, began his public career in the local government of Düsseldorf. He became a member of the city council of Düsseldorf in 1915 and lord mayor of Düsseldorf in 1924. He was a member of the German National People's party (DNVP). He was dismissed by the Nazis in 1933, arrested, and then permitted to live in retirement. He had contacts with the leaders of the uprising against Hitler in 1944. After the capitulation, he was appointed the administrative president of the North Rhine province, and the next year was appointed chairman of the zonal advisory council in the British zone. He was also elected president of the Landtag of North Rhine-Westphalia. He was one of the founders of the CDU. In the postwar period, he had business connections with the *Vereinigte Stahlwerke* and with the Rhenish-Westphalian Electricity Works. He was federal minister of the interior from 1950 to 1953. Dr. Lehr was born in 1883 in Celle, the son of an army officer, and was educated at the Universities of Marburg, Berlin, and Bonn, taking his final examination for the doctorate of law at Heidelberg. He died in 1956.

The late *Professor Dr. Hermann von Mangoldt* (CDU–Schleswig-Holstein) was chairman of the committee on basic rights, a deputy member of the constitutional court committee, and a member of the main committee. After World War I, von Mangoldt studied constructional engineering and jurisprudence in Danzig and law in Königsberg, where he sat for the state examination in 1930. Afterward he worked as an independent tutor in Königsberg. In 1935 he went to Tübingen, where his professional prospects were at first prejudiced because he did not join the Nazi party. However, he was finally appointed professor. He was drafted into the navy in 1943, but was discharged in 1944 on grounds of health, after which he was appointed at Kiel University as a lecturer in the Institute for World Trade. He later became professor, director of the Institute for International Law, and rector of Kiel University. He was a member of the first Landtag of Schleswig-Holstein and was minister of the interior from April to August, 1946. He was the leader of the CDU faction in a number of committees of the Landtag of Schleswig-Holstein. Dr. von Mangoldt has written the most authoritative of the commentaries on the Basic Law. He was born in 1895 at Aachen and died in 1953.

Dr. *Josef Schwalber* (CSU–Bavaria), one of the leading federalists, was a member of the committee on governmental organization. He belonged to the Bavarian People's party from 1929 until his arrest in 1933, and from that time was politically inactive until 1945, when he took part in founding the CSU in Bavaria. He had practiced law in Dachau from 1929 to 1933 and was elected Bürgermeister of that town in 1946. He subsequently became a member of the Bavarian Landtag and Staatssekretär in the ministry of the interior, and, later, Bavarian minister of education and culture from 1951 to 1954 and a member of the Bundesrat for Bavaria. He was born in 1902 in Fürstenfeldbruck and was educated at the University of Munich, where he studied law and political science.

Dr. *Walter Strauss* (CDU–Hesse) was deputy chairman of the committee on distribution of powers and of the constitutional court committee. From 1927 until he was compulsorily retired in 1935, Dr. Strauss was in the civil service, first in the judicial system in Berlin and later in the Reich ministry of economics. He held an economic advisory position until 1943 and afterward worked in a factory. After the capitulation he worked as a manager of hospitals. He later became Staatssekretär in Hesse and a member of the directorate of the Länderrat. In 1947 he became deputy director of the bizonal economic administration and, later, chief of the legal section. After the establishment of the Federal Republic, he became Staatssekretär in the ministry of justice. He was born in 1900 in Berlin and pursued studies in history, economics, and jurisprudence at Freiburg, Heidelberg, Munich, and Berlin. He passed the referendar's examination for the civil service in 1923.

Professor Dr. *Adolf Süsterhenn* (CDU–Rhineland-Palatinate), who was a member of the council of elders and the main committee, as well as a deputy member of the committees on governmental organization and basic rights, took up the practice of law in Cologne in 1932 and was a Center party representative in the city council. He was chairman of the constituent assembly in Rhineland-Palatinate. After 1946 he was minister of justice and, from 1947, also minister of education and culture in Rhineland-Palatinate. He is now president of the constitutional court of that Land. He was born in 1905 in Cologne and studied jurisprudence at the Universities of Freiburg and Cologne.

Frau Dr. Helena Weber (CDU–North Rhine-Westphalia) was a member of the committee on basic rights. From 1909 to 1916, Frau Dr. Weber taught in Bochum and Cologne. In 1917 she became director of the social school of the German Catholic Women's League in Cologne. In 1919 she was elected to the Weimar National Assembly, and in the same year became referendar in the civil service. In 1920 she was appointed Ministerialrätin in the Prussian ministry of welfare. Until 1933 she was a member of the Reichstag and also, for some time, of the Prussian Landtag. She was dismissed from public office in 1933 and compelled to retire. After serving as a member of the Landtag in North Rhine-Westphalia for a short time in 1945, she was appointed to the zonal advisory council and was chairman of its committee for culture. Frau Dr. Weber was elected to the first Bundestag. She was also an alternate for the German delegation to the Assembly of the Council of Europe. She was born in 1881 in Elberfeld. She passed the intermediate teachers' examination in 1900 and, after studying at Bonn and Grenoble, passed the higher teachers' examination in 1909. She has been active in Catholic welfare organizations throughout her career. She holds the doctorate h.c. from the University of Münster.

SPD

Professor Dr. Carlo Schmid (SPD–Württemberg-Hohenzollern) was the leader of the Social Democratic delegation in the Parliamentary Council, chairman of the main committee and of the Occupation Statute committee, and a member of the council of elders and of the committee on basic rights. He was associated with Tübingen University, first as a student, and later, between 1929 and 1939, as a lecturer in international law. In 1946 he became full professor at Tübingen. In the postwar period he was successively the head of the provisional government, the deputy president of the Land, Staatssekretär and minister of education and religion, and Staatssekretär and minister of justice, as well as a member of the Land legislature from 1946 to 1949 in Württemberg-Hohenzollern. He was the author of the constitution of Württemberg-Baden. He was also chairman of the South Württemberg Social Democratic party and a member of the Social Democratic national executive. He was elected vice-president of both the first and second Bundestag and has been a member of the German delegation to the Council of Europe's consultative assembly. Dr. Schmid's wide cultural interests are reflected in his translations of Baudelaire, Rostand, and Calderon, and such publications as his *Römisches Tagebuch.* He was born in 1896 in Perpignan, France, the son of a German scholar and a French mother. He studied law at Munich and Tübingen Universities.

Professor Dr. Ludwig Bergsträsser (SPD–Hesse) was a member of the committees on basic rights and rules and procedure. He became honorary lecturer at Greifswald in 1910 and, in 1920, was appointed to the research section of the Reich archives. He published several works of his own, including *The History of Political Parties in Germany,* and was given the task of compiling a history of the Frankfurt Parliament. He was dismissed in 1933 on political grounds. Active politically since 1907, he joined the Democratic party after 1918, becoming, in 1919, Reichstag member for the Potsdam constituency. When the Democratic party changed into the State party *(Staatspartei),* he joined the SPD. During the Nazi period he was active in the resistance. After 1945 he was Regierungspräsident of Darmstadt. He was a member of the Hessian Landtag and was chairman of the Hessian constituent assembly. He was a member of the first Bundestag. Dr. Bergsträsser was born in 1883 in Altkirch, Upper Alsace. He was educated at Heidelberg.

Dr. Rudolf Katz (SPD–Schleswig-Holstein) was deputy chairman of the committee on governmental organization and a frequent participant in the meetings of the main committee. In 1923 he worked as a legal consultant in Lübeck, and in 1924 established himself as a lawyer and notary in Hamburg-Altona. In 1929 he was a Social Democratic member and head of the Social Democratic faction in the Hamburg city council, and a member of the Schleswig-Holstein Städtetag. Because of his Jewish origin, he left Germany at the beginning of the Nazi period and went to Nanking, where he became the League of Nations adviser in munici-pal affairs to the Chinese government and a member of the Chinese National Economic Council. He went to the United States in 1935, where he became an assistant at Columbia University and, in 1938, the editor of *Die Neue Volkszeitung* in New York. He was also a member of the editorial board of the *New Leader,* and secretary of the German labor delegation affiliated to the American Federation of Labor. He be-came an American citizen in 1941. In 1946 he returned to Germany with Bürgermeister Brauer as a delegate of the American Federation of Labor. In December, 1947, he became a member of the Schleswig-Holstein Landtag and was appointed minister of justice, thereby regaining his German nationality. He is vice-president of the federal constitutional court. Dr. Katz was born in 1895 in Falkenburg, Pomerania. He studied law and political science, completing his studies at Kiel in 1920.

Dr. Walter Menzel (SPD–North Rhine-Westphalia) was a member of the main, finance, and electoral law committees. After his assessor examination in 1927, he became a government assessor at the police

Präsidium in Essen. In 1931 he was Landrat in Weilburg-an-der-Lahn. In 1934 he settled in Berlin as a lawyer. In 1945 he became an adviser to the U.S. military government, and subsequently was made General-Referent for the interior in the Westphalian provincial administration. From 1946 to 1950 he was minister of the interior in North Rhine-Westphalia. He was also a member of the zonal board of the Social Democratic party. He was elected to the first and second Bundestags and is chairman of the Bundestag committee on constitutional matters and parliamentary secretary for the SPD in the Bundestag. Dr. Menzel was born in Berlin in 1901, and studied jurisprudence, political science, and economics in Berlin and Freiburg.

Herr Adolf Schönfelder (SPD–Hamburg) was first vice-president of the Parliamentary Council and deputy president of the council of elders. He was also a member of the main committee and the committee on rules of procedure. Herr Schönfelder was educated in an elementary school and apprenticed as a carpenter, following his trade until 1905. He became a trade-union secretary and the chairman of the Central Union of German Carpenters. In 1919 he was a member of the Bürgerschaft of Hamburg. In 1919 he was elected to the senate of Hamburg and appointed chief of police. In 1933 he was arrested on a charge of high treason, which was subsequently dropped. In June, 1947, he became deputy Bürgermeister of Hamburg. He was elected to and became president of the Bürgerschaft. He was born in 1875 in Hamburg.

Herr Jean Stock (SPD–Bavaria) was a member of the main committee, the electoral law committee, and the finance committee. He was self-taught in economics and politics. He was apprenticed as a printer and took the master printer's examinations. He joined the printers union (Free Trades Union) and the Social Democratic party in 1911. After World War I, he became secretary of the Free Trades Union. In 1919 he was town councilor in Aschaffenburg. He was a member of the Bavarian Landtag. He was manager of the Aschaffenburg Social Democratic newspaper until 1933, when he established his own printing business. After 1933 he was arrested on various occasions. Finally in 1943 his business was closed, and in 1944 he was imprisoned in Dachau. Upon his release from Dachau in 1945, he became Oberbürgermeister and Landrat of Aschaffenburg and, later, Regierungspräsident in Lower Franconia. From 1946, he was chairman of the Social Democratic faction in the Bavarian Landtag. Herr Stock was born in 1893 in Gelnhausen, Hessen-Nassau.

Herr Georg-August Zinn (SPD–Hesse) was chairman of the constitutional court committee and a member of the committee on basic rights and the editorial committee. From 1929 to 1931 he was a Social Democratic member of the city council of Kassel. In 1931 he began the practice of law in Kassel, which he continued until he was drafted into the army in 1941. He had joined the Social Democratic party as early as 1920, and from 1924 to 1926 was chairman of the Social Democratic Students' League in Berlin and, after 1928, a leader of the Social Democratic party in Kassel. The Nazis arrested him on various occasions after 1933, but Zinn continued secret organizational work for the Social Democratic party. In 1945 he joined the Hessian judicial service and was given charge of the state personnel department. In 1946 he was appointed minister of justice for Hesse. He was elected to the first Bundestag in 1949, but he resigned his Bundestag membership in 1951 when he was elected minister-president of Hesse. He has retained the portfolio of minister of justice. He was born in 1901 in Frankfurt-am-Main. He studied law and political science in the Universities of Göttingen and Berlin.

FDP

Professor Dr. Theodor Heuss (FDP–Württemberg-Baden), leader of the Free Democratic party in the Parliamentary Council, was a member of the council of elders, the main committee, and the committee on basic rights. Heuss was inspired by Friedrich Naumann to take an active part in the German liberal movement, and he became editor, from 1905 to 1912, of Naumann's *Hilfe* in Berlin. From 1912 to 1918 he edited *Die Neckar Zeitung* in Heilbronn, and a leading literary and political journal of the time, *März*. After 1918 he edited the weekly *Deutsche Politik* in Berlin. From 1920 until the Nazis took power, he lectured at Berlin's Hochschule für Politik. He represented the German Democratic party (DDP) in the Berlin city council, and from 1924 to 1928 and 1930 to 1933, in the Reichstag. The Nazis excluded him from public office in 1933 and publicly burned two of his books. Under an assumed name, he wrote cultural essays for the *Frankfurter Zeitung* until the Nazis also put a stop to this. After the capitulation he returned to journalism, publishing the *Rhein-Neckar Zeitung* in Heidelberg. Later he was appointed minister of education and cultural affairs in Württemberg-Baden. In 1948 he became chairman of the FDP of the Western zones of Germany. Dr. Heuss has twice been elected president of the Federal Republic. He has published a number of books on politics, literature, and art. He was born in 1884 in Brackenheim into a family of Neckar River boatmen. He was married by Dr. Albert Schweitzer in 1908 to Elly Knapp, the daughter of the famous German economist.

Dr. Max Becker (FDP–Hesse) was chairman of the electoral law committee and a member of the constitutional court committee. Dr. Becker began the practice of law in Kurhessen and became a lawyer and notary in Hersfeld in 1913. After World War I he joined the Young People's Liberal Union, and in 1919 became a member of the German People's party (DVP). His first public office was as a member of the

Kreistag in Hersfeld from 1919 to 1921, and from 1922 to 1933 he was a member of the provincial Landtag of Hessen-Nassau. In 1945 he became a member of the Magistrat and, in 1946, of the city council of Hersfeld. Later he was elected to the Hessian Landtag. He was elected to the first and second Bundestags. He is now a vice-president of the Bundestag. He was a member of the German delegation to the Council of Europe. He was born in 1888 in Kassel and studied at Grenoble, Berlin, Halle, and Marburg.

Dr. Thomas Dehler (FDP–Bavaria) was a member of the main committee, the committee on governmental structure, and the editorial committee. Before 1933, Dr. Dehler practiced as a lawyer in Munich and Bamberg. He took an active part in politics from an early age, becoming a member of the German Democratic party (DDP) as a student in 1919. In 1924 he helped to found the Reichsbanner movement to protect the republican democratic form of government in Germany. He was finally arrested in 1938 and sent to the forced labor camp at Rositz in 1944; after some time, his friends were able to obtain his release because of ill health. Following the capitulation, he set out to form a non-party anti-Fascist organization, "Democratic Bloc" and, in Bavaria in 1945, founded the Free Democratic party (FDP), of which he is Land chairman. In the meantime he had been advocate-general in Bamberg and public prosecutor in the denazification court of appeal. He resigned when Loritz became minister-extraordinary. In 1947, he became president of the higher Land court in Bamberg but, in the same year, refused the post of minister of justice because his party wished to remain in opposition to the CSU government. In 1948 he was elected president of the Bavarian constitutional court, but refused the post because it would have debarred him from political activity. He is a member of the Bavarian Landtag. He became a member of the first and second Bundestags and was named federal minister of justice in the first Adenauer coalition. His controversial views ultimately led to his resignation and assumption of leadership of the FDP in the Bundestag.

The late *Dr. Hermann Höpker-Aschoff* (FDP–North Rhine-Westphalia) was a leading member of the finance committee. In 1921 he became Oberlandesgerichtsrat in Hamm and a member of the Prussian Landtag, representing the German Democratic party (DDP). He was also a member of the Reichsbanner. He became Prussian finance minister in 1925, from which post he was dismissed by the Nazis in 1933. He lived in retirement until he was drafted into service in 1939 to work in the German administration in the Eastern occupied territories dealing with Polish assets. Because of this employment, the British military government refused to sanction his appointment in 1946 to be the finance minister of North Rhine-Westphalia and the finance member of the zonal advisory council. He became the first president of the federal constitutional court. He was born in 1883 in Herford and studied law at the Universities of Jena, Munich, and Bonn. He died in 1954.

DP

Dr. *Hans Christoph Seebohm* (DP–Lower Saxony) was a member of the main committee, the finance committee, and the council of elders. He was employed in the Prussian ministry of commerce from 1931 to 1933. After employment as a works director and general manager in coal and ore mining companies, Dr. Seebohm was appointed manager of a mining company at Dortmund-Bentheim and was on the board of directors of a Brunswick machine-building works. After the war he became chairman of the Brunswick chamber of commerce and industry and was a member of the boards of various metal industry corporations. In 1945 he joined the Lower Saxony party, which later became the German party (DP), in which he has been a member of the directorate and the deputy chairman. He was elected to the Landtag of Lower Saxony in 1947. From 1946 to 1948, he was minister for reconstruction and labor and health in the government of Lower Saxony. He was leader of the German party's delegation to the Parliamentary Council. Dr. Seebohm was elected to the first Bundestag in 1949, and in that year became federal minister of transport, an office which he has held to the present. He was born in 1903 at Emanuelssegen, Upper Silesia. He was trained as a mining engineer at Freiburg, Munich, and Berlin.

Z

Herr *Johannes Brockmann* (Z–North Rhine-Westphalia) was a member of the council of elders, the main committee, and the committee on governmental organization. After qualifying as a teacher, he taught in the state schools from 1911 to 1933. He was vice-chairman of the Catholic Teachers' Union for Germany until 1933 and Bürgermeister of Rinkerode from 1929 to 1933. He was a member of the Prussian parliament from 1913 to 1925. After having been disqualified for public employment at the start of the regime, he was arrested and imprisoned by the Nazis in 1944. He became zonal chairman of the Center party and leader of the Center faction in the Landtag of North Rhine-Westphalia after 1945. He was elected to the second Bundestag. He was born in 1888 in Paderborn.

Frau *Helene Wessel* (Z–North Rhine-Westphalia) was a member of the committees on distribution of powers and rules and procedures. In 1915, Frau Wessel became secretary of the Center party in Dortmund-Hörde, and in 1928 was elected to the Prussian Landtag. In 1939 she became the chief welfare officer in the central office of the Catholic Welfare Union. In 1945 she was chosen deputy chairman of the German Center party and subsequently represented that party in the Landtag of North Rhine-Westphalia. She was elected to the first Bundestag, in which she was chairman of the committee on public welfare. She was elected chairman of the Center party in 1949 and resigned from this position in January, 1952, in order to devote her time to the neutralist *Notgemeinschaft für den Frieden Europas,* of which she was joint chairman with Dr. Gustav Heinemann. In 1953, she and Dr. Heinemann founded the All-German Peoples' party to promote a neutral, united Germany. This was dissolved in 1957, and Frau Wessel, Dr. Heinemann, and others joined the Social Democratic party. She was born in 1898 in Dortmund. She attended commercial school and, later, a social welfare school, and passed the state examination in youth welfare. She holds a diploma as welfare officer from the German Academy for Social Work in Berlin.

KPD

Herr Max Reimann (KPD—North Rhine-Westphalia), the leader of the Communist delegation, was a member of the council of elders, of the main committee, and of the electoral law committee. He was a miner in the Ruhr. He joined the KPD in 1920. By 1933 he had become the Communist party secretary of the Essen district, and was also a district leader of the Revolutionary Trade Union Organization (RGO). After the Nazis came to power, he took an active part in the resistance. He was forced to flee to Czechoslovakia. In 1939, attempting to escape to England, he was captured by the Gestapo and imprisoned in the concentration camp at Sachsenhausen, where he remained until the end of the war. He was Communist district leader in the Ruhr in 1945, and since then has successively been KPD chairman for the British zone and for Western Germany. He was a member of the bizonal economic council. During the Parliamentary Council proceedings he was sentenced to three months' imprisonment by a British military tribunal for making a subversive speech. He was elected to the first Bundestag. His parliamentary immunity was suspended in July, 1950, because of his suspected complicity in the kidnapping of a fellow Communist member of the Bundestag. He was born in 1898 in Elbing, East Prussia.

BIBLIOGRAPHY

GERMANY AFTER 1945

Documents

1. *Bericht über den Verfassungskonvent auf Herrenchiemsee vom 10. bis 23. August 1948.* Munich: Richard Pflaum Verlag.

2. "Die Stellungnahmen der Ministerpräsidenten zu Dokument Nr. I, Dokument Nr. II, Dokument Nr. III," in *Kommentar zum Bonner Grundgesetz.* Hamburg: Hansischer Gilden Verlag, 1950.

3. *Parlamentarischer Rat: Stenographischer Bericht: Verhandlungen des Plenums.* Bonn: Bonner Universitäts-Buchdruckerei Gebr. Scheur G.m.b.H.

4. *Parlamentarischer Rat: Stenographischer Bericht: Verhandlungen des Hauptausschusses.* Bonn: Bonner Universitäts-Buchdruckerei Gebr. Scheur G.m.b.H.

5. *Parlamentarischer Rat: Sach- und Sprechregister zu den Verhandlungen des parlamentarischen Rates und seines Hauptausschusses 1948.* Bonn: Bonner Universitäts Buchdruckerei Gebr. Scheur G.m.b.H.

6. *Parlamentarischer Rat: Grundgesetz für die Bundesrepublik Deutschland (Entwürfe)—Formulierungen der Fachausschüsse, des allgemeinen Redaktionsausschusses, des Hauptausschusses und des Plenums, Bonn 1948/49.* Bonn: Bonner Universitäts-Buchdruckerei Gebr. Scheur G.m.b.H.

7. *Parlamentarischer Rat: Schriftlicher Bericht zum Entwurf des Grundgesetzes für die Bundesrepublik Deutschland erstattet von den Berichterstattern des Hauptausschusses für das Plenum.* Bonn: Bonner Universitäts-Buchdruckerei Gebr. Scheur G.m.b.H.

8. "Parlamentarischer Rat: Stenographischer Bericht: Verhandlungen

der Fachausschüsse." (Available only in typescript in the archives of the Bundestag.)

9. *Grundgesetz für die Bundesrepublik Deutschland mit Wahlgesetz, Besatzungsstatut, Bundesverfassungsgerichtsgesetz und Konvention zum Schutze der Menschenrechte.* 15th ed. Munich and Berlin: C. H. Beck'sche Verlags Buchhandlung, 1955.

10. *Wahlgesetz zum ersten Bundestag der Bundesrepublik Deutschland vom 15. Juni 1949; Geschäftsordnung des Deutschen Bundestages vom 6. Dezember 1951 in Handbuch des Deutschen Bundestages.* Stuttgart: Buchgestaltung und Druck Chr. Scheufele, 1952.

11. *Certain International and U.S. Policy Documents Regarding Germany.* Published by Office of the United States Political Adviser for Germany, 1949. Includes documents of the Crimean and Potsdam conferences of heads of state, the Allied Control Council reparations plan of March 28, 1946, the Byrnes-Bevin agreement on the fusion of the US/UK zones in Germany of December 2, 1946, United States government statements and proposals at Council of Foreign Ministers, Moscow, March–April, 1947, and London, November–December, 1947.

12. *Germany, 1947–1949: The Story in Documents.* (U.S. Department of State Publication 3556.) Washington: Government Printing Office, 1950. Includes the major quadripartite, bipartite, tripartite, and American documents of the period on constitutional and political developments, German war potential and maintenance of security, reparations and restitution, economic rehabilitation, educational and cultural developments.

13. *Documents on German Unity.* Vol. I. Published by Office of the U.S. High Commissioner for Germany, 1951. Includes relevant extracts from the Crimean and Potsdam agreements, papers of the Allied Control Council ("CONL" and "CORC") and of the Council of Foreign Ministers ("CFM") on quadripartite occupation government in Germany.

14. *Documents on the Creation of the German Federal Constitution.* Published by Office of Military Government for Germany (U.S.), 1949. Includes decisions of the London conference on Western Germany of June 1, 1948, minutes of the meeting of the military governors and the ministers-president of the Länder of July 26, 1948, the Chiemsee draft constitution, the draft of the Basic Law adopted in third reading of the Parliamentary Council main committee, the military governors' memorandum of March 2, 1949, counterproposals of the committee of seven of March 10 and 17, 1949, resolutions of the SPD and CDU/CSU factions of the Parliamentary Council of March 30, 1949, decisions of the U.S., U.K., and French

foreign ministers of April 5, 1949, revised version of the Basic Law and resolution adopted by the Social Democratic party on April 20–21, 1949, the military governors' letter of approval of the Basic Law of May 12, 1949, texts of the drafts of the electoral law of February 24, 1949, and May 16, 1949, communications exchanged by the military governors, the Parliamentary Council, and the ministers-president on the electoral law between March 2, 1949, and June 15, 1949.

15. *Basic Law for the Federal Republic of Germany*. Bonn-Petersberg: Allied General Secretariat, 1951. Contains parallel texts in English, French, and German.

16. *Draft Basic Law passed in First Reading in November/December 1948*. Published by Office of Military Government for Germany (U.S.), 1949.

17. *Constitutions of the German Länder*. Published by Office of Military Government for Germany (U.S.), 1947.

18. *Reports of the Meetings of the Bundestag and Bundesrat to the Office of U.S. High Commissioner for Germany, 1949–1953*. Prepared by CURT S. GOLDSMITH.

19. *Comparative Federal Constitutions*. Published by Office of Military Government for Germany (U.S.), 1948. Contains texts of the constitutions of Switzerland, Canada, Australia, the United States, the Soviet Union, Yugoslavia, the Weimar Republic, South Africa.

Books

ABENDROTH, WOLFGANG. "Zum Begriff des demokratischen und sozialen Rechtstaates im Grundgesetz der Bundesrepublik Deutschland," in *Aus Geschichte und Politik: Festschrift zum 70. Geburtstag von Ludwig Bergsträsser*. Düsseldorf, 1954.

Amtliches Handbuch des Deutschen Bundestages. 2. Wahlperiode. Darmstadt: Neue Darmstädter Verlagsanstalt G.m.b.H., 1953.

BARZEL, RAINER. *Die deutschen Parteien*. Geldern/Ndrh.: L. N. Schaffrath, 1952.

Bundesrecht und Bundesgesetzgebung: Bericht über die Weinheimer Tagung des Instituts zur Förderung öffentlicher Angelegenheiten in Frankfurt a.M. am 22. und 23. Oktober 1949. Frankfurt a.M.: Wolfgang Metzner Verlag, 1950.

CLAY, LUCIUS D. *Decision in Germany*. New York: Doubleday & Co., 1950.

DENNEWITZ, BODO, et al. *Kommentar zum Bonner Grundgesetz*. Hamburg: Hansischer Gildenverlag, Joachim Heitmann u. Co., 1950——.

DÖMMING, K-B. VON, FÜSSLEIN, R. W., and MATZ, WERNER. *Enstehungs-*

geschichte der Artikel des Grundgesetzes: Jahrbuch des öffentlichen Rechts der Gegenwart. New Series, Vol. I. Tübingen: J. C. B. Mohr (Paul Siebeck), 1951.

Elections and Political Parties in Germany, 1945–1952. Published by Office of the United States High Commissioner for Germany, 1952.

Germany Reports. Published by the Press and Information Office of the German Federal Government, 1953.

GIESE, FRIEDRICH. *Grundgesetz für die Bundesrepublik Deutschland (Kommentar).* 3d ed. Frankfurt a.M.: Verlag Kommentator G.m.b.H., 1953.

GILLEN, J. F. J. *State and Local Government in West Germany, 1945–1953.* Monograph of the Historical Division of the Office of the United States High Commissioner for Germany, 1953.

GLUM, FRIEDRICH. *Das parlamentarische Regierungssystem in Deutschland, Grossbritannien, und Frankreich.* Munich: Verlag C. H. Beck, 1950.

———. "Kritische Bemerkungen zu Art. 63, 67, 68, 81 des Bonner Grundgesetzes," in *Um Recht und Gerechtigkeit: Festgabe für Erich Kaufmann.* Stuttgart and Cologne, 1950.

IPSEN, H. P. *Über das Grundgesetz.* Hamburg: Hamburg Universität, 1950.

LITCHFIELD, E. H., *et al. Governing Post-War Germany.* Ithaca, N.Y.: Cornell University Press, 1953.

MANGOLDT, HERMANN VON. *Das Bonner Grundgesetz (Kommentar).* Berlin and Frankfurt a.M.: Verlag Franz Vahlen Gmbh., 1953.

MAUNZ, THEODOR. *Deutsches Staatsrecht.* 3d ed. Munich and Berlin: C. H. Beck'sche Verlags Buchhandlung, 1954.

MÜNCH, FRITZ. *Die Bundesregierung.* Frankfurt a.M.: Alfred Metzner Verlag, 1954.

NAWIASKY, HANS. *Die Grundgedanken des Grundgesetzes für die Bundesrepublik Deutschland.* Stuttgart and Cologne: W. Kohlhammer Verlag, 1950.

NETTL, J. P. *The Eastern Zone and Soviet Policy in Germany.* Oxford: Oxford University Press, 1951.

PILGERT, H. P. *The West German Educational System.* Monograph of the Historical Division of the Office of the United States High Commissioner for Germany, 1953.

PLISCHKE, ELMER. *The West German Federal Government.* Monograph of the Historical Division of the Office of the United States High Commissioner for Germany, 1952.

Political Parties in Western Germany. Published by Office of Military Government for Germany (U.S.), 1949.

SÄNGER, FRITZ. *Handbuch des Deutschen Bundestages.* 1. Wahlperiode. Stuttgart: J. G. Cotta'sche Buchhandlung, 1952.

WEBER, WERNER. *Weimarer Verfassung und Bonner Grundgesetz.* Göttingen: Verlag Karl-Friedrich Fleischer, 1949.

———. *Spannungen und Kräfte in Westdeutchen Verfassungssystem.* Stuttgart: Vorwerk, 1951.

Articles in Periodicals

Abbreviations:

AOR—Archiv des Öffentlichen Rechts

SJZ—Süddeutsche Juristen-Zeitung

JZ—Juristen-Zeitung (successor to *Süddeutsche Juristen-Zeitung*)

DV—Deutsche Verwaltung

DVB—Deutsches Verwaltungsblatt (successor to *Deutsche Verwaltung*)

NJW—Neue Juristische Wochenschrift

RSW—Recht, Staat, Wirtschaft

DRZ—Deutsche Rechts-Zeitschrift

ABENDROTH, WOLFGANG. "Zwiespältiges Verfassungsrecht in Deutschland," *AOR*, Vol. LXXVI (1950–51).

APELT, WILLIBALT. "Betrachtungen zum Bonner Grundgesetz," *NJW*, No. 13 (July 1, 1949).

———. "Erstreckt sich das richterliche Prüfungsrecht auf Verfassungsnormen?" *NJW*, No. 1 (January 1, 1952).

———. "Verfassung und richterliches Prüfungsrecht," *JZ*, No. 13/14 (July 15, 1954).

ARNDT, ADOLF. "Das Bundesverfassungsgericht," *DVB* (May 15, 1951; January 1, 1952).

BERGER, HANS. "Der Verfassungentwurf von Herrenchiemsee," *DV*, No. 4 (November 15, 1948).

———. "Zur Entstehung des Bonner Grundgesetzes," *DV*, No. 12 (June 15, 1949).

DERMEDDE, C. "Der Bund und die Länder," *DV*, No. 12 (June 15, 1949).

DIRKS, WALTER. "Bundesrepublik Deutschland," *Frankfurter Hefte*, No. 6 (June, 1949).

DREHER, EDUARD. "Das parlamentarische System des Bonner Grundgesetzes im Vergleich zur Weimarer Verfassung," *NJW*, No. 4 (February 15, 1950).

DÜRIG, GÜNTER. "Art. 2 des Grundgesetzes und die Generalermächtigung zu allgemein polizeilichen Massnahmen," *AOR*, Vol. LXXIX (1953–54).

FECHNER, ERICH. "Über einige Neuerscheinungen zum Problem des Naturrechts," *DRZ*, Vol. IV, No. 5 (March 5, 1949).

FÜSSLEIN, R. W., and MATZ, WERNER. "Zur Enstehungsgeschichte des Grundgesetzes," *AOR*, Vol. LXXV (1949).

GLUM, FRIEDRICH. "Literatur zum Bonner Grundgesetz," *SJZ*, No. 12 (1950).

GREWE, WILHELM. "Das Grundgesetz," *DRZ*, No. 14 (July 20, 1949).

———. "Das bundesstaatliche System des Grundgesetzes," *DRZ*, No. 15/16 (August 15, 1949).

———. "Die Bundesrepublik als Rechtsstaat," *DRZ*, No. 17/18 (September 15, 1949).

HERMENS, F. A. "Der Proporz als Verhängnis der Bundesrepublik," *Neues Abendland*, Vol. VII, No. 4 (April, 1952).

HÖPKER-ASCHOFF, HERMANN. "Die Abgrenzung der Verwaltung zwischen Bund und Ländern, mit besonderer Berücksichtigung der Finanzverwaltung," *DV*, No. 4 (November 15, 1948).

———. "Das Finanz- und Steuer System des Bonner Grundgesetzes," *AOR*, Vol. LXXV (1949).

HUBER, ERNST R. H. "Bundesexekution und Bundesintervention: Ein Beitrag zur Frage des Verfassungsschutzes im Deutschen Bund," *AOR*, Vol. LXXIX (1953–54).

IPSEN, HANS PETER. "Die Nachprüfung der Verfassungsmässigkeit von Gesetzen," *Beiträge zum öffentlichen Recht* (Sonderveröffentlichung der *Zeitschrift für ausländisches und internationales Privatrecht*) (1950).

JERUSALEM, FRANZ W. "Die Grundrechte des Bonner Grundgesetzes und ihre Durchsetzung in der Rechtsprechung," *SJZ* (1950).

KERN, EDWARD. "Die Rechtsprechung," *DV*, No. 12 (June 15, 1949).

KLEIN, FRIEDRICH. "Bonner Grundgesetz und Rechtsstaat," *Zeitschrift für die Gesamte Staatswissenschaft*, Vol. CVI (1950).

KRATZER, JACOB. "Zustimmungsgesetze," *AOR*, Vol. LXXVII (1951–52).

KRAUSS, GÜNTHER. "Die Verfassung Deutschlands, 1945–1954," *Die öffentliche Verwaltung*, Vol. VII, No. 19/20 (1954).

LEIBHOLZ, GERHARD. "Die Struktur der neuen Verfassung," *DV*, No. 4 (November 15, 1948).

———. "Volk und Partei im neuen deutschen Verfassungsrecht," *DVB* (April 1, 1950).

———. "Parteien Staat und Repräsentative Demokratie," *DVB* (1951).

———. "Der Parteienstaat des Bonner Grundgesetzes," *RSW*, Vol. III (1951).

LOEWENSTEIN, KARL. "Verfassungsrecht und Verfassungsrealität: Beiträge zur Ontologie der Verfassungen," *AOR*, Vol. LXXVII (1951–52).

MANGOLDT, HERMANN VON. "Grundrechte und Grundsatzfragen des Bonner Grundgesetzes," *AOR*, Vol. LXXV (1949).

———. "Das Verhältnis von Regierung und Parlament," in *Deutsche Landesreferate zum III. Internationalen Kongress für Rechtsvergleichung in London 1950* (Sonderveröffentlichung der *Zeitschrift für ausländisches und internationales Privatrecht*).

———. "Das Verhältnis von Staatschef und Regierung," in *Deutsche Landesreferate zum III. Internationalen Kongress für Rechtsvergleichung in London 1950* (Sonderveröffentlichung der *Zeitschrift für ausländisches und internationales Privatrecht*).

MAURER, J. H. "Die Krise des Föderalismus," *Neues Abendland*, No. 7 (July, 1952).

MENGER, C-F. "Zur verfassungsrechtlichen Stellung der deutschen politischen Parteien," *AOR*, Vol. LXXVIII (1952–53).

MENZEL, WALTER. "Die verfassungspolitischen Entscheidungen im Grundgesetz," *DV*, No. 12 (June 15, 1949).

MERCKER, REINHOLD. "Zwei Jahre Rechtsprechung des Bundesverfassungsgerichts," *Bundesanzeiger*, No. 206 (October 24, 1953); No. 226 (November 24, 1953); No. 243 (December 17, 1953).

PRASS, DR. "Die Bundesorgane," *DV*, No. 12 (June 15, 1949).

RABUS, GÜNTHER. "Die innere Ordnung der politischen Parteien im gegenwärtigen deutschen Staatsrecht," *AOR*, Vol. LXXVIII (1952–53).

RIDDER, HELMUT K. J. "Finanzausgleich und Grundgesetz: Bemerkungen zum Urteil des Bundesverfassungsgerichts vom 20. Februar 1952," *AOR*, Vol. LXXVIII (1952–53).

ROHWER-KAHLMANN, HARRY. "Verfassungsrechtliche Schranken der Zustimmungsgesetze (Art. 84, Abs. 1)," *AOR*, Vol. LXXIX.

SCHÄFER, HANS. "Bundesaufsicht und Bundeszwang," *AOR* (1952–53).

SCHEUNER, ULRICH. "Die institutionellen Garantien des Grundgesetzes," *RSW*, Vol. IV (1953).

SCHMID, CARLO. "Regierung und Parlament," *RSW*, Vol. III (1951).

SCHNEIDER, HANS. "Die Gesetzgebung des Bundes," *DV*, No. 12 (June 15, 1949).

———. "Die Zustimmung des Bundesrates zu Gesetzen," *DVB* (1953).

———. "Fünf Jahre Grundgesetz," *NJW*, No. 25 (June 24, 1954).

STRAUSS, WALTER. "Die rechtsprechende Gewalt im Bonner Grundgesetz," *SJZ*, No. 8 (August, 1949).

STRICKRODT, GEORG. "Das Bundesratsmandat—gebunden und frei," *Frankfurter Hefte* (1949).

THOMA, RICHARD. "Über die Grundrechte im Grundgesetz für die Bundesrepublik Deutschland," *RSW*, Vol. III (1951).

ULE, DR. "Die Grundrechte," *DV*, No. 12 (June 15, 1949).

WEBER, WERNER. "Zur Problematik von Enteignung und Sozialisierung nach neuem Verfassungsrecht," *NJW*, No. 11 (June 1, 1950).

WESSEL, DR. "Die Verwaltung," *DV*, No. 12 (June 15, 1949).

WOLFF, BERNHARD. "Die Ermächtigung zum Erlass von Rechtsverordnungen nach dem Grundgesetz," *AOR*, Vol. LXXVIII (1952–53).

ZINN, GEORG AUGUST. "Der Bund und die Länder," *AOR*, Vol. LXXV (1949).

Newspapers (period from June 1, 1948, to August 1, 1949)

Die Welt
Der Telegraf
Flensburger Tageblatt
Die Neue Zeitung
Der Tagesspiegel
Der Kurier
Die Zeit
Die Neue Züricher Zeitung
Die Allgemeine Zeitung
Der Tag
Der Morgen

Press Services:

DPD—Deutscher Presse-Dienst
DENA—Deutsche Nachrichten Agentur

Manchester Guardian
New York Times
The Times (London)
New York Herald Tribune
Christian Science Monitor

Combat
Le Monde

Other Publications

Monthly Reports of the United States Military Governor in Germany
Monthly Reports of the Control Commission for Germany (British Element)

Quarterly Reports of the United States High Commissioner for Germany
Weekly Bulletin issued by the Press and Information Office of the German Federal Government

GERMANY BEFORE 1945

Books and Articles Consulted

ANSCHÜTZ, GERHARD. *Die Verfassung des Deutschen Reiches.* 12th ed. Berlin: Verlag von Georg Stilke, 1930.

APELT, WILLIBALT. *Geschichte der Weimarer Verfassung.* Munich: Biederstein Verlag, 1946.

BERGSTRÄSSER, LUDWIG. *Geschichte der politischen Parteien in Deutschland.* Mannheim: J. Bensheimer, 1932.

BRAUN, OTTO. *Von Weimar zu Hitler.* New York: Europa Verlag, 1940.

BRECHT, ARNOLD. *Federalism and Regionalism in Germany: The Division of Prussia.* New York: Oxford University Press, 1945.

———. *Prelude to Silence: The End of the German Republic.* New York: Oxford University Press, 1945.

BRÜNING, HEINRICH. "Ein Brief," *Deutsche Rundschau,* Vol. LXX, No. 7 (July, 1947).

BRUNET, RENÉ. *The German Constitution.* Translated by J. GOLLOMB. London: T. Fisher Unwin Ltd., 1923.

BULLOCK, ALAN. *Hitler: A Study in Tyranny.* London: Odhams Press Ltd., 1952.

CLARK, R. T. *The Fall of the German Republic.* London: Allen & Unwin, 1935.

DARMSTÄDTER, F. *Bismarck and the Creation of the Second Reich.* London: Methuen, 1948.

ECKHARDT, ERNST. *Die Grundrechte vom Wiener Kongress bis zur Gegenwart.* Breslau: Verlag Mund H. Marcus, 1913.

EYCK, ERICH. *Bismarck and the German Empire.* London: Allen & Unwin, 1950.

———. *Geschichte der Weimarer Republik.* 2 vols. Zurich and Stuttgart: Eugen Rentsch Verlag, 1954, 1956.

FORSTHOFF, ERNST. *Lehrbuch des Verwaltungsrechts.* Munich and Berlin: C. H. Beck'sche Verlags Buchhandlung, 1951.

GIESE, FRIEDRICH. *Die Verfassung des Deutschen Reiches.* 8th ed.. Berlin: Carl Heymanns Verlag, 1927.

GREWE, WILHELM. "Der Schutz der Menschenrechte in Deutschland," *Proceedings of the International Congress for Comparative Law in London, 1950;* German section published under auspices of Kaiser Wilhelm Institut für ausländisches und internationales Privatrecht. Berlin: de Gruiter & Co., and Tübingen: J. C. B. Mohr, 1950.

HEADLAM-MORLEY, AGNES. *The New Democratic Constitutions of Europe*. Oxford: Oxford University Press, 1928.

HEADLAM-MORLEY, JAMES W. *Bismarck and the Foundation of the German Empire*. Putnam, 1899.

JELLINEK, WALTER. *Verwaltungsrecht*. Berlin: Verlag Julius Springer, 1928.

JEPSEN, CHARLES H. "The Influence of the Multi-Party System on Representative Government in Germany under the Weimar Constitution (1919–1930)." Unpublished Ph.D. dissertation, Bodleian Library, Oxford University, 1953.

NIPPERDEY, HANS CARL. *Die Grundrechte und Grundpflichten der Reichsverfassung*. Berlin: Verlag Reimar Hobbing, 1929.

REDSLOB, R. *Die parlamentarische Regierung in ihrer wahren und in ihrer unechten Form*. Tübingen, 1918.

RITTER, GERHARD. "Ursprung und Wesen der Menschenrechte," *Historische Zeitschrift*, Vol. CLXIX, No. 2 (1949).

ROSENBERG, ARTHUR. *History of the German Republic*. London: Methuen, 1936.

SCHEELE, GODFREY. *The Weimar Republic*. London: Faber, 1946.

SCHNEIDER, HANS. *Das Ermächtigungsgesetz vom 24. März 1933: Bericht über das Zustandekommen und die Anwendung des Gesetzes*. Bonn: Bundeszentrale für Heimatdienst, 1955.

SMEND, RUDOLF. *Bürger und Bourgeois im deutschen Staatsrecht*. Rede gehalten bei der Reichsgründungsfeier der Friedrich Wilhelms Universität, Berlin, January 18, 1933. Berlin: Preussische Druckerei und Verlagsaktiengesellschaft, 1933.

STAMPFER, FRIEDRICH. *Die vierzehn Jahre der ersten Deutschen Republik*. 3d ed. Hamburg: Verlag Auerdruck G.m.b.H., 1953.

STEINBERG, S. H. *A Short History of Germany*. Cambridge: Cambridge University Press, 1944.

STRESEMANN, GUSTAV. *Diaries, Letters and Papers*. Edited and translated by ERIC SUTTON. London: Macmillan & Co., 1940.

TAYLOR, A. J. P. *The Course of German History*. London: Hamish Hamilton, 1945.

THOMA, RICHARD. "Grundrechte und Polizeigewalt," in *Verwaltungsrechtliche Abhandlungen: Festgabe zur Feier des fünfzigjährigen Bestehens des Preussischen Oberverwaltungsgerichts 1875–1925*. Berlin: Carl Heymanns Verlag, 1925.

VALENTIN, VEIT. The German People: Their History and Civilization from the Holy Roman Empire to the Third Reich. New York: Alfred A. Knopf, 1952.

VERMEIL, EDMOND. La Constitution de Weimar et le principe de la démocratie allemande. Strasbourg: l'Imprimerie Alsacienne, 1923.

WHEELER-BENNETT, J. W. Hindenburg, the Wooden Titan. London: Macmillan & Co., 1936.

———. The Nemesis of Power. London: Macmillan & Co., 1953.

urges prompt implementation of
London agreements, 15–16
position of, on draft Basic Law, 97,
100
unwillingness of, to upset German
compromises on draft Basic Law,
97, 100
urges delivery of foreign ministers'
communication, 106
insistence of, on need for federal
electoral law, 143–44
see also Military governors
Ruhr
French attitude toward, 2, 8, 13, 97
Russian attitude toward, 2
International Authority of, 6, 13, 16
coal, iron, and steel reorganization
in, 6

Saar, French control of, 4, 97
Saltzman, Charles E., 6
Schäfer, Hermann, 20
Schäffer, Fritz, 86, 154
Schleicher, Kurt von, 37, 117–18
Schleswig-Holstein
representation of, in Parliamentary
Council, 19
geographical constitution of, 39
parties' strength in, 52
tax revenues in, 90
Schlör, Kaspar, 209
Schmid, Carlo, 27, 40, 42, 53–54, 64, 66,
69, 93–94, 125, 137, 157, 178, 180,
182, 186, 189–90, 192–93, 206, 208,
210–12, 214, 216, 269
Schönfelder, Adolf, 19, 85, 191
Schools, differing patterns of, in West
German Länder, 196
Schräge, Josef, 190
Schumacher, Kurt, 105, 107, 145–46
Schuman, Robert, 13, 97
Schwalber, Josef, 64, 66, 206, 268
Scientific research, promotion of, 65–
66
Seebohm, Hans Christoph, 191–93, 206,
216, 274
Selbert, Elisabeth, 196, 216
"Senate," as form of upper house of
legislature, 46–47
Senate, United States, 28, 51–52, 57, 143
Simple majority electoral system, 138
arguments in Parliamentary Council
for, 139

elements of, in electoral law, 141–42
in United States, 143
increase of number of deputies to be
directly elected under electoral
law, 145–46
effect of, on party system
outside Germany, 148
in Germany, 151–53
Smend, Rudolf, 167
Social Democratic party (SPD)
character of, as party, 156–57
representation of, in Parliamentary
Council, 19
views on
London agreements, 14
"provisional nature of Basic Law,"
22
federalism, 41–42
Land representation in Bundesrat,
51–53
composition and powers of Bundesrat, 42, 45, 48–50, 55–56
civil servants in Bundesrat, 53
administrative responsibilities of
federation and Länder, 69, 72–
74
division of legislative powers, 42,
58–59
legislation on taxes, 80–83
administration of taxes, 42, 83–86
parliamentary executive, 124
presidential executive, 125
president's powers, 126
"minority" chancellor, 127
"constructive vote of no-confidence," 128–29
natural rights, 178
police powers, 63–65
promotion of scientific research, 65
judicial review, 183–84
economic and social rights, 188–98
strength in elections from 1946, 52,
122, 141, 152
American attitude toward possible
government of, 99–100
complaints of Allied "pressure" on,
100
reaction of, to military governors'
intervention
in Basic Law, 95–96, 101–3, 107–8
in electoral law, 145–47
isolation of, after foreign ministers'
communication of April 6, 1949,
104